# Shattered Triangle

by

William P. Messenger

authorHOUSE®

*AuthorHouse™*
*1663 Liberty Drive*
*Bloomington, IN 47403*
*www.authorhouse.com*
*Phone: 1-800-839-8640*

*Published by AuthorHouse 5/17/2012*

*ISBN: 978-1-4772-0173-2 (sc)*
*ISBN: 978-1-4772-0174-9 (hc)*
*ISBN: 978-1-4772-0175-6 (sc)*

*Library of Congress Control Number: 2012907959*

*This book is printed on acid-free paper.*

*"Nulla dies umquam memori vos eximet aevo"*
*No day shall erase you from the memory of time"*
Virgil's "The Aeneid"

# Acknowledgments:

The quote above is only a partial sentence from the great poet, but as pure poetry, the words stand on their own. They reflect the depth of love, and memory's power to endure even as the ages pass. Here, Virgil offers an antidote to the greatest ravage of time—forgetting.

In many ways this book is about memories: recalling our past and the ones we have loved, both living and dead. Contrary to the old song, it is not easy to remember. But there are people involved in this endeavor who must never be forgotten.

It is with humility, love and grace that I dedicate this book to

**David Tortel**

His inspiration, encouragement and friendship enabled me to give this story life. Without him it would not even be a memory. Thank you, my friend.

I owe a huge debt of gratitude to others who assisted in the preparation of this book.

**Adolfo Batres** was a superb and invaluable resource regarding the Los Angeles Police Department.

**Perry Leiker, Taylor Lilly and Marilyne Sherwood** read through multiple and various drafts, a truly unenviable task. They offered sage advice, made corrections and suggested modifications that made this a better work.

**Frank Hicks** provided a quiet place to write without distraction.

Thanks to all of you.

# Chapter 1
## (2000)

The day of the funeral, I arrived thirty minutes early. I wanted to speak with Fr. Giovanni Lozano before the service began. I also needed to collect my final thoughts, for I had been asked to deliver the eulogy. My mind was on grief. It is arguably the deepest of human emotions, made more difficult by the fact that in spite of our continued efforts, it remains always inconsolable, leaving our best sentiments to languish among the insipid poetry of sympathy cards. So what do you say to someone who confronts the death of a loved one? What do you say when the survivors are your friends?

My entire journey to the church that morning was one of struggle, fighting mightily to keep myself in check, at times unable to withhold my tears, all the while wondering what private thoughts I might share with my friend. As I approached the church, I knew I would have only minutes before the arriving crowd would inundate him, thereby by vanishing any opportunity for personal affection. Over the previous few days we had spent many hours together, but emotions would be different that morning—for both of us. Right then we would need each other.

I entered the sacristy and greeted him.

"Hello, Giovanni. How are you today"? Geez, what a stupid question. I might as well be writing for a greeting card company!

"I'm fine for the moment, Tom. Thanks". Giovanni was the priest. If he was not in good shape for the funeral, the whole congregation was in trouble. "No. Actually, I'm not fine. In all my years, I have never had to face anything like this".

"Neither of us has, Gio". That was his favorite nickname. "The hearses are already out front. They are preparing to unload the four coffins".

"I don't think I could do this without you, Tom. Your being here…. I can't tell you what this means to me".

"Don't even try. I couldn't be anywhere else. You are my best friend, and I support you today as I always have. But I came here early to draw strength from you. I don't have your faith, Gio, and I'm not sure I can get through the service, let alone the eulogy".

"You don't need faith, Tom. You need only speak from your heart. I know it won't be easy. Still, I have a lot of confidence in you. You'll do just fine".

"Thanks, Gio". I knew he was trying to encourage me even though he, himself, felt weak. At the same time he was not being condescending. He knew the trouble I would have controlling my emotions and trying to speak with any coherence. He was facing the same difficulty, himself, but for me, the size of the congregation would only complicate the situation. Public speaking is second nature to Giovanni, whereas I am unaccustomed to any stage. He knew that the crowd would likely unnerve me, easily disturbing an already confusing range of feelings.

"We'll both get through this, Tom", he continued.

I found his manner and confidence quite steadying.

Beyond the sacristy door lay a cavernous church that would soon fill beyond capacity with individuals angry, confused and fearful. Irrespective of religious tradition, the believers among them would be searching for the hand of God. Scattered among these faithful would be humanists and agnostics with concerns a little less sacred. They do not seek consolation or escape through the intervention of the divine or the mystery of an afterlife. Being more down to earth, their challenge embraces paradox. How does one make sense of a senseless tragedy? Shortly, Giovanni would need to marshal all his intellectual forces and attempt to craft a meaningful narrative that would address all these diverse views. For now, words were superfluous.

We reached out and cocooned ourselves in an embrace of such depth that it divorced the bonds of time and space. We were not alone, yet we were unaware of the funeral directors and altar servers who passed by in respectful quiet. Though lasting only moments, time was as immobile as an unwound watch. Silent sobs. Tears both of love and sadness streaming onto each other's shoulders. I may not have possessed faith, but in this embrace I found peace. As we stepped back, I could feel Giovanni's strength. He could feel my love. We were both ready.

*     *     *

In my experience, most funerals attract a reliable core of mourners, if only family members and close friends. But accidental death, violent murder and young lives cut suddenly short create a uniquely abrupt, if however brief, pause in people's lives. These are the deaths that stir throngs into attendance—tending to draw numbers that rival a rock concert. Today's funeral was no exception and my expectations about the crowd proved correct. There was a reason the attendance was standing room only.

Giuseppe Lozano, a candidate for the U.S. Senate, returned home one evening to find his wife, two teenage daughters and 11 year-old son, all murdered in their family home in Los Angeles. That was a week ago.

As the police lieutenant assigned to investigate the killings, I would have been at the church anyway. But my attendance today was not just part of my job. I knew the family only too well, and now I watched as the priest, my best friend, presided over this traumatic service with a restrained elegance. How he could appear so calm, I do not really know, for he was both brother-in-law and uncle to the deceased.

The two of us have long approached death from different vantage points. I am a cop, a detective. I routinely see death, frequently the result of violence. Over the years I have become nearly immune to the feelings associated with other people's loss. The most bloody and senseless have become almost commonplace for me. Other than committing myself to solving the crime, I see no rays of hope in the violent end of life, and words of solace do not come easily.

Giovanni is no stranger to any of life's transitions, either. Having been a priest for twenty years, he is certainly as familiar as I am with the inevitable passage known as death. During his years in ministry he has consoled more grieving people than he cares to remember. So death, itself, poses no particular strain for him. Then again, this was not just death. It was unexpected, violent, senseless—and personal. And no one, not even a priest, is prepared for that. Yet, it was to Giovanni that I looked to gather strength for my own part in the service.

Although we grew up together and I knew him as well as he knew himself, I could not imagine from what depths he would summon the fortitude to lead this funeral. I doubt that he would find comfort this morning even in the hauntingly beautiful requiems of Mozart or Fauré. But then, Giovanni always had an untapped, interior calm. As the tower bells struck the hour, he processed down the aisle and the service began.

\*      \*      \*

Today's funeral, with its perturbing placement of caskets, evoked another in my memory. I had been on the police force for only a few years, and Fr. Giovanni was a young priest. It fell upon him to pastor another family through a tragedy with eerie similarity. That situation was a case of mistaken identity—not of person, but of address.

In Los Angeles, several numerical street names appear duplicated and are therefore easily confused, as in 109th Pl. and 109th St. It does not help that they are parallel, occurring one after the other and in numerical order between 108th and 110th. The only distinguishing characteristic is their designator.

This confusion served as a remote cause of that other catastrophe. A woman, her daughter and two grandchildren were all killed, the result of a drug deal gone wrong, a drug deal that did not involve the victims. The dealer sent his henchmen to an address. The correct house number, the correct street number—the wrong suffix. They broke in and killed four innocent people, sparing only a grandchild they did not find.

As I entered the church on that long ago summer day, it dawned on me that I had never attended a funeral with more than one body. I had, of course, been to memorial services commemorating multiple dead, such as those held on national holidays and occasions following plane crashes, earthquakes or other natural disasters. When I walked into the church, that day, I was taken aback.

Regardless the size of the church, there is something unsettling about the vision of multiple caskets at a single service, especially when children are coffined beside adults. That service was held in a large church, with several hundred people in attendance. Visual attention was drawn to the area between altar and pews, and the disparity among the caskets was incongruous, leaving the threat of unreason to claim the day.

The funeral mass took place on a particularly hot summer morning. Who ever thought of building churches in Los Angeles without air-conditioning? Fill them to capacity in the middle of July and you are guaranteed a sweltering experience. Even if the congregants do not pass out from heat exhaustion, how can they steel their attention on hymns, readings, sermons and prayers? How can they possibly focus on some uncertain promise of eternal life?

In my recollection, however, Giovanni kept all the intruding forces at bay. His engaging style personalized each element of prayer, leaving everyone in attendance to feel as though the priest was speaking directly to his or her own emotions. Even a non-believer would have to admit that Giovanni channeled a powerful and transcendent faith, at the same time displaying remarkably imminent compassion. He gently shepherded the family and congregation that morning, offering sensitive insight into God, the Scriptures, life and death. He enabled all present to think through the unthinkable and find trust in the hands of God. Something more was being required of him today.

5

# Chapter 2
## (1960)

We were six years old when Giovanni and I first met. It was the summer the Lozano family moved into our modest, Pasadena neighborhood, a little north of Los Angeles, and I had just finished kindergarten. My own parents had moved directly from Houston, Texas, to Pasadena in 1952, and were already living in our family home when I was born in 1954. As a result, I grew up knowing all the other children in the neighborhood.

In the 1950's and '60's there was not much to say about Pasadena, other than that it was the home of the annual Rose Parade and college football's Rose Bowl Game. The city rambled along the foothills, sheltered on one side by the San Gabriel Mountains and over-shadowed on the other by the big city of Los Angeles. It enveloped a wide diversity of neighborhoods, but never quite gelled them into a community. Not unintentionally, racial, and to some extent ethnic, zones were created, erecting invisible barriers between people. It was believed that these divisions made for a secure environment in which to raise children. In truth, the divisions simply made it easier for people to harbor false and negative attitudes toward the larger and more diverse populace.

Perhaps the greatest legacy of the civil rights movement and its subsequent legislation was the integration of previously segregated neighborhoods. Only by living next door to one another do we come to understand our commonality, that we struggle for the same kind of life and share the same concerns for our children.

The city fathers did not want to admit it, but in its early days Pasadena's biggest draw was that it served as a bedroom community for Los Angeles. Almost everyone worked in L.A. and the length of the daily commute threatened the city's future growth. In order to ease and speed the traffic between the two cities, the nation's first freeway was built, and Highway 11 became known as the Pasadena Freeway. It meandered along the Arroyo Seco, a major tributary of the Los Angeles River, at the break neck speed of 45 miles per hour. Well, it was break neck in its day, especially considering the winding turns necessitated by the decision to parallel the riverbed.

Over time, with the injection of Federal dollars, the highway number was changed to Interstate 110, the speed limit was raised, a concrete divider added and other attempts were made to make driving the freeway safer. But the twists and turns remain. I still like driving along the Pasadena Freeway late at night when there is little traffic. I push the pedal a little closer to the floor, inch the speedometer beyond the posted limits and test my ability to cut corners and straighten a winding road.

\*     \*     \*

The Lozano family was a good fit for our neighborhood. Marjorie Collins, who lived next door to us, was the neighborhood's unofficial social chair. So after the move was completed, she quickly organized a welcome party at the local park. A decision by enlightened city planners many years previous, resulted in a good size multi-purpose recreation area with plenty of playground space, thus freeing the children from the boredom of adult conversation, and the restrictions of overly cautious parenting.

Since it was summer, we were in the midst of daylight saving time, which meant long afternoons and evenings to play outside. For the adults, this time of year was perfect for parties and this occasion provided an opportunity to begin to know their new neighbors. Most of the fathers were drinking beer and playing cards or horseshoes. A few of the mothers drank vodka, and, of course they were all talking and laughing. We kids did not stick around the tables long enough to figure out what they were talking about. It just seemed like the same stuff as always, and, as always, we were completely uninterested. After inhaling our food, we were off, hoping to be forgotten for a few hours.

The Lozanos were the first Italians I had ever met. Of course, at six years old, I didn't even know what Italians were. All I noticed was that their names were a little different.

Luciano and Carmela Lozano had three children. Their first-born was named Bianca, but the family always called her "Bella", an affectionate Italian nickname meaning beautiful. The family was completed with the arrival of twin boys, Giuseppe and Giovanni.

My own family was slightly smaller. My parents, Thomas and Susan had only two children. My mother had miscarried on two occasions, and I ended up with no brothers and only one younger sister, Karen. This did not mean that there was no sibling rivalry.

Although I loved my sister in my own way, I never nicknamed her, "Bella". Fortunately, neither did my parents. Equally gratifying was that they didn't call her "princess". There was no need. I think she thought of herself as the heiress to some mythological throne. Whether due to those imaginary pretensions or her general psychological make up, she was extremely dramatic, and it probably didn't help that she was "daddy's little girl." My father, of course, did not call her that. Nonetheless, he clearly favored her. But, since I tended to live in a world of my own making, I really did not care. I spent sufficient time outside the house that I was not bothered by family favoritism.

\*    \*    \*

The day the Lozanos moved in was the first weekend of July. I was playing in the front yard, and so I was the first to meet the new kids. I had heard of twins and seen them on television shows, but never in person. The Lozano boys were identical. Actually, that is an understatement. Had they not been banded at birth, even their parents would have been unable to tell them apart. Every feature of their tiny bodies was an exact duplicate. Any distinguishing characteristics would not emerge for years, and those markers would not be physical, displaying themselves, instead, as differences in personality. The day their family moved in, I really thought I was seeing double, for the boys were certainly more alike than different. But then, their personalities were only beginning to develop.

Giovanni and Giuseppe were six years old that summer, the same as I. Specifically they were one month older. Although we got along almost instantly, a sense of bonding would come later. Before their arrival, I was the kid in the neighborhood that the others followed, for I possessed the qualities that they all admired. I was the fastest and took the greatest risks—hallmarks of a genuine leader. This enabled me to determine the games and set the rules. If there were any disagreements, I was also the judge. So it was probably not by accident that I, or my team, usually won.

At first, with the arrival of the twins and their sister, not much changed. Everyone liked the new kids on the block and I continued to be the leader. Still, they were wildly popular among the other kids, and this meant that their opinions also counted and had to be considered. The Lozano children changed the dynamic of the group just by being there, and they each possessed creative imaginations from which they invented new games. Suddenly I was learning new rules. This would have been threatening except that neither of the twins wanted to be the leader. I remained unchallenged and in charge of our neighborhood gang.

*　*　*

Looking back, our games may not have been all that creative, but we were a relatively poor neighborhood and we did not have the latest toys. Since our childhood predated the advent of personal computers, we never had anything like a Gameboy, an Xbox or Playstation. Many of our games were modeled on the shows we watched on television, especially the westerns.

For us, jumping off a roof (when our mothers were not watching) was the equivalent of a cowboy jumping from a cliff onto his horse. Garages and sheds became bomb shelters in war games. We raced around cars, under fences and behind homes to avoid being eaten by invading aliens from Mars.

We crafted rubber band guns with pieces of wood and clothespins. For us, there was dexterity in playing cowboys and Indians. It was necessary to learn how to shoot straight with these guns. I can even recall the thrill of making the first rubber band rifle, stretching the band to its very limit, then firing to see how far it could be launched and with what accuracy I could hit a target. Through it all, the stings from a rubber band hitting its mark left no lasting damage and no one ever lost an eye.

The Christmas we all received metal cap guns—six shooters, replete with holsters—was a real treat. All of a sudden the race was on to see which of us would become the fastest draw. Who would play the part of Billy the Kid or Wyatt Earp? Even the girls got into the act, competing for the role of Annie Oakley. However, being the fastest draw was not good enough. These guns made a great sound, but provided no proof we had actually hit someone. We had to guess who's imaginary bullet landed first. Fortunately for me, I was still the judge. As I recall, it was surprisingly easy to convince the other kids that they were just a tad slower on the draw.

In spite of our fertile imaginations for creating new games, we lacked an appreciative command of language. The result was that we named things rather simply. At the end of our street stood the largest tree within miles. It was believed to be about 100 years old and was a perfect landmark. We called it "The Big Tree". Equally compelling was our name for a large mound of dirt left over after the construction of a local high school. It stretched the length of a parking lot and we called it "The Big Hill". At least when someone said we should meet at one of these locations, we all knew where to go.

The big hill was the sight of another of our games. Come to think of it, the game had no name. In fact, it was less a game than an adventure. We would race our bikes up the side and then along the top of the hill, pretending we were on some mission as a government secret agent. The more adventurous among us would accept the dare to ride off the top of the hill, pretending to dodge bullets from enemy spies and hoping to land upright on the ground below. Occasionally, we ended up with a few scraped knees, or bent bicycle rims, but no serious damage. As I look back on it now, the hill probably wasn't even that big, but it looked huge through 6 year-old eyes.

As for the tree, well, it fell over in a storm one night. Nobody ever thought that was possible. For days we would all ride our bikes to the corner, stare for a while and share our memories and incomprehension. It was like holding a wake over the death of a friend. Eventually a city crew came, cut it up and hauled the tree away.

*     *     *

In September, Giovanni, Giuseppe and I started elementary school. About one-half the kids on the block went to the same parochial school we did. This gave me a leg up on the leadership role, though it didn't much matter for the first three years. The only leadership required occurred on the playing field, usually as team captain, and I, unfortunately, did not excel in every sport. During those years we all got to know the rest of the students quite well. We were in a large class, consisting of two rooms, each with 56 kids. In the first three years, the two classrooms were separate and we only mixed at recess and lunch.

By the time we started fourth grade, the sisters created homerooms, keeping us together for some of our lessons, but creating mixed classes for others, like reading and arithmetic. This mixing enabled us to get to know the other kids even better. The sisters also thought we should elect class presidents. Although there were a lot of kids, I won the first election, just barely beating out a popular girl named Nancy. When I look back on it, I probably won as much for being class clown as for my leadership skills. I caused just enough trouble to keep the days from becoming sheer tedium, and the rest of the kids awarded me with the presidency.

Neither of the twins ran for president that first election, but throughout our school days they presented me with sufficient competition in other areas. Giovanni was always a little smarter than I. At the end of each year it was anyone's guess which of us would come home the winner of more academic awards. For some reason, we also found ourselves in annual competition for the religious award. I never quite figured out how the nuns decided that one. It was based partly on grades, but also included our conduct in church and overall religious devotion. As it turned out, Giovanni usually won. I guess he was destined for the priesthood.

Where Giovanni was always a little ahead of me in academics, Giuseppe was always a little more popular socially. He was elected class president two different years, in sixth grade and again in eighth. If he had run in fourth grade, I would not have had a chance. Giuseppe was a natural for politics. Like his brother there seemed to be some kind of pre-destination at work.

Not for me. My future was anything but determined, at least from my actions. Where the twins managed to fulfill everyone's expectations, I was odd man out. Being a bit of a troublemaker, no one would have pegged me for a life in law enforcement. Perhaps it was the tendency to be rambunctious that left my mom hoping that I would go with Giovanni to the seminary. I have a different take. My frequent trips to the principal's office gave me insight into the criminal mind. I think all three of us ended up exactly where we belonged.

# Chapter 3
## (1968)

In elementary school much of our learning was sheer rote. The number of children in each classroom, coupled with the variances in learning ability, necessitated the teachers repeating everything three or four times. Since Giovanni, Giuseppe and I possessed good memorization skills, we were among those students who grasped information the first time around. Preparing for exams usually meant just showing up for class. In fact, it seems that the only time we opened a book at home was to do some written work that we had to turn in the next day. In my case, this created a sense of boredom in the classroom and may have contributed to my behavioral problems—that, and the fact that I loved the attention.

Life began to change for us in high school, though, as it does for most adolescents. We attended St. Francis High School in La Cañada, a city bordering Pasadena. It is an all boys school founded by the Capuchin Friars, an order of Franciscan priests, and it draws its student body from a wide area of Southern California, mostly the San Gabriel

Valley. Since St. Francis is a college preparatory school it demands adherence to rigorous academic standards. For the first time in our lives we actually had to study. That meant developing decent study habits with less time for play, except in the case of organized sports, such as baseball and football. Along with new academic challenges, there were personal and social hurdles to overcome.

It was during these years that the three of us began to mature and show the characteristics that would define us later in life. It was also in high school that Giovanni and Giuseppe developed into distinct persons. There were still no telltale physical characteristics by which to distinguish them, but they were clearly on the verge of becoming unique individuals. Since I spent so much time with the twins, I had learned to differentiate them by the same recondite observations their family members used. Also, I had become much closer to Giovanni than I would ever be to Giuseppe.

Perhaps it was our newfound study habits, perhaps it was less time outdoors, but as we began to read more, each of us became bona fide bibliophiles, our choice of material being a somewhat prescient indication of things to come.

Both of our families were poor. Not destitute, just poor. Whenever we would complain, our parents always reminded us of the Great Depression and how much they had to do without. One of my mother's favorite admonitions was,

"At least you have a roof over your heads and food on the table. It might not be good food, but it's food".

My mother seemed to believe that we should appreciate, or at least realize, that we were so much better off than they had been at our age. As if any children are that astute!

It was much the same in the Lozano household, and because of this, Giuseppe always said he wanted to be rich someday. It was not surprising, then, that he cultivated a keen interest in economics and American history. From this information he generated an encyclopedic knowledge of the robber barons and tycoons who built the banking, oil, steel, and railroad industries. In his own mind I think he fancied himself one of them, or at least hoped to become a modern day version.

Every American boy is enthralled by trains. Owning an electric train set, building the tracks and designing the routes is one of the great experiences of childhood. As Giuseppe began to learn more about the history of the railroads, he grew more than just enthralled. He became truly captivated. His boyhood interest in electric train sets gave way to the history and imagery of the real American railroad. Occasionally we would test his comprehension, quizzing him about the differences between Cornelius Vanderbilt on the East Coast and the big four on the West Coast—Leland Stanford, Collis Huntington, Mark Hopkins and Charles Crocker. These were names that most people only associate with cities and institutions named after them, of particular note being Stanford University, Huntington Library (founded by Collis' nephew Henry), and Crocker Bank (now Wells Fargo). Giuseppe found himself transported into a past from which he could detail the personal histories of each of these men. In all honesty, the books Giuseppe read were tilted more toward romanticism and imagination than truth. They played off the mystique of the rugged and wild West, with danger lurking around every bend. Brave settlers battled relentless forces of nature, the American Indian, greedy landowners, outlaws, and frequently each other. True to reality or not, there was something entrancing about those stories of the American railroad and Giuseppe was swept away.

On his sixteenth birthday Giuseppe gave himself a gift. He had managed to save enough money to buy a 1944 mint condition U.S. stamp commemorating the 75th anniversary of the completion of the first U.S. transcontinental railroad. He had the stamp laminated onto a money clip. I do believe this was his most prized possession. Although he rarely had more than a few dollars, he carried it everywhere and showed it off with devotion and pride.

Giuseppe's detailed focus on the big four led him to possess a proficient recall of their business practices, a skill that would serve him well in years to come. It did not matter that they were not particularly intelligent or skilled businessmen. It did not matter that they were crooks. These men truly earned the "robber" part of their moniker. Nobody manipulated the American public and government better than the "Big Four". Unfortunately, that was the skill that most embedded itself in Giuseppe's mind. He had found himself some heroes, and emulating them would lift him from his perceived poverty.

My own interests were decidedly different. One day my father gave me a copy of an Earle Stanley Gardner novel, one in a series of Perry Mason stories. It was titled "The Case of the Perjured Parrot". I was hooked. I proceeded, admittedly without much discrimination, to read every Perry Mason novel. I next read the "D.A." series, also by Gardner. I have often been told that I should have become a lawyer, and I admit to enjoying the clever courtroom tactics of the literary Mason. Still, my fear of public speaking prevented me from seriously considering that career path. Besides, I found myself drawn more to the character of Paul Drake, the private detective who frequently worked for Mason.

I followed these two series by reading some of Arthur Conan Doyle's Sherlock Holmes mysteries. Then I was introduced to Agatha Christie. As much as I enjoyed the Miss Marple stories, it was her archetypal detective, Hercule Poirot who captured my imagination. I saw my own attention to detail reflected in his investigative style and some of my friends suggested that I measured up well to Poirot's arrogance! Regardless, there was an upside for me. My fascination with these imaginary detectives of literature led me to forsake the disciplinary foibles of my childhood. I did not surrender all indiscretion, but I began to see things through the lens of law and order. At this time I decided to pursue a career in law, not as a lawyer, but as a cop. Eventually, I would accidentally stumble into the specific profession of detective.

While Giuseppe took a practical approach to reading, and I succumbed to the world of literary fiction, Giovanni tacked in a spiritual direction. Maybe it was the weight of all those religious awards he won in elementary school, but whatever the reason, he immersed himself in the lives of the saints. At the time that we attended high school, this did not seem as strange as it might today. Besides, some of those saints led very earthy existences before "getting religion". The great St. Augustine was even downright bawdy. Unfortunately, the published books Giuseppe read, such as "Butler's Lives of the Saints", tended to sterilize the stories making the subjects a little too ethereal. As such, it took an adroit reader to discover the truly salacious tidbits, usually nestled between the lines, or in publications not recommended by the Catholic Church. Giovanni was just such a reader.

Whenever he picked up an indication that there was more to the story than Butler let on, he tenaciously followed the clues until he uncovered the lascivious truth. Being a good friend, he would always pass that information on to me. But that knowledge exhausted my interest in saints. It was the only thing I had in common with them. I did acquire one additional benefit from Giovanni's preoccupation with ancient Christians. When I looked closely at some of their lives, I had reason to hope that even I could make it to heaven, despite the doubts of my parents and teachers.

*     *     *

Navigating the waters of adolescence was not easy. Where once we never questioned our parents, instead trusting them in everything, we suddenly discovered their fallibility. We had no doubt that our parents loved us. At the same time, they were old-fashioned and did not understand our generation. And they were way too strict. Being a Moran or Lozano meant unreasonable curfew hours and much less freedom than other kids in our school. There was a constant struggle afoot for each of us to become not just a man, but to become our own man. Even our sisters had to fight for the independence and maturity that would enable them to embrace womanhood with distinction.

During these years, while my sister was an emotional wreck, I kept most of my feelings under a tightly clenched control. My memory may be faulty, but I only recall raising my voice to my father on two occasions. Usually, when I needed an emotional outlet, I could vicariously rely on the Lozano family. The twins were going through the same process as I, but they did so with an Italian flair.

While Mr. and Mrs. Lozano came from Italy, Giuseppe and Giovanni were born in the United States. Yet, there was no need to teach the twins how to be Italian boys. They are bred to be hot-blooded and anyone who has ever seen Italians argue has seen that in action. They are the only people who can split eardrums merely saying "hello". Indeed, Italians have lifted simple communication to an unparalleled art form, seemingly shouting their way through every conversation. And when they get upset, the beauty of their anger is that it rarely erupts into physical blows. Setting aside the history of Julius Caesar, this may explain why modern Italians are useless when it comes to war.

I must admit that I enjoyed conflict at the Lozano residence. I learned a lot about what to say when I was angry and even how to say it. But I could never quite garner the courage to speak to my father the way the twins did to theirs. Of course, not everyday was filled with tension or fighting. It would take us many years to appreciate it, but our parents demonstrated their love for us in ways we could not then comprehend. Sadly, little things tend to get lost in fading memories. But I remember both our families permitted us more freedom than we acknowledged at the time. And we could always turn to our parents for help, no matter the problem. Even on occasions when we least deserved it, they were always there for us.

\*     \*     \*

None of us steered a very straight course when it came to the subtleties of dating. It seemed there were too many rules and the girls, like our sisters, were overly sensitive at this age. We were not. Our interests were oriented in a much more simple direction than the girls. Giuseppe stood out the most in this area. Even given his insensitivity and tendency toward self-absorption, he managed to emerge as a real player. It was that extroverted personality of his. On top of that, he exuded incredible sex appeal, and the girls responded accordingly. He was not able to maintain any relationship for long, but neither did he seem to care. He got what he wanted.

Still, Giuseppe was surprisingly reticent about sharing his exploits. It may have been the fact that the three of us were so close, but when any of us did speak about our conquests it was never of the locker room variety. The bragging that went on there was mostly wishful thinking. At home, in the privacy of our own conversations, we could be more honest, even giving voice to our insecurities. That was not acceptable in public.

Since Giuseppe and Giovanni were identical twins, one might have expected them to exhibit the same sex appeal. Not so. Forget about the pretty face and ripped abs. Like his brother, Giovanni had those. But sex appeal is something more than surface attraction. It percolates from every pore. Giuseppe had it. Giovanni did not. He was too wrapped up in his saints. I remember him being very put out one day. He had just finished reading about Catherine of Siena, some fourteenth century saint.

"You know, Gio", I began. "She's way out of your league. First of all, she's dead. And second, that book says she committed herself to chastity when she was seven. How fucking ridiculous is that"!

"Leave me alone, Tom".

The anger flashed in his eyes. It was so funny to see him get upset over something so stupid. But I knew his buttons, so I continued.

"No. I'm serious, Gio. What do you see in all those saints, especially the women? They're barely human. You couldn't even get a good lay out of most of them. And you certainly can't now"!

Giovanni turned his back on me, but I just kept talking.

"Now, Joan of Arc, there was a babe for you. I could see myself getting a roll with her! Imagine all that power and determination bundled into an exquisite French charm. And at her age, she probably had strong legs and firm breasts. Sure beats any of the girls we meet. Can you imagine what it would be like to spend the night with her? Not much sleep, I'll bet"!

"You're disgusting, Tom".

"Wait a minute", I drolled. "You really do get turned on by these women, don't you? I'll bet you've had dreams about Joan of Arc yourself. Or Theresa, the one they call 'The Little Flower'. Yeah, you'd like to deflower her"!

Giovanni picked up a shoe and threw it at me.

"Fuck you, Tom. You're such an asshole".

That was a rare slip of the tongue for Giovanni. Unlike me or Giuseppe, he rarely cussed. His language was impeccably clean. I was actually surprised at how easily the words left his lips.

"Just because you don't believe in anything or anyone."

"Oh, I believe", I said with a grin.

"Just get out of my room".

I should have been more sensitive toward my best friend, but what the hell? We were kids and sometimes it was fun getting each other upset. Unfortunately, it wasn't much of a challenge with Giovanni, and it quickly became boring. So I left him to his reading and went home.

By this time we were all three very different. Giuseppe was sensual. Giovanni was spiritual. I was somewhere in between, and just floated along until our junior year.

I first saw Debbie Rayburn when we were seventeen. At the time, I thought I had met the love of my life. Her first boyfriend, Mark Warren, was the son of a Calvary Chapel minister. Very fundamentalist and very strict. In those days, the organization was just getting started as an evangelical church. Calvary Chapel was founded by Chuck Smith in 1965, and like many modern day church movements, it was far removed from the authenticity of Jesus Christ. George Warren was one of Smith's premiere proteges, and in 1970 he became senior pastor at a new facility. It seemed somewhat odd to start a Calvary Chapel ministry in the Pasadena area. All of the worlds major religions were already represented. There were Jews, Buddhists, Hindus and Muslims. And among the Christians, most were committed to serious and traditional denominations. There were Catholics, along with other mainline churches such as Episcopalian, Lutheran, Methodist and Presbyterian, even Orthodox. And there was a smattering of congregational churches, including Oneonta, a church that takes its name from a city in New York, the birth place of Henry Huntington. By this time I was no longer committed to the Catholic Church. Still, I took St. Paul seriously when he cautioned about people preaching a false gospel. I just couldn't see what Calvary Chapel had to offer. Besides, it was hypocritical.

George Warren preached about God's love, but condemned all those who did not believe as he did. This included everyone who was not a baptized Christian, especially those who dared call God by a different name, whether it be Yahweh or Allah or anything else, and he seemed to have a particular hatred for Catholics. As for sexuality?

Well, if I thought that the Catholic Church repressed sexuality, it was nothing compared to Calvary Chapel. Rather incongruously, it was

Mark who literally wrestled Debbie's virginity away from her. That was OK, since it was before she and I met and since we connected on more levels than just sex. Or at least we thought we did. We certainly shared a lot of things in common, that is, until her religion entered the picture. Debbie's family belonged to the same Calvary Chapel where Mark's dad preached. Eventually, my being Catholic would prove to be a problem.

St. Francis High School had an all girls sister school, Flintridge Sacred Heart Academy, also in La Cañada. Students from other schools were welcomed to our joint activities, such as dances and football games. For me and Debbie, our first few dates were at these events, so our parents did not even know we were seeing each other. One day she invited me over to her house for dinner and I met her family for the first time.

Her mother was very nice and welcoming, but overly exuberant.

"Hello, Tom. Debbie has told us all about you and we are so happy you are here. You must relax and just be part of our family".

God! I was not looking for another family. Still, I was raised to be polite, so I responded,

"Thank you, Mrs. Rayburn".

She continued, "Debbie tells me that you're Catholic. You must come to church with us some Sunday".

Mrs. Rayburn was not given to subtleties and she was just a little too sunny for me.

"To tell you the truth", I said, "I don't go to church very often".

"Then you really must come along with us. You can learn all about the bible". She was so saccharine, I could feel the nausea welling up inside me.

"Mom", Debbie said. "Leave him alone. He just came over to have dinner". She turned to me and softly said, "Sorry. She tends to be very religious".

With the condescension only a parent can muster, Mrs. Rayburn looked at Debbie and said,

"Listen, young lady. Everything you have is a gift from God. You should appreciate it. The least we can do is listen to his word and live the way he tells us in the bible".

The rest of the evening went decidedly better. Debbie had two sisters and a little brother and they were all pretty cool. Her brother was only eight years old and was the center of attention during the meal. We managed to avoid talking about religion, and Debbie's mom accepted me even though I did not go to church. I kept my deeper beliefs to myself. Still, as the weeks went on, Mrs. Rayburn continued to press me to go to church with their family.

I had already begun to question my faith in God, or at least in the Church. By this time religion no longer meant much to me. I just didn't think that either faith or God were all that important. Period. Debbie's mom changed that, for she convinced me of one thing. I might not have wanted to be Catholic anymore, but I sure wasn't going to switch to an even more ridiculous church, either.

It was not so much the emphasis placed on the bible, or even the anti-Catholicism that got to me. Calvary Chapel was like the Worldwide Church of God (sadly, also based in Pasadena) and Jehovah's Witnesses. These groups believe in the bible, but only on their own terms. In spite of what various churches claim, nobody really takes the bible literally. They all interpret. But with these groups, only their interpretations are valid. It is not coincidental that all three have predicted the end of the world, and they have all been wrong. I still can't believe intelligent people buy all that crap. I mean, really. If someone makes a big deal about knowing when the world will end and then it doesn't happen? How do you not just laugh at them and walk away? Sure, people laughed at Noah and walked away, but when the rains came, Noah had the boat. Chuck Smith had nothing.

Debbie was dominated and manipulated by her mother. As a result we broke up and she went back to her ex-boyfriend. My brief relationship with Debbie convinced me of the futility of religion. To this day, I wonder what Mrs. Rayburn, or pastor Warren, for that matter, would have done had they known that Mark and Debbie were sexually active in high school. As for me, when I look back on high school, I realize that I did not get anything out of religion. All that happened was I lost a girlfriend.

As it turned out, I never officially left the Church. In fact, I started going back to Mass regularly, allowing my religious practice to become more and more routine. I easily cruised into a world of agnosticism, but did not quite have the energy to become an apostate. I figured that even if I did not want to believe in the Church anymore, I did not have the desire to fight it, either. I also did not relish the thought of engaging in that conflict with my parents. It was much easier to preserve familial peace by going to church on Sunday and being bored.

Giovanni and I remained very close in spite of my drifting away from God at the same time that he was becoming ever more enveloped by him. It was while we were in college, that the strength and depth of relationship would be tested—among all three of us.

# Chapter 4

## (1972)

During our senior year of high school, the twins and I began sorting our various options for university. By this time I knew that I wanted to be a cop, but I also wanted to go to college before entering the academy. Giuseppe wanted to study business, and Giovanni had already decided to pursue priesthood. It soon became clear that wherever we went, we would each go alone.

Financially, our families were of limited means, which meant that none of us would be able to afford college without scholarships. In that regard, we were all well suited. In eighth grade, the sisters administered an I.Q. test to our class. For some reason we were never given the official results, although the three of us scored somewhere near the top of the class. It may have only been legend, but someone claimed to have discovered that my score was equaled only by one of the girls, Jill Thompson. I took that to mean that the two of us had the highest scores, although the same phrase could have been used if we each had the lowest. Since Jill was a very smart girl, I assumed the former. Of course, the results of an I.Q. test do not guarantee anything. At the end of that same year, I took home only the English award, with Giovanni taking the prize for both mathematics and, as usual, religion.

More than any I.Q., it was our classwork in high school that prepared us for college entrance exams, known as the SAT. We all scored in the top percentile, and that was of great assistance to both Giuseppe and me in receiving scholarships for college. Because Giovanni entered the seminary, his SAT result was less important as also was his inability to pay full tuition. The Church is always in need of priests. In those days, at least, it frequently overlooked academic deficiency in favor of perceived spirituality. It also was willing to compensate for any financial limitations by picking up the total cost of education. None of us wanted to leave California, so in the fall of 1972 Giovanni entered St. John's Seminary College in Camarillo, Giuseppe went to Stanford University in Palo Alto, and I was off to the University of California in Berkeley.

*     *     *

Giuseppe decided to pursue a business major, and given that the business world is so competitive, he minored in psychology. In theory this would give him an advantage in dealing with competitors or rivals. He attended Stanford at a fortuitous time. During these years there was turmoil over the university's nickname and mascot for the sports teams. In 1930, an "Indian" became the official mascot for Stanford athletics. The image used was not flattering, depicting a Native American with a small head and large, bulbous nose. In 1972 a group of Native American students presented a formal petition to university officials to remove the "Indian" as the official mascot. By agreeing to the request, the administration handed the student body a guaranteed subject for forum discussion. How would the Stanford teams be known in the future?

Stanford and UC Berkeley are major rivals, being located in Northern California across the bay from each other. As such, I have always found it difficult to sympathize with the plight of Stanford students. But even I realized that naming the school team was important stuff. Yes, there were other subjects of concern in those days. The moon was becoming an ever more familiar landscape with six successful manned landings between 1969 and 1972, and the United States was embroiled in what seemed like an unending conflict in Vietnam, eventually costing more than 50,000 American lives. But choosing a nickname and mascot for Stanford sports was what really mattered—and Giuseppe was ready.

A promising moniker emerged at the top of the list. Since the university was founded by Leland Stanford, one of the Central Pacific's "Big Four", it seemed perfect to name the teams "The Robber Barons". It clearly had a catch to it and would have distinguished Stanford's mascot among the nation's top tier universities, many of which have rather ordinary nicknames, frequently invoking some local animal. UC Berkeley settled for the nickname Golden Bears, even though the Grizzly Bear from which the name was taken is colored brown.

Being a participant in the effort to rename Stanford's teams proved a dream come true for Giuseppe, and he was in his element. He dazzled the other students with information about the university's namesake. His knowledge was reverential, almost devotional. At times, it was even positively personal. His arguments in favor of the Robber Barons selection were passionate, lucid and convincing.

There were other submissions, which included the less imaginative and un-intriguing Trees, Sequoias, Railroaders, Spikes and Huns. When the vote was taken Robber Barons decisively won among the students, only to be rejected by the university's administration, choosing instead to revert to the pre-1930 name. To this day the Stanford sports teams are hopelessly called "The Cardinal"—simply one of the school colors, and their mascot is a tree. In spite of the student body being rebuffed by the administration, Giuseppe surfaced as a credible leader among his peers. At this time, his star was only a flicker, but it was rising.

In the charter for Stanford University we find the following: "The trustees... shall have power, and it shall be their duty...[to] maintain on the Palo Alto Estate a farm for instruction in Agriculture and all its branches." As a result, the university has frequently been referred to simply as "The Farm." Of course, it is not a farm. It is a first class university and the breadth of its academic endeavors reaches into all aspects of life. But it is not the only great university in California.

Across the bay from Stanford stands the crown jewel in the University of California system, UC Berkeley. The University of California system is internationally renowned, and unrivaled by any other in the world, both for its size and for its academic credentials. UC Berkeley is known as the system's flagship campus, in part because it was the first, and also, at least from my perspective, because it is the best of the nine campuses (a tenth one is planned for an opening in the city of Merced, in 2005).

UC Berkeley shares with Stanford a place of preeminence among the world's academic universities. Both are first class research and teaching institutions, consisting of top ranked scholars including, among others, Nobel Laureates, MacArthur Fellows and Pulitzer Prize winners. While Stanford meanders along more than 8,000 acres of Palo Alto, UC Berkeley rises into the hills above Oakland, providing wonderful vistas of the vast expanse of water, across which stands the city of San Francisco. Spanning the top of the bay, the Golden Gate Bridge provides a welcome invite to visitors entering the hub of Northern California life.

*　　*　　*

Intercollegiate sports has long been a significant part of university life in the United States. In the early 1970's, select major universities on the West Coast comprised the Pacific-8 Athletic Conference. There were two schools in the state of Washington (The University of Washington and Washington State University), two in Oregon (The University of Oregon and Oregon State University), and four in California (The University of Southern California, The University of California Los Angeles, and, of course, Stanford and Berkeley).

The rivalry and quality of athletics set the Pacific-8 Conference apart from all other conferences in the nation. To this day, the Conference leads all others in the number of national athletic championships, with three of the schools, (USC, Stanford and UCLA), holding the top three positions among all the universities in the U.S. The greatness of this competition sometimes leads to an overly exuberant display of school spirit among players and, especially, among fans. Over the years, Berkeley has emerged as a bit of a scourge in the conference. Even I have to admit that the sportsmanship at CAL, as the university is called, is not something to be proud of. While preparing his team for an upcoming football game, the coach at one rival university referred to UC Berkeley as "the most hellacious people in the history of the game." He was right.

Although Stanford has more championships than Berkeley, there is an area where the students at UC Berkeley set themselves apart, allowing to shine through an enviable depth of character. While the Stanford students were fixated on a name for their sports teams, we Berkeley students addressed the genuinely critical issues of our day. Our predecessors had carved out solid ground for activism with the Free Speech and Anti-Vietnam War protests beginning in the 1960's. That anti-war militancy continued into the 1970's and it was joined by calls for curriculum reform and the establishment of ethnic studies programs. At the same time UC Berkeley students championed women's rights, opening both the California Marching Band and the Faculty Club to women. Eventually, this led to Barbara Christian becoming the first black woman to be granted tenure at Berkeley. Throughout the 1960's and 1970's, Berkeley was the gold standard of activism. As a result, it frequently found itself setting the direction for other U.S. universities on rights issues.

Those were exciting times at Berkeley, but I did not share my involvement in these activities with my parents. I once referred to my mother and father as religiously conservative and socially liberal. I suppose, in hindsight, that I was trying to see reality the way I wanted it to be. I was no longer religious myself, and could not care less about my parents' religious practice. But I wanted them to be politically liberal. They were, but only to a point. My father greatly disappointed me when I discovered that he supported banning communist speakers from college campuses. I admired my father and I did not expect him to fear the ideas and speech of other men. I realized then, that change does not come easily. Fear is not only rooted in ignorance. It is channeled by whoever frames the exchange of ideas. Communism was never the threat to our country that politicians, both Republican and Democrat, claimed. What I found in my disillusion was that my parents were just like the rest of the nation, apprehensive and afraid.

As I began to question authority in college, I experienced my first identity crisis. I wanted to be a cop, but what I saw of law enforcement, specifically university police and national guardsmen, was not encouraging. These were authoritarian thugs cut from the same cloth as those who wantonly massacred the college students at Kent State University in 1970. I believed in law and order, but that belief was rooted in the freedoms of the Constitution, not the ranting cries of anarchy by a dictatorial president. I was convinced that it was possible to instill the rule of law without peering through the visor of a riot helmet. Instead of changing career paths, I poured myself even more deeply into the study of public policy and criminology, securing my degree in public administration. If I was going to be a cop, I would be different than the ones who corralled and beat demonstrating students.

*　　*　　*

Giuseppe had no such crisis of identity. Early on he exhibited a unique variation of the Midas touch and he executed it with exquisite perfection. He turned no objects to gold by mere contact. That is only a gift of legend and myth. Rather, he wove complicated concepts into effortless comprehension. Not that he did not work. He studied long hours and dedicated a great deal of time to his projects. It's just that the world of business came easily to him. No study and no task proved too difficult. The ease with which Giuseppe mastered his subjects, quickly made him a resource for the other students and served to create a personal mythology around him, one that he had no desire of discouraging. Yet, there was also a downside.

Giuseppe began to think that everything in life should come as easily to him as his studies. He also thought everyone else should serve and fulfill his expectations. As skewed as his perspective was becoming, he was well suited for this evolution. His fascination with the railroad magnates of the 19th century superseded a mere romanticizing of the past. He saw a part of himself in the industrialists of old. More than that, Giuseppe understood that a fundamental driving force of capitalism, some might even claim *the* driving force, is greed. That was a commodity he possessed in abundance.

To be fair to the robber barons, some of them used their wealth to accomplish a great deal of good. A somewhat misguided appreciation of their beneficence is demonstrated in the argument that without wealth, that same good could not be achieved. There might, for example, be no Stanford University. At the very least this is shortsighted. Good deeds cannot redeem the exploitation of workers, or the corruption of governmental institutions. Nor can they justify illegal or amoral business practices.

If such criticism results in class warfare, so be it. The rich have only themselves to blame. During the reign of the robber barons, the relatively few wealthy Americans who existed, basked in a sufficiently bright limelight that their forays into philanthropy appeared more magnanimous than they actually were. In subsequent years, a number of studies taking a closer look at endowment practices concluded that charity is not really part of the lifestyles of the rich and famous. Their generosity is somewhat convoluted, in that the endowments they make tend to benefit mostly themselves or their social peers who are also financially well off. In the truest sense of the word, it is not charity.

In the case of Leland Stanford, there was also a more sinister element at work. Although he was to serve as Governor of California, and then as a U.S. Senator, it is likely that he, along with the other three members of the "Big Four", was fated to go to prison, spared only because the records of their Contract and Finance Company were destroyed. An "accident", of course.

Giuseppe would take no such chances, learning, as he did, more about business practices from the heroes of his adolescence than he ever did in the classroom. Once he began to build his own empire, there would be neither trials nor threats of prison. The trail of his business success would officially be clean. All records would be sanitized long before they were recorded, and, therefore, would not need destruction.

*     *     *

Giuseppe was the only one of the three of us to join a fraternity. He pledged the Stanford chapter of Sigma Alpha Epsilon (ΣAE), the nation's largest fraternity. Most fraternities had changed quite a bit by the time we went to college. Many were still involved in philanthropic endeavors—just enough to effect the requirements of their charters; not enough to achieve the visions of their founders.

Giuseppe's fraternity had fallen into the habit of engaging in no philanthropy at all during the semesters. Toward the end of the academic year, usually in March or April, they would call the priest at the university's Catholic Community and ask if they could help with the community's weekly ministry to the poor in Palo Alto. They figured that such minimal outreach was sufficient to maintain legitimacy. Not unlike me, Giuseppe had no particular need for religion, so this annual trek to serve the poor was the closest he came to any church while away from home.

Most of the university's fraternities were not, as depicted in the movie "Animal House", dens of iniquity. Still, the average house party concluded the following morning after more than a few fraternity brothers had slept with newly encountered sorority sisters. This part of fraternity life definitely appealed to Giuseppe, for the sex appeal that oozed from him in high school, while effective, was really rather juvenile. In college, however, it evolved into a winsome, if still only superficial, charm. He grew taller, trimmer and more dashing, with a Cary Grant sway in his walk and a Frank Sinatra timbre to his voice. In another era people would have called him debonair. He could have almost any girl he wanted and frequently did. Then again, not all college girls are easy—not even at Stanford.

Yolanda Cummings was beyond gorgeous. Simply put, she was stunning—rich brunette hair sparklingly cascading to her shoulders. It never looked wet, yet had a moist quality with just enough droplets to keep it from being straight while still lacking enough to call it curly. She had sea-green eyes and a thin nose turning up almost imperceptively at the tip. Her figure was just shy of perfect, making it all the more enticing. Yolanda enjoyed an elegant, graceful lilt to her bearing. She was soft spoken, yet self-assured. When she smiled, she did not light up the room. She ignited it. Everything about her manner was contagious. It was impossible to be in her presence without feeling completely beguiled. Perhaps, as the saying goes, blondes really do have more fun.

Perhaps even, as the Germans claim, redheads have three times the sex drive of other women. What matter? When it comes to marriage and motherhood, every man wants a brunette.

With all that Yolanda had going for her, and with every male student aching for the opportunity to date her, one might have expected her to cast a shallow persona. To the contrary, Yolanda was one of the most astute members of Stanford's student body. Her intellect was a match for any faculty member, not to mention the other students, and her mind was an information and knowledge trap. More to the point, she was not deceived by Giuseppe's charisma. Intrigued, perhaps even enchanted, but not in the least fooled.

I thought then and still do today that in charm, in physical beauty, and in intellect, Yolanda was the perfect match for Giuseppe. Beyond that, her response to his many advances was to remain just out of reach. She was not really resistant. Quite the opposite. Her coy and flirtatious manner was a way to keep him interested and at the same time under control. Giuseppe was marionette to Yolanda's puppeteer. She would eventually surrender, but on her own terms.

*   *   *

Giovanni's alma mater, St. John's Seminary College, was the most unusual of our three institutions. It was built on a hill overlooking its companion graduate school and the city of Camarillo. The graduate school was called St. John's Seminary. It was built in the 1940's and looked a place out of time—very monastic, enveloped by a quaint, old-world aura and charm. It was here, during four years of graduate study that the seminarians were immersed in the subjects that would directly impact everyday parish life. Here they were taught the various disciplines of theology, as well as Scripture, Canon Law, Pastoral Counseling, Liturgy, Preaching and Church History.

Although the college campus was only completed in 1965 and had a distinctly visual appeal, St. John's was not a contemporary institution. From the hill on which it stood, it was as anachronistic as Brigadoon. The difference being that Brigadoon dissolved into the Scottish mist at nightfall, not to return for a hundred years. Mist or no mist, St. John's was here to stay.

In previous days at the seminary, as the evening sky shrouded the hilltop, one could gaze over the city of Camarillo, and glimpse only a few flickers of light seemingly mirroring the stars of the early night. But times and populations change, and by the 1970's, the mirror was shattered. Camarillo began to resemble a mini metropolis with the lights of the city obscuring the heavenly luminaries.

Camarillo, itself, is part of a region known as the Pleasant Valley—an expanse of incredibly fertile farmland in the state of California. A virtual paradise, it was once home to large citrus groves, and rich walnut and avocado orchards. A wide variety of vegetables are still grown in the valley, and to this day it produces the sweetest and most flavorful strawberries in the entire nation. Sadly, much of the land has been paved over for roads, homes, churches, schools, shopping centers, even some of Joni Mitchell's lamented parking lots. The treasured trappings of modern life.

*     *     *

For Giuseppe and me, college was a time to find our place in the real world. For Giovanni it was a time to retreat from reality. My own religious bias may not leave me entirely objective, but it seemed that much of his seminary training was divorced from life as it truly was; life as it should have been—even in a seminary college.

St. John's was a closed institution and during most of Giovanni's time he was cloistered in Camarillo far from family and friends. It would be unfair to compare it to a prison. After all, occasional jailbreaks occurred even in places as famed as Folsom or Alcatraz. By contrast, no one ever escaped St. John's. Technically, of course, the seminarians were not in prison or sequestered behind bars. Neither were they monitored by armed guards. What restrained them was the force of their vocational aspirations. Some decided against becoming priests, and they simply left. Those who remained were set free for one weekend every five or six weeks. Students who drove themselves to the seminary were required to register their vehicles and keep them unmoved in the parking lot. This, in the 1970's.

As with any closed institution, the seminarians tended to develop a myopic vision of life, with insignificant events over-arching reality. This created a rather strange disconnect at St. John's. The college required a major in philosophy, and yet the students focused their attention not on the progress of the human race or events in the outside world, such as the war in Vietnam, but primarily on what was happening within the institution, itself. At St. John's there were no anti-war protests and no marches for equality. Those were freedoms the administration would never extend and the student body would never demand. In retrospect, it seems to me that the seminarians were so focused on the goal of ordination that no one considered whether he might actually, as an individual, have an impact on society at large—an attitude rather peculiar for a group of men studying philosophy. No lectures in the classroom and no preaching in the chapel ever questioned that lack of vision.

At St. John's there were no intercollegiate sports, so the students could not even argue over naming a school mascot. The closest they came to college sports were intramural competitions and the annual football rivalry with the "old men" in the graduate school.

The seminarians at St. John's were expected to be respectful and dutiful at all times—to surrender their minds in the classroom and their spirits in the chapel. In the end, there is more than one way to be a prisoner.

\*     \*     \*

An isolated existence can, however, distill certain elements of humor. In keeping with the old adage, "familiarity breeds contempt", such close confines can often lead to a refined sarcasm. One such example occurred at the faculty dinner table and it involved two unique professors. The first was a philosophy professor from the Deep South—Louisiana, to be specific—by the name of Fr. Frank Hopkins. He fancied himself a southern gentleman. This meant that he never raised his voice, nor did he whistle in public (that was simply too crude and plebeian). The second was a history professor, Monsignor Joe Theophilus. An odd little character, he was a sports family scion, though, he himself, commanded no competence in physical exercise. What he lacked in athletic ability, however, he compensated with intellect. In this he proved a mental gymnast, truly a brilliant man, with a humor tending toward the sardonic.

During his first year, Giovanni was assigned to wait table for the faculty. He was on duty one evening when a classic white wine was served with dinner. In a soft tone of voice, Hopkins attempted to interrupt a professorial discussion, pointing out that the wine was not chilled. No one paid him any heed. Again he noted that the wine was not cold enough. Still no response. Refusing to raise his voice, yet successfully achieving annoyance, Hopkins made a third attempt, saying,

"This wine would be much better if it were chilled."

Having heard enough about the wine, Theophilus turned his head, and without interrupting his train of thought, tacked on the phrase,

"Put it next to your heart, Frank"!

It was a funny enough comment, but it also suggested that Msgr. Theophilus had no particular affection for Fr. Hopkins. Giovanni could not ignore the humor, but he kept his laughter to himself, not wanting to give away the fact that he was eavesdropping on the faculty discussion. Still, humor was not Giovanni's only observation. He was taken aback by the fact that there was tension among the professors.

Giovanni was so driven by an idealistic concept of religion and priestly life, that he thought every priest liked every other priest. That there was always perfect decorum among them. He was so intent on removing human foibles from his own life, that he was not prepared to witness them among his mentors, and he thought that night's humor out of place.

It was this same attitude of Giovanni's, this desire to seek some ridiculous perfection, that motivated him to constantly try to convert me. From my side, it was probably the biggest annoyance and source of conflict between us during our college years. I just wanted Giovanni to leave me alone. On the other hand, discovering unpleasant realities among the faculty, coupled with their biting humor, may have humanized him a bit.

Over the next three-and-a-half years, Giovanni had come to admire Msgr. Theophilus, and thought him to be probably the most intelligent man he had ever met. He looked up to the monsignor and considered him a genuine role model. He had even come to appreciate his sense of humor.

As with other institutions of higher learning, St. John's was accredited by the Western Association of Schools and Colleges. Giovanni had a classmate, Bob Carrington, who was a bit of a clown with a penchant for not thinking before he spoke. At times this led to very funny humor, at other times, it was just obnoxious.

Bob had been selected to escort the WASC committee around campus during one of its periodic visits. Giovanni mentioned that in a discussion with Msgr. Theophilus who expressed concern that he might say something out of place.

"Not to worry", Giovanni assured him. "Bob said he is going to bite his tongue".

"Well", replied Msgr. "Let's hope he doesn't break the skin. He might poison himself".

Of course, Giovanni laughed. He wanted to develop the same kind of humor, which I found interesting, because Giovanni was never sarcastic while we were growing up. Still, sarcasm seemed to develop as an integral part of seminary life.

At the end of each year, the graduating seniors were treated to a roast. One year there was a student named George Mellman. He was a noted gossip. Other students often joked that if anyone wanted to broadcast a secret, they should first tell George.

At his graduation roast, three students dressed up in a single outfit, so that their heads protruded from the top. They walked up on stage and each one in turn introduced himself, saying:

"I'm George Mellman".

"No. I'm George Mellman".

"No. I'm George Mellman."

The skit was a huge success, and George was appropriately mortified. The next morning he showed up to class, looked at his classmates, and with wonderful religious flare, simply cried out,

"Judases!"

The seminary was sufficiently dull that anything out of the ordinary could pass for excitement. On the property stood an old tower from which St. John's received its water supply. It had a disgusting taste as it exited the faucets, a taste that could only be masked by bringing the temperature near freezing with a great deal of ice. As Camarillo continued to expand, the seminary finally surrendered its dependence on the well and tapped into the city's main water supply. This improved the taste of the water, and also occasioned the demolition of a landmark.

The day the water tower was to be dismantled and removed, most of the students formed a gallery on the field to witness the end of an era. In a bid for attention, one student, Jack Johnson, walked along the line of students handing out imaginary papers and barking,

"Programs. Get your programs here".

He did not garner quite the attention he had hoped. According to Giovanni, Jack was not the most creative individual. A few minutes later he asked,

"When does it come down"?

Bob Carrington, replied,

"Read your program".

Bob got the laughs, Jack, the chagrin.

I think the seminary, for all its value, had a corrupting influence on Giovanni's personality. By the time he graduated, he had developed a new sense of humor, but it was still crude, far from the refinement of Msgr. Theophilus. In Giovanni's case, the humor was becoming increasingly cruel. It is one thing to make another person the subject of a joke. It is quite another to make him the butt of the joke.

Giovanni would never admit it, but I think it was in the very nature of St. John's. For if the overly familiar character of the seminary did not steer the students to contempt, it certainly instilled in them the same kind of sarcasm that possessed the faculty. I, for one, did not like the way this side of Giovanni's personality was developing.

\*  \*  \*

In those days, St. John's was a bastion of tradition. Watching 200 adult males promenading the grounds in Roman cassocks was to be transported back in time. It was as if each man was auditioning for a role in "Going My Way", or one of the other early Hollywood films depicting Catholic priests. An expected sight in a pre-WWII seminary, it was nothing short of bizarre by the 1970's. As incongruous as it may seem, given that the wearing of the cassock was so insignificant on a grander scale, the issue became almost the equivalent of the Berkeley protests. Naturally, there was no rioting. There were no sit-ins or taking over administration buildings. But there was controversy.

It is hard to believe, but some students actually enjoyed the cassock. Limited by their inadequate imaginations they engaged in a flight of fancy, seeing themselves as dashing young clerics. They were young, but most were hardly dashing. And they were not clerics. That would not come for several years. While these men were playacting the role of priest, other students had practical reasons for liking the cassock. No one could see beneath the black robe, so they could get away with wearing gym shorts instead of trousers. This left them ready to bolt the classroom after the final bell to claim the best courts for basketball, tennis or handball. First come, first served. Indeed, the cassock had its useful side. Still, it all looked so silly.

The proposal under debate, the suggestion that caused such upheaval at St. John's, was that the cassock be worn only for religious services in the chapel. During the rest of the day, a simple clerical shirt would be the norm. It was suggested that this be a trial experiment for a few months. Who could object? Oh yes, that would have to be Msgr. Theophilus. He expounded the theory that there is no such thing as an experiment. If this change were initiated it would become permanent and he was opposed to the whole idea. Giovanni and a number of other students knew he was correct about experimentation, but they were angling for a permanent dress code change, and this was an important first step. They organized and persuaded the majority of the students around the trial concept. The faculty agreed. The cassocks were finally on their way out, and none too soon.

It was sad to see intelligent people, especially my friend, spend so much time on something so picayune. But that was the nature of the institution. There wasn't anything else going on. If nothing else, the seminary enabled Giovanni to develop a crafty style of argument. Few of his peers could make the distinctions he did.

*     *     *

Individually the three of us all did well during these years. We were each successful academically, we built solid social lives in our new environments and our future goals emerged with incontrovertible direction and clarity of purpose. Still, the differences that began to surface among us in high school became ever more apparent.

We would not find the cause in the simple fact of physical separation. For the first two years of college, Giuseppe and I carpooled to and from campus, taking turns on the use of the car while at school. I spoke with Giuseppe on the telephone occasionally and frequently with Giovanni. No, the emerging distance was internal to each of us. It was sometimes warm, often cool and the origins clearly pre-dated college life.

By the time we were sixteen, I had begun to notice the circumference of Giuseppe's world shrinking. From the way he used his friends, to the way he interacted with his family, it appeared that the only thing that mattered to Giuseppe was Giuseppe. It was obvious that he knew what he wanted and how to get it. That was not the problem. It reflected a narcissism that perhaps was not so identified at the time. I suppose our families and teachers all chalked it up to youth and immaturity, but the result was that it went unchallenged and so unchecked.

At the same time, Giovanni was becoming less and less a doppelgänger. An opposite world was being formed around him, one that was expanding. Giovanni developed a profound interest in the poor and volunteered to help with various church outreach programs. At first I thought this was due to the service requirements of our Confirmation program. But it was more than that. Giovanni really did care about other people.

As usual, I was somewhere between the twins. I was not as self-centered as Giuseppe, nor was I as altruistic as Giovanni. In terms of service projects, I did only what was required. I suppose Jesus would have called me "lukewarm." Due to my interest in law, I was beginning to see the world comprised not exactly of opposites, but in ever clearer terms of right and wrong. I could see that the way Giuseppe treated other people was wrong, and there was something very right about Giovanni's commitment to service. I admired him for it, but I could not divorce this service from the religion that was developing a progressively strong hold on him. At that age, I guess a middle ground appealed to me. Or perhaps it was just my way of avoiding any real commitments. At any rate, these differences became more pronounced in college.

Giovanni developed an almost missionary zeal for the Catholic Faith. He felt a need to convince me that I was wrong to not believe in God, and he was determined to bring me back to the church. He wanted to save me. I found his fanaticism almost as annoying as he found my irreverence. If I did not care about my immortal soul, why should he? Giovanni's labors were fruitless. My approach to religion was more disinterest than it was objection. I simply did not see the need. Still, his insistence irritated me. But I knew his vulnerabilities, I still knew which buttons to push. At times I am sure I succeeded in my efforts to be offensive and obnoxious while commenting about faith, especially my ideas about God. But I had had enough. There were occasions when our arguments became so vociferous and tinged with disgust that I was sure our friendship was at an end. However, given the opportunity to calm down, we discovered affection to be far more powerful than anger. Each argument ended with a commitment not to talk about religion again. And each commitment was broken—until we graduated. Giovanni shed his zeal in graduate school, and I softened my reciprocal attacks on his beliefs.

Something deeper and more intangible separated me from Giuseppe. During our long rides to and from university, Giuseppe would often ride for hours without speaking. This was not the comfortable silence of close friends who can wordlessly relax in each other's company without the need for verbal communication. Neither was it the silence of friends who have just completed an argument and desire to be anywhere but in each other's presence. Giuseppe and I were just drifting apart, as if we had little in common. We clearly did not have much to say to each other. Our values were no longer the same. I was not interested in Giuseppe's desire and plans to become a millionaire, and his concerns were far from the world of public policy or law enforcement. Our families and our mutual love for Giovanni were all that held us together. It would remain that way over the years to come, and it would be enough.

# Chapter 5
## (1976)

Destined as he was to be a priest, Giovanni moved seamlessly through the seminary system. He experienced very little anticipation that summer, for following vacation, he returned to the familiar city of Camarillo to begin his graduate studies at St. John's Seminary. The graduate school was called the Theologate. Giuseppe, on the other hand, was filled with excitement. He would be moving some 3,000 miles, all the way across the country, to seek a master's degree in business from Harvard University. As for me, at the end of college I was finished with my formal academic education and ready to become a cop.

I had given a lot of thought as to which department to join. Pasadena's police force was too small for my liking. The same was true for most of the cities in Southern California. Since I did not want to move away, I really had only two choices—The Los Angeles Police, or the Los Angeles County Sheriff.

Growing up in Pasadena we were quite fortunate to have our own police force. It was a small department, and for the most part, the officers and the community were on good terms. Incidents of police violence and abuse were rare. That was not the case everywhere else.

At St. Francis High School I met kids from all over Southern California, and heard horror stories about the Los Angeles Sheriff Department. This is the agency that runs the jail system, covers all the unincorporated areas of the County of Los Angeles, and is contracted out to provide law enforcement for some of the smaller cities that do not have their own police force. Many of the sheriff officers hold only a high school diploma. Lack of education, however, is not the real problem, for the same can be said of police in many departments. From the stories of my classmates, it appeared as though the LASD had very low admission standards. Simply put, these guys were goons. It was as if the officers had escaped Germany following WWII, changed their names at Ellis Island, and immediately went to work for the Los Angeles Sheriff Department. Or course, when I say they escaped Germany, let me clarify that these were not men fleeing the Nazis in fear of their lives. They were the Nazis.

The Los Angeles Sheriffs had a contentious relationship with many of the communities they policed. Within the various divisions of the department it is still not uncommon to find secret gangs of sheriffs, replete with code names and unique tattoos. This cannot be dismissed with the observation that LASD is the largest sheriff department in the nation, nor the fact that they must patrol such a vast territory. As much as any despotic regime, the LASD defines quotidian corruption. Most of my friends would have preferred no policing at all to what they experienced with the Sheriff Department. My limited choice was easily whittled down to one.

*    *    *

"Through these doors pass the world's finest police officers". So reads a plaque donated to the Los Angeles Police Academy by the graduates of 1968. Without question I have a strong bias in favor of the LAPD. That predisposition aside, the plaque is not mere hyperbole. The Los Angeles Police Academy is the paragon of law enforcement training. And yet, as deserved as the reputation is, it was a long time aborning.

Until the 1960's, the perception of the city of Los Angeles was captive to its formal name: "El Pueblo de Nuestra Señora de la Reina de Los Ángeles del Rio de Porciúncula"—"The Town of Our Lady Queen of the Angels of the Porciúncula River". In either language, that is a mouthful. The simple truth is that few people took Los Angeles seriously. Overshadowed by New York and Chicago to the East, and San Francisco to the North, Los Angeles was slightly more than a town or pueblo. This image was reinforced by the fact that until 1964, no buildings in the city could be taller than the 32-story City Hall. To some extent the reputation of the Los Angeles Police Academy mirrored the importance of the City of Los Angeles.

The Academy is built in the hills of Elysian Park, just a few minutes from downtown Los Angeles, right next to baseball's Dodger Stadium. And yet, before the 1960's most Angelenos would have been hard pressed to say where it was. This, even though there was sufficient signage including the "Academy Road" exit from the Pasadena Freeway.

Hollywood, "The entertainment capital of the world". Though truly a self-serving and self-proclaimed phrase, no one can ignore the impact of Hollywood on American culture, and on the world. Already well established as a center for film, Hollywood was a perfect fit for the new medium of television, providing an opportunity to visualize the serial stories of radio. As the city's renown grew, the studios took an interest in portraying life in Los Angeles.

The proximity of the Los Angeles Police Academy to the television industry made it a natural element for such shows as the groundbreaking and dramatic "Dragnet", the success of which led to "Adam 12". Unlike the rather silly "Car 54, Where are You?" that buffooned police work in New York City, the two Los Angeles dramas realistically portrayed the life of the city's police, including both the boredom and the theatrics, and brought their stories into the living rooms of the American public. They were so popularly received, that people around the nation who would never dream of visiting Los Angeles, were made to feel like natives with the ability to identify the city's culture, street names and landmarks.

Los Angeles has long been a center for media attention, in part due to the residence of so many famous actors and Hollywood power brokers. So it is no surprise that the LAPD, and by extension the Academy, would draw significant scrutiny. This is a level of analysis not accorded the Sheriff Department, which is not headquartered within the city of Los Angeles. The rise in the city's stature, the environment of Hollywood, and various policies created by Darryl Gates, the soon-to-be Chief of Police, all converged to make the Los Angeles Police Academy the quintessential training center that it has become.

I entered the Academy in July of 1976. Four months of grueling training followed. During that time I proved myself physically fit, but then again, no one graduates who is not. Donut shops are a luxury for sworn officers already on patrol, not for cadets. One of the training requirements involves a near-constant running up and down the hills of Elysian Park and double-timing to classes. Coupled with the rest of the training and security background checks, these four months successfully weeded out those unfit for or incapable of the rigors of police life. Throughout my training, I was a competent member of my class. Though not the smartest, I still competed academically. I spent extra time on the shooting range, and upon graduation I had achieved the level of sharpshooter. I also was awarded the medal for most physically fit.

*    *    *

The following June, during my rookie year on the force, a friend of mine, Officer Tim Harkin, was married and the ceremony took place at the Academy. On the grounds is an alluring area called "The Rock Garden". Unofficially, police officers and cadets refer to it as the "baby maker". In the center is a large staging surface perfectly designed for wedding ceremonies. The Rock Garden is tiered in both directions with numerous secluded sections where couples have been known to disappear for lengthy periods of time. Since the entire area is unlit, there is a guarantee of privacy, and no one goes in search of the wayward. Hence, the nickname.

It was at Tim's wedding that I met my wife, Emily Cartwright. She was the Maid of Honor and I was a groomsman. I was paired with an attractive woman, but it was Emily who caught my eye. On my part, it was love at first sight. Emily, not so much. The more time we spent together that evening, and the more I tried to impress her, the more conceited she found me. Emily was not seeing my best side, and needless to say, we did not avail ourselves of the sequestered recesses of the Rock Garden. As I recall, they were fairly well occupied that night anyway. However, there must have been something I did right that evening, because Emily agreed to see me again. Hoping to give her enough time to forget what she did not like about me, I suggested a date a fortnight later. I was determined to be on better footing. In that I proved successful, and we dated regularly for the next two years.

I always expected to fall for someone like Yolanda Cummings. Emily was surprisingly different. To begin with, she was blonde, not brunette and she was not overly-buxomed. She was also a little on the short side for me. After all, I stand 6' 1", and she barely measured 5' 5". But whatever she lacked in physical attributes, she counterpoised with personality. Truth be told, had it not been for Emily, I probably would have sunk into a chasm of superficiality.

Emily was British and had come to the United States to study journalism. Upon graduation, she was hired as a columnist for the Los Angeles Herald Examiner. Once the largest circulating afternoon newspaper in the country, it had already begun to wane in popularity. Preferences were changing. The commute to and from work left people's energy depleted by the time they returned home in the evening; it was much less demanding to get the news from television; broadcast stations made greater efforts to address local as well as national and international stories. The end result was the decline and eventual disappearance of the afternoon newspaper. The Herald Examiner would shutter its doors in 1989, but for the time being, Emily was a prized commodity. Her specialty was international affairs, providing unique insight into the mind and activities of Great Britain. This proved of particular value during the Falkland Islands War between Argentina and the United Kingdom. Emily brilliantly articulated the case for British sovereignty over the islands.

Emily and I were married in the summer of 1979. Giovanni was not yet a priest, and I wanted him to be best man. But since he had just been ordained a deacon that May, he was able to preach and to perform marriage ceremonies. I figured that having him officiate was even better. Actually, I wanted him to be both best man and officiant, but he considered that too pretentious. In the end, I asked Giuseppe to be best man. Giovanni has always been at his best while preaching, even at the beginning of his career. That day he did not disappoint, but delivered a stunning and provocative homily, surpassing my highest expectations.

My career in the LAPD was as much the luck of timing as anything else. By the time I graduated the Academy, drug and gang violence had become epidemic in Los Angeles, particularly in the poorer parts of the city. The most notable example is the area known as South Central, primarily populated with minorities and the very poor. In 1971 President Richard Nixon declared his now infamous "War on Drugs". Darryl Gates, who would become Chief of Police in 1978, made this his personal obsession. It was also to prove a springboard for my own career.

I was initially assigned to the 77th Station for my year of probation. The required reassignment upon completion of that first year, found me transferred to the Southeast Division. During two years of patrol I received recognition for making arrests and getting guns and drugs off the street. My success in this endeavor led my captain to tap me for our division's C.R.A.S.H. unit. The acronym stood for "Community Resources Against Street Hoodlums". In our division it was particularly successful.

Two gangs, known as the Crips and the Bloods turned the streets of South Central into a war zone. The roots of the conflict between these two gangs were multi-faceted, but the fighting was continually fueled by drugs. This all resulted in numerous drive-by shootings that often left innocent bystanders, frequently children, as the victims. Gates used the C.R.A.S.H. units indiscriminately. Although never officially voiced or formally written, we had one objective and one only: to get gang members off the streets by any means. If that meant planting evidence on the suspects we questioned, even guns and drugs, well, so be it. Our justification was simple. A suspect might not be guilty of a particular crime, but none of these gang members was an innocent, either. As my mother used to tell us when we were punished at school for something we did not do, "This makes up for the times you were guilty and didn't get caught". A hopeless Irish Catholic. On the streets of Los Angeles, planting evidence was easy. In spite of any protestations, prosecutors and jurors were more likely to believe cops than gang bangers.

Like many other officers, I took my lead from the Chief. At the time, I was filled with esteem for Darryl Gates, thinking he was a godsend for the city of Los Angeles. Gates understood the realities of the street and realized that law enforcement agencies were ill-prepared for the new breed of criminal that infested the city. These gang members had become more heavily armed, and hostage situations were becoming more common place. Even before being appointed Chief of Police, Gates developed "SWAT". Originally he wanted to call it "Special Weapons Attack Team." However, as one might say in today's parlance, that was politically incorrect and so he settled for the equally intimidating, though less controversial name, "Special Weapons and Tactics." Regardless of the moniker, it achieved the same goals and even served as the inspiration for a short-lived television show of the same name.

Once gates became Chief, he proved himself a no-nonsense leader. He used the tools at his disposal and he got results. He established the C.R.A.S.H. units which, in my opinion, were significantly responsible for the reduction of gang violence. He employed the awesomely intimidating battering ram as a weapon against suspected drug houses. It was actually capable of knocking down entire walls. One of Gates' lasting legacies is the Drug Abuse Resistance Education program, known as "DARE". It targets school children in an attempt to educate them about the dangers of drugs.

I first came to the attention of Chief Gates because of the C.R.A.S.H. unit. Quite often Gates, himself, would be present in the wee hours of the morning serving search warrants, especially when the battering ram was being used. It was clearly his pride and joy. We would gather our unit to prepare our "Game Plan" operation and also to debrief after a raid. Gates liked the way that I, as investigating officer, commanded presence. He found me articulate. He also liked the way I gathered intelligence on the local gangs.

For my part, I was not just a young cop, starry-eyed with admiration. In those days I completely bought into the concept of fighting fire with fire. I did what I had to do in order to clean up the streets, and I was successful, evidenced by the fact that Gates took note of my work. There was, however, a toll.

My involvement with C.R.A.S.H. coincided with the demise of my marriage. Emily wanted children, I was hesitant. Still, we could have worked through that problem. But she could not accept what was happening to me, what she referred to as a change in personality and corruption of values.

I had never intended to become a detective. In March of 1982, Gates called me into his office.

"Moran, you've been doing excellent work in C.R.A.S.H".

"Thank you, sir".

"We need people like you. However, I think you can do more. Have you ever thought about taking the detective exam"?

"Frankly, no, sir. I like what I do".

"You've got a future, Moran, and I see you moving up. Don't get me wrong. You've made a huge contribution in C.R.A.S.H. But you have natural instincts that are under utilized. It's time you started looking at the big picture. Look, Moran, I'm not going to bullshit you. I am just as self-centered as my enemies claim. But I see things. I have a vision.

"It's only a matter of time before we wrap up this gang problem. On the horizon are larger issues. Do you think anybody really cares about South Central? So a few blacks kill each other off. Tourists don't visit that area and the smart people move out. We set up C.R.A.S.H. to placate Washington and keep the reporters busy. And it worked. But the average person? He cares about bigger crimes. About the rich, the famous, and of course, his own safety.

"It's one thing when violence erupts in South Central. But when homes are broken into on the West Side; when celebrities get killed; when banks are robbed in Hollywood and downtown; that's what the public really cares about. And we're going to see a lot more of that. So forget about South Central. We want to keep the white voters happy.

"Moran, you could develop into a first rate detective. You have all the necessary qualities. And who knows where you go after that? There are no limits".

I started to speak, but he raised his hand and continued,

"I don't want an answer right now. Give it some thought. I'm sure you'll make the right decision".

"Thank you, sir".

"Oh, Moran. When you talk this over with your wife, make sure she knows where you stand. Don't let her be a problem. I've read her work in the paper. She doesn't think the way we do. Be sure you're the one who makes the decision".

"I understand, sir".

Gates did not do well with small talk, so it was a brief, and one-sided, meeting. One thing was obvious, though: He was not extending an invitation. I knew what he wanted.

So how does a young officer respond to the Chief? Is it even possible to turn him down? That evening I told Emily about the meeting, and I expected her to be thrilled. Things had been strained between us lately, for quite a while, actually, and I naively thought this would be good news. I could hardly wait to get home and share it with her.

"Emily, you won't believe what happened today. I had a private meeting with Chief Gates".

She knew this was an unusual experience for a young cop. Still, she barely cocked her eyebrows as she asked,

"What about"?

"He wants me to take the detective exam".

There was an unexpected and prolonged silence. She looked away, then turned back and stared into my eyes.

"Do you have any idea what's wrong between us"?, she asked.

Well, I thought to myself, that was one possible response.

"Don't start with the children", I said.

"This has nothing to do with children. And honestly, right now I'm glad we don't have any kids. They might turn out like you! No. It's not about kids. It's all about you".

I mustered just enough sarcasm to say, "That's encouraging. Thanks".

"Don't you see what's happened to you"?

Raising my voice just a tad, I replied, "What are you talking about, and what the hell do you mean, 'it's all about me'"?

"When we met you were a young, enthusiastic police officer. You were driven by idealistic principles. You believed that everyone deserved the protection of the law and the benefit of the doubt. Remember that little principle about being innocent until proved guilty? What you have become is a jaded, racist cop who thinks nothing of planting evidence on suspects. And now, your corrupt and imperious chief wants even more from you".

"Maybe I am jaded. Maybe I'm even racist, but you don't see what I see everyday. Young black punks who think nothing of killing each other or even innocent bystanders in the midst of their turf war and their bid for power. I'm not saying they're all bad. I admit there are some good black people. But where I work the criminals are all black. That's just the way it is. It changes how you see things".

I went over to the cabinet and took down a bottle of scotch.

"You want some"?, I asked.

She just shook her head, then continued,

"We've both changed over the last few years, Tom. In part I blame myself. The man I married would have never called a suspect a "nigger", and the woman I thought I was, would have never let him".

"For God's sake, Em. They even talk that way to each other. There's not a one of them wouldn't rat out another with just such language. That word is often the last thing a victim hears before being blown away by another gang member".

"And that, somehow, makes it right for you"?, she asked.

I really did love Emily, but I hated the way she argued. She was always so cool, straight forward and wickedly insightful. She rarely raised her voice. She was content to lay out her arguments in a logical fashion, as if she were a lawyer in a courtroom. Every concept detailed with exquisite calm and precision. So many times I wished that she had just a drop of Latin blood in her; Puerto Rican, or Peruvian, maybe. Even a little Italian would do. At least that would have reminded me of the Lozano household. Not Emily. Maybe it was her journalistic temperament. Maybe she was just too British. Whatever the reason, she had all the public emotion of Queen Elizabeth. She always left me so frustrated. And humbled.

I took a drink and walked across the room. I sat down, and leaned forward. I decided to try her style. Remaining calm and trying to speak softly, I said,

"You're right, Emily. We have changed. You knew I was a cop when you married me, and you used to want me to succeed. Now I come home and tell you that the chief has shown an interest in my career. I expect your support, and instead you tear down everything I've achieved".

"Just what is it that you think Gates really wants, Tom? You think he's interested in your career? I hate the man, but I have to admit he's smart. Can't you see that he's just using you? He knows that if you stay where you are and maintain your current activities, you will eventually get caught doing something illegal, and your career will be over. Then he will have lost the chance to use you. Gates sees the way you've given into corruption. If he pulls you out now, he can rescue you. Then you'll owe him and he can get you to serve his own personal agenda. He doesn't give a shit about you or your talents or your career".

"You know, Emily, I really thought you would be pleased about this".

"Then you're more blind than I thought. This is not our first conversation about this, Tom. I'm tired of trying to get through to you. You come home at all hours, and sometimes I don't know if you're coming home at all. This is not the life, not the husband, I want".

"You think I'm cheating on you, Emily"?

"I know you're not cheating, Tom. Quite the opposite. I've known for some time that your work is your first love. Unfortunately, it's also your only love. At least if you were cheating, I'd know you still had a soul".

"What happened to 'for better or worse'"?, I asked her.

"This isn't worse. It's worst. And it's not part of the bargain. Go ahead. Take Gates' offer. But don't expect me to hang around and watch you sink even deeper into the corruption you cops euphemistically call 'justice'".

I had gone numb inside and was half-surprised to find that I had nothing left to say. I had gone home with a sense of pride at being singled out by chief Gates. A destiny, an opportunity I had not planned, was being set into motion. It was compelling and exciting. To call Emily's reaction an emotional let down would be disproportionate understatement. She and I were supposed to craft a future together through shared hopes and dreams and joys. Instead, our future disintegrated within minutes. Or so it seemed. I suppose I already had a premonition that the marriage wouldn't last. This only served to convince me.

Others might marvel at the dedication and drive that made me a successful cop. That night I began a self-examination and experienced my own personal revelation. Is it all really worth it? Altruism may be good in the abstract, but there is a toll for keeping the streets safe and peaceful. I don't mean the sacrifice of one's physical life. I have seen wonderful cops cut down in the line of duty. That's heroic, and it is a price most people are reluctantly willing to pay. But there is another price for keeping the peace, one that we conveniently ignore. As such it goes unaddressed and unappreciated. Far from the fear that one might die in uniform, it is not fear at all. It is apathy and neglect, and it is the worst part of being a cop.

Emily was correct when she said she was glad we did not have kids. Each time a cop is required to work into the wee hours of the morning, denied the opportunity to kiss his kids goodnight, forced to cancel days off or vacations with the family, lives are diminished. It really is no surprise that the rates of infidelity, alcoholism and divorce are so high among police officers. My revelation that night was that peaceful streets aren't really worth the cost.

Emily was right about me, too. I had lost something I believed in. I was becoming what I hated most about the cops on campus, what I despised about the Sheriffs. And suppose she was right about Gates, too? I had to find my way back. Whether or not I was being used by the Chief, I realized that I needed a change. A change of work and a change of direction.

For me and Emily the damage was already done and we never did recover. We struggled through a few more months before she finally left. I cannot fully measure what I lost. But I was determined to take and pass the detective exam. That would be my exit strategy. I wanted out of C.R.A.S.H. and out of South Central. I still wanted to make the city safe. But from now on it would be on my terms. I would fight crime with my brains and intuition, not the despicable and illegal practices that made so many of my fellow officers criminals themselves; that had made me a shadow criminal.

Emily awakened me to the corruption of power that consumed the chief and she was right on target about Gates using me. That was really not unusual, though. If I were an older cop, I might not have been surprised. Anyone who looks closely at Gates' career, discovers that he used everyone. His concern was never the City of Los Angeles or the LAPD. He was, arguably, the most ambitious chief in LAPD history. He was all about himself and the power that he wielded. He had no compunction about using people to advance his career or bolster his self-esteem. I decided this was going to be my chance to figure out just how smart I really was. I would find a way to dodge the Chief's corruption and still do my job.

As it turned out, Gates only lasted another ten years himself. During much of that time he was caught up in public relations nightmares of his own making. His personal racism led to injudicious comments. These led, subsequently, to castigation from community groups, the media and the city's politicians. There are many comments to choose from, but perhaps the most insensitive and offensive of all was in response to the allegation of excessive force and police brutality after several people died as a result of police choke holds. Gates' response?

"Blacks might be more likely to die from choke holds because their arteries do not open as fast as they do on 'normal' people".

How charming! This comment did not come from the public relations office or even a street cop. The was the chief, himself. Like most institutions, police officers take their cues from the top, and Gates created an environment that fostered racism and abuse at all levels.

Ultimately, that same racism would bring down Gates' own career as it morphed through simple arrogance into unbridled hubris. In 1992, following the verdict in the Rodney King beating, a riot broke out in the city. Instead of taking charge or even putting a priority on the crisis, he headed off to a pre-arranged fundraiser, telling reporters that the situation would soon be under control. In truth, Gates could not care less. He succeeded in resurrecting the spirit of Emperor Nero. But this incarnation was no more beneficial for the city of Los Angeles, than the first was for Rome. The flash point of the rioting was the intersection of Normandie and Florence in South Central. That may have been the reason Gates displayed such supercilious scorn. He was wrong, anyway.

The rioting continued for more than six days with more 3,500 fires set and more than 1,000 buildings destroyed. Professional sporting events, from basketball to baseball, from horse racing to wrestling, were all cancelled, postponed or moved to other venues. Concerts were cancelled along with community events. Public transportation in and out of the city was suspended and Los Angeles International Airport was shut down for six days. Not exactly what a prescient observer would call being under control soon.

To be fair, Gates was not responsible for the rioting. Still, he never faced judgment nor did he have to account for creating a department that was steeped in racism. It was his disdain for minorities, especially African-Americans, that would inevitably led to events like the beating of Rodney King. The riots were the beginning of the end for Gates. I think everyone in the city knew they would be better off without him, no matter who would be chosen as his successor.

# Chapter 6

While I was enduring the rigors of the police academy, the supervision of probation, the gangs and drug wars of South Central, Giovanni was safely sequestered in the Seminary graduate school. Sequestered might be an exaggeration for there was much more freedom than he had experienced in college. To begin with, most of the students drove their own cars and were free to use them without first seeking permission. Technically, there was a 10:00 PM curfew, but it was never enforced. Occasionally, the Dean of Students would remind everyone that it existed, but those reminders were tongue-in-cheek.

Not much was required of the seminarians. They were expected to go to class, complete their work, attend daily Mass and other chapel exercises, and meet regularly with their spiritual directors. Even with the physical freedom, there was a great deal of structure, particularly in terms of class and chapel. It was supposed that an environment of such formation would instill the discipline necessary to be holy priests. And it worked for some.

The academic requirements were rigorous. As Giovanni likes to note of the faculty, it was the age of giants. The two Scripture professors were both internationally recognized scholars. Most of the professors held doctoral degrees from institutions as diverse as the North American College in Rome, Catholic University in Washington, D.C. and the University of Southern California in Los Angeles. The faculty also ranged widely in age, with the professor of Church History, Newman Eberhardt, having seemingly walked the shores of Gethsemane with Jesus, himself!

A key component of graduate life at St. John's was the field education program, designed to expose the seminarians to a variety of pastoral work situations. Each Saturday, the seminarians would gather in small groups to share experiences from the previous week's assignments. One student in each group would write out and present a "verbatim", a detailed retelling of an experience from field education. This would then be discussed and evaluated by the other students and the professor. Fortunately, not every experience made it into the verbatim reports. Giovanni tells a story that originated in his third year and never made it to the weekly meetings. Actually, it was not really verbatim material, because it happened after the day's assignment was complete.

Giovanni was assigned to the drug rehabilitation center at Camarillo State Hospital. This was a lockup center for drug addicts, and one of the more difficult field assignments, for even the seminarians were not allowed to leave the lockup during their hours of work. Giovanni never before realized just how slowly time passes between the ticks of the clock. The program was supposed to help addicts, so that after a 30, 60 or 90 day stay they could exit as productive members of society. A key component was created by the misguided psychology that the best way to help people addicted to drugs is first to tear them down and then build them up again according to some predetermined idea of health and productivity. As a result, the treatment center included an exercise called the "hot seat".

The group would gather in a circle, with a chair in the middle. Everyone was expected to take turns sitting on the hot seat. While in that position, no question, no insult, no offense was out of bounds. It was an excruciating experience, because the individual could not evade the intrusions of the group without subjecting himself to even more intense criticism and vicious ridicule. This was followed by the obligatory, though hardly comforting, hug from all the members of the circle. Although the intent of this exercise was to force people to face the truth in their lives, according to Giovanni it was difficult to see how this was a positive in the treatment of the patients. It seemed at odds with his theological training and with the compassion that Jesus demonstrated in the Gospels.

Giovanni was not assigned to the drug center alone. Another classmate went with him. As it turned out, the other student was also an Italian, Marco Romano. I know, it sounds like he was destined to be a priest, too. Marco was an older student, having been an accountant before entering the seminary. As a student at St. John's, Marco became the source of unending bizarre and humorous stories. He was a very friendly and entertaining guy, but really not cut out for priesthood. He had a difficult time adjusting to the seminary and figuring out what he wanted to do with his life.

There was an infirmary on campus for the care of the sick. It was not uncommon for Marco to complain about being ill in the morning. This enabled him to skip chapel and classes, and have an infirmarian deliver meals to his room. It was a wonder to see his remarkable recovery in late afternoon, just in time to head out for a nice dinner in town. This explained how Marco could flirt with obesity, given that the seminary food held no culinary attraction.

In spite of the fact that Giovanni's sense of humor and outspokenness seemed to turn off some of the other students, he had a need to be liked and accepted. He was also generous to a fault, and found it difficult to say no to anyone. At least, that was the Giovanni of seminary days. The following occurred after a field education day at the state hospital.

Giovanni was driving. On the way home, Marco made the suggestion:

"Let's not go back to the seminary yet. Let's go to dinner at Ottavio's".

"We went out to dinner last week, Marco. Besides, I don't have any money".

"That's OK. I'll pay. You don't realize what the drug center does to me. I can't relate to those people and it leaves me uncomfortable. Besides, I would really like some Italian food tonight".

The Belvedere Family opened Ottavio's as a small pizza restaurant in 1969 and it quickly became a mainstay of Camarillo life, popular among the locals for serving a variety of family style meals along with Italian beers and wines, all at reasonable prices. In Giovanni's second year of graduate school, the restaurant moved to a new location, still in Camarillo. The move enabled the owners to expand the premises to four rooms serving over 200 customers.

On the seminary menu that night was a frequent, and always revolting, item. Officially, it was supposed to be some sort of beef short ribs, but these ribs were unlike anything that anyone ever had. The seminarians simply called it "buffalo butt". So Giovanni had a choice: Buffalo butt, or Lasagna. Easy decision.

"OK, Marco. But I insist on paying you back when I get some money".

Giovanni was generous himself, but did not like being in anyone else's debt.

When they arrived at the restaurant, Marco immediately ordered a bottle of Chianti. Giovanni had but one glass before the bottle was emptied. Marco started to order a second bottle.

"Whoa"! Giovanni protested. "We don't need another bottle. Besides, you practically drank the last one by yourself".

"I know, but I'm Italian and we grew up drinking wine at dinner. This is like water to me".

"Marco, that's such bullshit. Don't forget. I'm Italian, too".

Nonetheless, a second bottle was ordered. Again, Giovanni only had one glass.

Once they got in the car, Marco came up with another idea.

"Let's stop off at the Two plus Two for an after dinner drink. It's on the way back to the seminary, anyway".

The "Two" was a favorite local hangout among the seminarians. It was tucked away at the far corner of a string of businesses, just a short drive from the seminary. The bartender was always a little more generous to the future priests and, as such, he secured their undying loyalty. Against his better judgment, Giovanni agreed.

"All right. But just one drink".

Once seated at the table, they ordered. Giovanni drank slowly, giving Marco the opportunity to order a second drink for himself. Beginning to relax a little, Giovanni agreed to another round. That actually meant two additional drinks for Marco. If the evening was beginning to deteriorate, Giovanni was not prepared for what happened next.

As he walked up to the bar to order a third drink, he encountered a drunken man and drunken woman celebrating their drunken 25th wedding anniversary. When a person is as loaded as these two, no one is a stranger. The woman looked at Giovanni and slurred,

"Don't I know you"?

"No", was his abrupt reply.

"Yes, I do. You're a singer. I know I've seen you before".

"You must be mistaken". Attempting to be a polite he continued, "I sang one time with a small combo at the Pierpont Inn".

The Pierpont is an inn and racquet club about ten miles north, in the city of Ventura. It sits beside the 101 Freeway overlooking the Ventura pier and a wide expanse of the Pacific Ocean. A couple of years earlier, Giovanni had been pressured by some classmates to sing a couple of songs, and it was highly unlikely that this woman and her husband were present that night. Nonetheless, she continued,

"That's where it was. It's our anniversary tonight. Will you sing for us"?

Giovanni has always had a decent voice, but he was not cut out to be an entertainer. After resisting repeated requests, he realized that the woman would not give up. So he relented. He nestled close to the couple, put his arms around their shoulders and began quietly to sing "The Anniversary Waltz". It is shorter and easier to sing than the more familiar "Anniversary Song", so it would be less likely to draw attention. At the conclusion, the woman slurred rather loudly,

"That was beautiful"!

Unknown to Giovanni, Marco took advantage of this rather brief time frame to order, and drink, yet another two drinks. It was now only about 8:00 in the evening, but with Marco having consumed a total of six drinks, plus the wine at dinner, Giovanni was anxious to get him back to the seminary. Whether due to Marco's insistence or influenced by his own drinks, Giovanni agreed to one final round. Needless to say, that meant two more for Marco. It's hard to believe, but after finishing those drinks, Marco continued to press on for more. This time, Giovanni stood his ground and insisted they leave.

"No, Marco. I'm leaving. Either you get in the fucking car, or take a taxi. I don't really care, but I'm going now".

Marco decided to go with him. After returning to the seminary, Giovanni went straight to his room, tired, frustrated and angry--mostly with himself. A few minutes later, there was a knock. He opened the door and another friend asked,

"What did you do to him"?

"Who"?

"Marco. He can barely stand up. He's falling against the walls"!

Given his size, that must have been a sight. But Giovanni was not interested. He simply said,

"I don't want to talk about it. I'll tell you tomorrow".

Not long afterward, Marco left the seminary.

*     *     *

Following his ordination in 1980, Giovanni was assigned to St. Hildegarde Parish in Los Angeles. His first meeting with the pastor, Fr. Henry Hansen, was pleasant enough. After all, Giovanni was excited to be a priest and filled with enthusiasm for his new ministry. It also seemed as though the pastor was happy to have a young priest assisting him. But this was not a forthright encounter, and it did not take long for Giovanni to realize that confrontation would be a staple of life in his first years as a priest.

Pope John XXIII had convened the Second Vatican Council in 1962 in order to make the Church more relevant to society and the world. The great rallying cry was to read "the signs of the times". Since an Ecumenical Council happens, on average, only once every hundred years, all around the world there was excitement in the air. Though no one could have predicted the full outcome of the Council, one effect was felt in priestly formation. Seminarians were being far better trained and readied for ministry than their predecessors. This was in no small part due to the wide range of field education experiences that were added to the formation process. The seminary was becoming more open, and theological courses were updated in keeping with the vision of the Council and the research of scholars. Of particular import was the advancement in biblical studies, which in turn, impacted every other area of theology. Seminarians, like the rest of the Church, had reason to believe that a new future was unfolding.

Fr. Hansen had thirty years experience as a priest. A more accurate evaluation came from one of Giovanni's professors:

"He has not lived thirty years as priest. He has lived one year, thirty times". Hansen had not adapted very well to the changing church. He was not fond of John XXIII. He had not read and, therefore, had no appreciation of the documents that emerged from the Council, especially the Constitution on the Sacred Liturgy, and he quite clearly was not prepared for his new associate.

Giovanni was more liberal than Hansen. But that was not the real problem. It was more that he did not read people well. For all his intelligence, he was not as perceptive as his brother. Giovanni assumed that everyone told him the truth and so he accepted them at face value. He certainly was no expert at detecting deception. He also believed that what he was taught in the seminary would be the reality in parish life. Specifically, he believed in collaboration and expected to be treated as an adult, equal to the priests he would work with. He naturally assumed, having met Fr. Hansen, that they would work well together. But naïveté has always been the bane of youth and youth is not defined merely in terms of age. It is as much a question of the mind as it is of time. After eight years in the seminary, Giovanni was a young twenty-six.

Giovanni continually looked for ways to make the people feel more comfortable in and around the church. He had an aversion to the clericalism that left so many priests expecting preferential treatment and demanding displays of respect in public. In his mind the priest is a servant who is also part of the parish community. The priest clearly holds a different role from that of the people he serves, but he is not better than the rest simply by virtue of ordination. Harking back to his college days, Giovanni disdained titles and symbols of respect, especially the Roman collar. One evening he returned from his day off to find Hansen waiting up for him in the kitchen.

"Father, can I talk to you for a minute"?, asked Hansen.

Imagine Hansen, twenty-seven years Giovanni's senior, calling him "father". How absurd! Giovanni knew something was up when he saw the pastor waiting for him, but felt he could handle whatever it was.

"Sure", was his response. He took a seat across the table and Hansen continued:

"You've been here two weeks and I have not seen you wear your Roman collar, not even on Sundays."

Giovanni was not prepared to give ground. He simply replied: "That's correct".

"You do own one, don't you"? There was sarcasm in the air even if it was not in Hansen's voice.

"Of course, I do".

"Well, I called the bishop's office today and asked them about it. They said that a priest could wear whatever he wanted on his day off or in his own room, but that he was supposed to wear the collar when on duty."

"You did what", Giovanni asked? There was no need to feign incredulity. He really was taken aback by the statement. It was like being thrust back into elementary school and confronted by a tattletale.

If it is possible to nuance a distinction between conceit and arrogance, then Giuseppe was clearly the former. By contrast, most of the arrogance born to the Lozano family in 1954 subsided in Giovanni. A little bit of Italian blood began to boil. He continued,

"Let's get something straight right now. If you want to know anything about me or why I do something, you ask me. I'm more than willing to answer questions about how I dress, or anything else for that matter. But the Bishop's office doesn't speak for me."

These two priests came from different worlds. In Hansen's day, no one questioned authority or would have responded to a pastor the way Giovanni did. And Giovanni, himself, was on the cutting edge of changes in the Church that had not yet taken root. Eventually, many pastors would come to see their associates in terms of collaborative ministry. They would share decision-making with their associates and with parishioners, but Hansen would never be one of them. For now, these days were still on the horizon. That night, Giovanni realized that he was not an associate pastor, he was an assistant pastor. And Hansen realized that both titles began with the same three letters. It would not be easygoing for either of them.

At the time of Giovanni's ordination, Cardinal Timothy Manning was Archbishop of Los Angeles. He was well-liked, but introverted, noted especially for his retiring and self-effacing manner. Manning was clearly a holy man given to prayer and frequent retreats, but he was ill-suited for leadership. He ceded his responsibility and authority, choosing to entrust (an uncertain word at best), administration to others. For all intents and purposes, Msgr. Benjamin Hawkes ran the bishop's office, a.k.a the Chancery. He was Vicar General and he was in charge of finances, but in truth, he ran the entire Archdiocese. Msgr. John "Archie" Rawden was personnel director. His jobs included being chairman of the placement board, the group responsible for priestly assignments. He was also responsible for disciplining those clergy who did not tow the party line. An older priest whom Giovanni greatly admired once observed that these two men managed to destroy an entire generation of priestly leadership through their authoritarianism and abuse of power. Nature's abhorrence of a vacuum pales when compared to that of autocracy. As a result, an obsession with control filtered through all departments of the Chancery.

One day the sisters at Holy Trinity Parish asked Giovanni to celebrate a Mass to conclude a women's day of recollection that they were hosting in the parish. The focus of the day was women's roles in church leadership. The Mass was held in the living room of the convent. Giovanni arrived that afternoon dressed in casual clothes, as was his custom. The setting for prayer was very informal. The coffee table served as an altar, a wine goblet was used as a chalice, the bread lay upon a dinner plate, and there were no church vestments to wear. Giovanni simply led the service in his street clothes.

Somehow, knowledge of the occasion made its way to the Bishop's office. At the time, John Ward, one of the auxiliary bishops, was in charge of the Liturgy Department. Ward was quite a large man, rotund as Santa Claus with the voice to match. On occasion, he even shared Father Christmas' personality. At other times he was sternly obtuse. He called Giovanni into his office.

"Father, I hear that you celebrated Mass for some sisters without wearing proper vestments".

"Yes, bishop. It was not in a Church. It was a simple house Mass at the end of a day of recollection".

"You know that the rubrics say you are to wear vestments when celebrating Mass"?

Ward possessed an unfailing devotion to the obvious. As such, he frequently posed questions as modestly veiled statements of fact. This supposedly eliminated any need for discussion. In this instance Giovanni could not care less. He reasoned that there were informal situations that were just as religious and sacred as church services. Besides, Jesus did not dress up in special garments for the Last Supper. Not unlike that celebration, this was a simple prayer in a simple room, lacking the formality of a Church environment. Still, he decided that he could not win the argument, so he chose the easy way out.

"The nuns had everything organized for the Mass and they didn't set out any vestments for me to wear".

Bishop Ward boomed out the question,

"Well, who wears the pants? You or the nuns"?

It would have been laughable were it not so misogynistic. Then again, this was the early 1980's. One by product of an all-male clergy is a lack of respect, or sense of equality, for women. Certainly in Los Angeles, the Catholic Church had no real use for women. The nuns served a useful purpose in hospitals and schools, but men were the brains and power behind the church. In those days the Sisters of the Holy Names of Jesus and Mary had a unique response. They are headquartered in Northern California, yet serve throughout the state. Taking their lead from the U.S. National Anthem, they referred to Oakland as the "land of the free" and Los Angeles as the "home of the brave".

Bishop Ward concluded the meeting after Giovanni agreed not to commit this transgression again. They probably both knew that something less than honesty had just transpired between them.

Three items converged to remake Fr. Giovanni Lozano. First was disillusionment with the intransigence of church authority. All institutions develop a life of their own, existing outside the control of individuals. Occasionally someone like John XXIII comes along with the will and the power to effect change. More often leaders simply succumb to the power of the establishment. Frequently a symbiotic relationship develops between the institution itself and the people whose sole self-worth is rooted in their being its agents. In the Los Angeles Archdiocese, Manning, Ward, Hawkes and Rawden were examples of this tragic but all too familiar reality. The kind judgment is that they lacked vision and desire. The alternative is to suggest impotence. Regardless, it led some priests to develop a dismissive attitude toward church authority, instead, becoming a power and law unto themselves. Eventually, Giovanni would join their ranks. Not so much in terms of power. That never interested him. But he would set about to make his own rules with little concern for official regulations.

The second element of Giovanni's transformation was on display while he was still in the seminary, though at the time it was still nascent. The students at St. John's used a term to describe certain of their peers, FKIA. Pronounced (fŭ - kī´ - a), it meant "fucking know-it-all". Although mostly a disparaging description, it could also be flattering. Or at least that is how some of the recipients received it. Actually, FKIA had more to do with attitude than it did real knowledge. That made the term more complicated for Giovanni. His friends would call him a FKIA as a matter of humor when he had them bested in a discussion; his enemies used it to identify something more arrogant. They were both right. Few seemed to realize that Giovanni's self-assurance masked an insecurity that had trailed him from childhood.

Giovanni always feared that he would not measure up to his parent's expectations or his brother's example. Giuseppe's outgoing personality put him much more at ease in the public arena. It is what made him a natural for political life. By contrast, Giovanni had to rely on his intellect and oratorical skills to appear comfortable before a crowd. Arrogance started out as a crutch, but ultimately cemented itself as a true personality trait. Eventually, it would also ground the third element of his metamorphosis--insensitivity. It was nearly impossible to see this one coming. Giuseppe, not Giovanni, was the insensitive one.

While in the graduate seminary, Giovanni had begun to develop a modestly liberal approach to religion. He had a classmate by the name of Michael Anderson. Although Giovanni was always smart and intelligent, there was no question that Michael was the brightest one in the class. He was the one who pushed theological concepts and classroom discussions past the limits of official Church teaching. He was practically a bête noir for certain professors, a mere irritation for others. Anderson reasoned that the whole point of a theological education was not to receive and parrot back official teachings. That could be accomplished by the mundane task of reading a book. No, the purpose of the classroom was to challenge ideas and develop good reasoning and articulation skills. And challenge he did.

There were times when Giovanni and the others welcomed Michael's interjections and subsequent discussions with the professors. There were other times when they were bored and feared that the discussion might extend the length of class time.

Nonetheless, Giovanni was intrigued and frequently fascinated by Anderson's ideas. He was particularly drawn to the way Anderson argued his points. As brilliant as the professors were, it sometimes seemed that Anderson was the one who prevailed in the discussions. I guess FKIA was a good way to describe him, too.

These classroom encounters, coupled with frequent discussions outside class, led Giovanni to begin questioning some established norms of church life and teachings previously perceived as absolutes. Even though Giovanni had always been an intelligent and forward thinker, more than a few observers considered Anderson a bad influence on him.

One area where Giovanni made a great deal of noise was around Satan and hell. His friend Anderson had written several articles challenging the existence of both, and the articles were truly compelling. At least Giovanni could find no flaws. Anderson detailed the theology of the early Church. He focused on how the early theologians viewed the life, death and resurrection of Jesus, noting that the majority of theological centers taught universalism, the belief that through Jesus, everyone goes to heaven. In one of Anderson's articles he even went so far as to suggest that teaching and reiterating the existence of a literal hell gave rise to atheism. If true, that would certainly be counter-productive for the Church.

Giovanni was persuaded. He began trying out his own arguments on family and friends. That was when he discovered that the average Catholic possessed a totally inadequate grasp of Church teaching, in part because most Catholics knew next to nothing of Church history. They simply thought they had to believe everything the pope, or the bishop, or the priest said. Since few had ever heard of a hierarchy of church doctrine or teaching, every church statement required the same assent. That may have been the moment Giovanni most appreciated his own seminary education. It certainly was the moment he rededicated himself to his studies. And it marked a shift from a moderately liberal intellectual to one approaching the borders of radicalism.

I had the opportunity to see these shifts first hand, because Giovanni always shared with me what he was learning in theology. Perhaps it was the combination of his intellectual metamorphosis and my willingness to listen. But during these days he was less and less concerned with my immortal soul. He did not specifically say so, but he seemed to think that God and I could sort out my salvation without having to return to the Catholic Church. It certainly made for more pleasant times between us.

The theological development around universal salvation led Giovanni to conclude that the existence of Satan is incompatible with a modern understanding of God. This led to many discussions between us about evil. For my part, I did not care about heaven or salvation. But I was a cop, and I was very concerned about evil.

"I see evil everyday, Gio. The streets are full of it. Drugs, rape and murder are commonplace. How can you say there is no evil? I've seen it in the flesh".

"I'm not saying there is no evil, Tom. All anyone has to do is look around to see that. And it may very well be enfleshed in the criminals you meet on the street. What I'm saying is that evil is not personified in a mythical being that people refer to as Satan or the devil. The whole idea is an affront to the goodness and the power of God. If God is both all-good and all-powerful, then there cannot exist a devil and there certainly is no hell".

"Gio, since I don't believe in God, it doesn't much matter to me. But you are part of a church that teaches there is a devil. And a hell. Isn't that a problem for you"?

"Oh, please. First of all, there is very little that people have to believe in order to be Catholic, and neither the existence of the devil nor of hell is one of them. Besides, church teaching is continually evolving. The concept of a devil had its place in history. It makes no real sense now. I want to change how people understand evil, itself, without the crutch of a Satan".

His arguments were well thought out, and even though these were new ideas for me, I found them compelling. I also admired that he wanted to make a real change in how people understood their faith. It was neither his liberalism nor his theology that proved the problem. He just went about it the wrong way. He seemed to develop a disdain for the unenlightened. That, in turn, led to an unexpected impatience on his part. So it was with some dismay that he related the following story.

One night after dinner, Giovanni went to his room. At about 7:30 the phone rang. Since it was his turn on duty, he answered. On the other end was a man who said,

"Father, I need you to come over and bless my wife. She's possessed by the devil".

Giovanni responded by saying,

"I'll come over, but I don't believe in the devil".

"Aren't you a Catholic priest", the man queried?

"Yes, I am".

"Then how can you not believe in the devil"?

"I'm trying something new," Giovanni replied. "I believe in God".

"Well. Then I guess I have the wrong the priest". The man hung up the phone.

That was such a smart ass comment. I started to laugh, but then said,

"Gio, you can't say those kinds of things".

"What do you care, Tom? You're not religious. You don't even believe in God."

"No, but you are my friend, and I want people to see you as a good priest".

"So what was I supposed to do? Go over, wave my hand and say some magical words"?

"That's not the point, Gio. Most people don't call the priest to say their wife is possessed by the devil. Something was going on. Maybe you could have helped. You have something to offer the church, and I want people to take you seriously. Besides, you could get in trouble with the bishop".

The exasperation on his face indicated that I was not getting through to him. Admittedly, stories like that were few and they were not public knowledge. But the personality behind the stories was very public. In a world where life was filled with ambiguity and the bureaucracy of the church brooked little opposition, Giovanni's future was going to be fraught with difficulty.

# Chapter 7

Couples who are forced into long distance relationships hold fast to the belief that absence makes the heart grow fonder. But those are merely the words of poets providing a comforting counter to the disquiet of modern life. The real truth is that absence makes the heart forget, and that was the challenge facing Giuseppe and Yolanda, especially considering Giuseppe's history with women. After graduating from Stanford, he was off to complete a business degree at Harvard on the east coast, while she would make her home in Los Angeles, pursuing an advanced degree in education from USC. Meanwhile, they had the summer, and saw each other regularly. It was a fortunate summer, for it seemed as though Giuseppe emerged a very different young man in the fall. Everyone knew he had an affection for Yolanda that went way beyond anything he demonstrated for previous girlfriends. Also, he never spent so much time with one person before. Apparently, she was not just another conquest. Giuseppe made a decision that summer that remained unknown to everyone else: Yolanda was the woman he wanted to marry.

In spite of steady dating for a couple of months, Yolanda continued to keep Giuseppe at bay. She had become quite fond of him, but was not willing to make any serious commitment. She knew that graduate school would keep them separated for at least two years. She was also unsure of his ability to remain faithful while they were apart. However, only Giuseppe realized that he had finally found the person he was willing to settle down with. It put a damper on his move to the east coast.

\*    \*    \*

Boston is a truly exciting city. Imbued with history and patriotism, it possesses an easily walkable downtown that exposes visitors to details of the colonial, and of the more recent, American past. Although many cities are centers for culture, or politics, or sports, few can compare to the way these elements all coalesce in Boston. And, there are other draws.

Boston is renowned for great seafood, including its own namesake clam chowder. And it offers an even wider array of culinary delights. From Charlestown, to Hyde Park, Boston is an epicurean treasure with foods introduced by immigrants from around the world. These days, with the Revolutionary War a distant memory and the East India Company long dissolved, one can even find a good cup of tea.

Boston is a college town unlike any other, and has a genuinely youthful allure. It seems that every couple of blocks one encounters another college or university. In fact, more than twenty exist within the city limits. Once outside the city proper, the greater Boston area embraces yet more institutions, such as Harvard and MIT, located in the city of Cambridge, and another fifty within an easy driving distance. This was to be Giuseppe's home for next couple of years. But, as charming and exciting as it was, it was not Los Angeles.

Not that Harvard was unattractive. The campus of the Business School cannot be more picturesque. Nestled along the Charles River, it is seductive for its synthesis of water, trees and greenery. Something simply not found in Los Angeles. Then again, the city of the Angels does have something Boston does not: the unrivaled Southern California weather.

In spite of having visited Harvard previously, and then continuing to correspond with other students, Giuseppe was not prepared for the harsh winters that characterize the New England states. Back in Los Angeles, whenever transplanted easterners would complain about the lack of snow, Giuseppe would respond like any native Angeleno: "We have snow. Where it belongs. In the mountains. Not outside our front door". Indeed, that has always been part of the charm of Southern California. Where else can one surf the waves at sunrise and ski the mountains at sunset? Opening his door in the morning, being blinded by an eclipse of white, and then trudging through snow to get to class was not his idea of winter and certainly not his idea of fun.

*    *    *

Giuseppe decided not to come home for Thanksgiving that first year. He would return a month later for Christmas, and the cost was too prohibitive to fly home twice. He did his best to convince Yolanda to fly to Boston for Thanksgiving, but she, and her family, would have none of it. They had a tradition of gathering the entire Cummings clan for all the major holidays, and no potential boyfriend would alter that. Still, she did agree to fly out and visit for a weekend.

Labor Day, while a national holiday, is not a major time for assembling family members. It tends to center around close friends and business and neighborhood barbecues. It was the perfect weekend for Yolanda to fly East. She had no plans in Los Angeles, the east coast weather was still pleasant, and she already missed Giuseppe, who had been gone for almost a month.

Yolanda hated flying. She hated the inconsistent weather patterns that are a staple of life when crossing a country as large as the United States. It was, therefore, not surprising that her flight experienced turbulence, particularly over the midwestern states. But the landing in Boston was smooth, and Giuseppe was waiting at the gate. Being once again on terra firma, and seeing his smile, calmed her nerves.

Giuseppe's apartment was not large, but there was clearly room for two. Besides, they had overcome prudish barriers during the summer, so sleeping together was natural and comfortable.

Yolanda had never been to east coast before, and Giuseppe suggested that Boston and its environs would keep them plenty occupied during her visit. Or, as Bostonians might say, "Who needs New York when you have Boston"? The days were a jumble of activity and the weekend proved too short a time together.

Giuseppe had never broached the subject of marriage with Yolanda. He knew that was what he wanted, but he kept it to himself. For now, he just needed to keep Yolanda interested. Still, Sunday evening he nearly derailed his future plans.

The day had been exceptional. Spectacular weather, a drive out to Salem to explore the history of the Witch Trials, and dinner at the Warren Tavern Restaurant in Charlestown. If Yolanda kept a diary, this would have been one of her perfect days. It was during drinks at McFadden's that Giuseppe committed his faux pas.

Despite dating throughout the summer, Yolanda's reluctance prevented them from officially entering into a relationship. After taking a drink of rich Irish ale, Giuseppe took her hands and spoke of the next two years.

"Yolanda, we are going to be apart for a long time. You know I really like you--more than any girl I have ever known. Would you be willing to try an open relationship while I'm here in Boston"?

It was a pregnant question, as was the pause, at once verifying Giuseppe's self-centeredness and validating Yolanda's reservations. How could he not have known that she would be insulted by such a suggestion? He may have wanted to marry her, but he clearly did not know her as well as he thought. Insulted or not, Yolanda realized that this needed to be discussed if they were to have any future together. And truth be told, she had fallen for Giuseppe.

She pulled back, sat up straight and said,

"I would not be here if I did not have deep feelings for you, Giuseppe. But I don't believe in open relationships. They don't work, and in the end they don't last".

"It wouldn't change how I feel about you or what our future will be".

"Of course it would. There is no commitment in an open relationship.

I don't pretend that you will pursue a celibate existence here in Boston. But if we are together, we are together. There can be no one else. There is no 'open' anything. Until you can make that commitment, we cannot be in a formal relationship, and our future will remain uncertain".

"Yolanda, can't we at least try it for a while and see what happens"?

"You don't listen very well, Giuseppe. You never did. You see things the way you want them to be and expect everyone else to cede to your desires. Well, I'm not everyone else. I really hope we have a future together, but it will not happen this way. The answer is no, and the discussion is over".

He had, indeed, blown the conversation and it made a segue awkward, but he heard something he wanted to pursue.

"Yolanda, are you saying that you want a future together--I mean a permanent one"?

"Why do you think I'm here, Giuseppe? I've known for sometime, now, that I want something more, something permanent. But I can't take that step until you're back in Los Angeles--until I know that you're ready, too. Besides, I think we need to complete our educational pursuits first".

Giuseppe's mind was always running at record speed. He could carry on multiple conversations at once. Or he could be in a conversation with one person, all the while thinking of something else. And no one would ever know. That was happening now. The evening was turning out even better than he planned. He really did want to marry Yolanda, but was not prepared to give up his freedom. At least not yet. Entering into an open relationship would have given him cover both in Boston and back home. This was just as good. He could tell everyone at home that he hoped for a future with Yolanda, and he could tell people in Boston that he had no commitments in Los Angeles. These two years could be a lot of fun! If he had been more amiable, he might have been dismissed as a scoundrel or a rogue. This was duplicity. I never trusted Giuseppe as far as Yolanda was concerned. It always seemed to me that she deserved better.

*    *    *

Then again, I wonder if my judgments of Giuseppe are too harsh. Sometimes I even suspect my own motivations. Neither of us was immune to the search for self-identity. It consumed a great deal of our teenage years and on into in our twenties. I always thought that Giuseppe's quest focused more on the self, than it did on identity. He seemed driven by what he wanted, not by what he was. This personal absorption frequently had a negative effect on his friends, and even more so on his family.

Then there was the competition between us--mostly unspoken, but nonetheless real. Giuseppe had grown into a more popular person than I. As his circle of friends was expanding, mine was contracting, at least my circle of genuine friends. I kept a tighter control over my emotions than he did. In fact, I kept a tighter control over everything. I was selective about what I shared and with whom I shared it. I was lucky and thankful to have Giovanni as a best friend. That was enough for me.

Giuseppe, on the other hand, seemed to rocket to the height of popularity. From my perspective, though, he did not possess a lot of depth. And yet, he seemed to leave everyone feeling that they had been given passage into the special recesses of his life. He was a master of superficiality. Or so I thought. Was I just jealous? Did Giuseppe have a personal comfort and self-confidence that I lacked? Were we just different people taking different paths in life? Whatever the answers, I was cautious of Giuseppe. It was the reason I worried for Yolanda.

# Chapter 8

Over the years, Giovanni and I continued our discussions about evil, our differing attitudes about the existence of God notwithstanding. On one level, evil was very real. I saw it in the faceless and random acts of street violence, Giovanni experienced it in the confessional admissions of people who had sinned. Still, it was not personal. For either of us.

Giuseppe was never a party to those conversations. Yet he was the one who would experience evil on a very deep and personal level. He watched its tentacles insidiously entangle and engulf the first true friend he had ever known. And at twenty-four he was not prepared for it. It would alter the dimensions of his personality.

Early upon his arrival at Harvard, Giuseppe had met a fellow business student, Jackson Carver, "Jacks" for short. They became fast friends, even though their backgrounds were very different. Jackson came from Louisiana and was the fifth of seven children, with no twins in their family. Though very bright, he had to work much harder at his studies than Giuseppe. They shared a discontent with religion, but unlike Giuseppe, Jackson had revoked any religious tradition at all, instead professing flat out atheism.

They shared similar goals for the future. Both wanted to start their own businesses and become millionaires. Jackson's interests lay in banking, Giuseppe's in electronics. They both were remarkable in their popularity.

Giuseppe was boisterous but not offensive. Reprising his days at Stanford, he regaled the Harvard students with his knowledge of the robber barons, expounding on their history and extolling what he termed their virtues. No one was more intrigued by these stories than Jackson.

By contrast, Jackson was quiet without being shy. In fact, quite the opposite. He may have been the single, easiest person to talk to. A magnetism radiated from him and he demonstrated a profound interest in each person he met. No matter who he was with he was truly engrossed in every conversation.

Though quite distinct from each other, the two of them were quite a pair. Their deepening friendship wove an intricate and peculiar pattern in the tapestry of the student body. Over the next two years they became almost inseparable. The more they shared their personal stories, the closer they became. Jackson had a unique insight into people. Sometimes he read them wrong, but he got Giuseppe right. Jackson saw a genuine goodness that his new friend had spent his life hiding. And he was able to inspire Giuseppe to live up to that vision. For a time.

Giuseppe had an easy life compared to Jackson. There were no personal or familial tragedies. No divorce and no unexpected deaths in the Lozano family. Even his perceived poverty was as much myth as reality.

Jackson, on the other hand, experienced a much more difficult upbringing. His family was genuinely poor. Two of his siblings died before the age of ten, and his father and stepmother were frequently out of work. Simply securing an education was not guaranteed, but Jackson possessed a keen intellect and he put it to good use. He excelled in school at every level. He was the first in his family to attend college, and the only one to go to graduate school. With no financial backing from home, his success was due to his intelligence, his fierce determination and his hard work.

Through their time together Giuseppe learned that Jackson, despite his intellectual prowess, was a very fragile person, given to bouts of depression. He was well liked by the other students, but not very astute when it came to recognizing trustworthy friends. As a result, he was frequently betrayed by others. He shared some deeply personal stories with Giuseppe, swearing him to silence. The events of his life gave Giuseppe insight into why Jackson was so vulnerable. Jackson did not know what trust really was. He enjoyed meeting new people and was always open to new friends, but his personal history left him easily manipulated by others, especially in situations he would never initiate. Giuseppe had spoken often about Jackson. But true to his promise, he refused to share certain details of his past with me and Giovanni.

Whenever Jackson slipped into depression, he would seek out a therapist. While they were in graduate school, the two friends became so close that Jackson shared with Giuseppe everything that happened in his therapy sessions--what he learned about himself and how he felt about people and things.

After graduating, both friends remained in Boston for another year. Giuseppe received an offer from a firm he had previously interned for, and Jackson secured a responsible position with a small local bank. He was sure it would be a good opportunity for him to learn some of the more subtle elements of the banking industry.

During the winter of 1978, Jackson had slipped once again into depression. Each weekend he would fly back to Louisiana, where he began seeing a therapist. He could, of course, count on the support of his friends, especially Giuseppe. But it was the therapy sessions that would allow him to confront his past. And it was those same therapy sessions that would create his greatest crisis.

*   *   *

Jackson had been fortunate in his choice of roommates. Like most major U.S. universities, Harvard draws students from around the globe. Ricardo Duran, from Spain, arrived at Harvard the same year as Giuseppe and Jackson. He came from a wealthy Spanish family in the city of Barcelona, in the Catalonia region of Spain. He was not a tall man, standing just about five feet, ten inches. His complexion was not very dark. More a light brown. He did not exude the machismo so frequently associated with Latin men. On the other hand, he certainly was not effeminate. Ricardo could best be described as nondescript. He did have a pleasant personality, though, and given Jackson's genial makeup, they were apt roommates. Their apartment was a fun and relaxing place for their friends to spend time.

As a roommate, Ricardo put no demands upon Jackson, so everything seemed perfectly normal. Of course, Jackson would think that, since he was always driven by a naiveté that did little to prepare him for reality. One day in late spring of 1978, just before completing their masters program, Ricardo overstepped the boundaries of normal male friendship. They had some friends over that evening. Not a party, exactly. Just a social gathering with some casual drinking and smoking.

After everyone left, Jackson started cleaning up. Ricardo walked over to him, and said,

"We can do that later".

As Jackson looked up, Ricardo took his shoulders, looked at him, and kissed him. Neither of them closed their eyes as they kissed. Ricardo could see unmistakable surprise in Jackson. Not, however, disgust, or a desire to pull away. Jackson had never known how to act when people made such advances. He told himself that he was not gay, but did not have the fortitude to speak up for himself. As such, he became a willing partner to this kiss.

Afterward, Ricardo said,

"We've wasted two years together. I have wanted to do that since the day we met".

Then he took Jackson's hand and led him into his bedroom.

Despite his close friendship with Giuseppe, Jackson locked away that experience, keeping it and other such events to himself. Until therapy. They were about to emerge and propel him into yet a deeper crisis.

\*     \*     \*

In Louisiana, Jackson sought out a therapist named Helena

Brockman. She was easy to find, since her husband, Anthony, was the Carver family's physician. At thirty-nine, Helena, herself, was fifteen years older than Jackson. Still, he was captivated by her beauty. In therapy, she displayed great tenderness. As Jackson shared the details of these sessions, alarm bells began to ring in Giuseppe's head.

Therapists are trained to deal with transference, the tendency to shift emotions, especially those from childhood, to the therapist. They are thus trained because transference is commonplace. So it was no particular surprise that Jackson had fallen in love with Helena. But that was just the beginning of the story.

Giuseppe was the one person in Jackson's life, where trust was not misplaced. Jackson was free to be himself with Giuseppe in a way he could not be with his family or any of his other friends. If Jackson asked him to keep something confidential, it was sealed forever. As such, Jackson did not just share generalities from his therapy sessions. He told Giuseppe everything he told Helena and everything she told him.

One night Giuseppe stopped by Jackson's apartment and suggested they go out for a drink.

"Sep, can we stay here? I really need to talk to you, but I don't want the distraction of a bar and I need to guarantee privacy. Besides, we can drink here. I've got some scotch".

"Of course, Jacks".

Jackson poured a couple of drinks and then began.

"Sep, you know that I trust you with my life".

"And I trust you, Jacks."

"Yeah", Jackson continued. "But in all the time we've known each other, there's something I've never shared. It's something I couldn't really face, myself. But I want to share it with you now".

Giuseppe was certainly intrigued, especially given the seriousness of some of the things that Jackson had told him in the past. He let him continue without interruption.

"I've been afraid for a long time that I might be gay. Things have happened to me that have been very confusing. I know that I've had two real girlfriends and that I've had sex with a lot of others. Part of that was my attempt to convince myself that I'm straight, and to provide cover with my friends back home. But some things have also happened with guys".

He proceeded to tell Giuseppe about the encounter with Ricardo.

"Ricardo was different from anyone else. Maybe because we were roommates and I never had any inkling that he was gay. Maybe because we were already friends. Anyway, what happened between us felt much more real than anything else, even my experiences with women. Sep, there was something honest about what happened with Ricardo".

Giuseppe did not react, and his look imparted no internal feelings, not even to the perceptive eyes of Jackson. The truth is, this revelation did not matter to him. Jackson had never done anything untoward, and Giuseppe had already learned to care for him. He recalled that while he was in college at Stanford, both the American Psychiatric Association and the American Psychological Association had delisted homosexuality as a disease. So he would accept Jackson regardless of his sexual orientation. He responded,

"Jacks. What difference does it really make? You're the same person you've always been. Everyone who cares about you now will still care about you. I know that it doesn't matter to me".

"Yeah, but you're from California. You don't know what it's like in Louisiana. There's a lot of macho shit down there and a lot of bigotry. You don't know my family, either. They may love me, but they would never accept my being gay. That's why I've always been so afraid and why I don't want it to be true. After Ricardo, I got depressed and went to therapy to try to figure things out".

Jackson paused to take a drink, then continued.

"Remember a couple of months ago, I told you that I fell in love with my therapist, Helena"?

"Yeah".

"Well, I didn't know how to deal with that, either. I mean, there I was, thinking I might be gay and telling this beautiful woman about my life and my experiences with both guys and girls. Then these feelings began to arise. Feelings of being attracted her. I didn't know where they were coming from. I was becoming even more confused, and I wondered what the fuck was happening to me".

Unbeknownst to Jackson, was that at the same time he was sharing his story with Helena, something very different was going on inside her mind. She would prove to be one of the most evil people Giuseppe had ever known or even imagined could exist. The fact that she was clever, made her all the more devious. And it put his friend in great danger.

Helena was in an unhappy marriage. The combination of children and financial liability meant that there was no easy escape. This created an emotional hell for Helena, and one would expect her to seek help from a therapist of her own. Instead, she sought escape through Jackson. He was so pliable that she could choose which finger to wrap him around. Even better, she could wrap him around one, unwrap him and then wrap him around another. She could do that in succession and then start the whole cycle over again.

In successive sessions, Helena encouraged Jackson to delve into his confusion. To relate to her every sexual experience he had ever had. In her "analysis", she zeroed in on Jackson's homosexual encounters, because she could manipulate them without raising any suspicions, thereby twisting them to fit her own agenda. Jackson continued,

"Sep, Helena really helped me. At first, I thought this attraction was only in my own mind. That it was just me. But over time she began to share experiences from her past. Things that happened to her that were very similar to mine. We really began to bond. One night in July we were at a party and we managed to talk most of the evening, into the wee hours of the morning. That night we kissed for the first time".

Giuseppe could not hold back his initial reaction.

"Jackson, she's your therapist"!

"I know. But wait. There's more. One of the things she did later in our sessions was to use hypnotherapy so that I could face things I had forgotten about or buried inside me. When I came out of it, I was so refreshed and tired. I was crying and couldn't stop. She held me and we cried together and kissed for a long time. That was the real beginning.

"She kept telling me how handsome I was, and that anybody would be lucky to have me. Through my tears I asked her about guys, and she said that just indicated that I was a real man. She was not surprised that men were interested in me, since most gay men don't want to be with someone effeminate and I was so strong.

"She assured me that I was a real man and kept repeating that I was handsome and sexy. She said anyone would find me attractive. While we were kissing, she put hand between my legs and massaged me while I fondled her breasts. Then she put her cheek next to mine and said, 'One day I will prove to you just how much of a man you really are'. When I got home that night I took care of myself. In my imagination it was only Helena's face I saw".

Giuseppe could see Jackson swirling in the middle of a whirlwind. He did not have his feet on the ground, and despite therapy, maybe even because of it, he had no true direction in his personal life. Like any new relationship, there was an almost uncontrollable excitement. Being involved with an older woman created a certain facade for him--the illusion of personal pride and self-respect. Jackson did not realize that these cannot be found in someone else, regardless of their age. The fact that Helena was sixteen years older than Jackson, did not make him more mature or more secure. To the contrary, it made him look even more jejune and desperate and it made Helena look pathetic.

Jackson continued his story.

"The next time I went in for therapy, we didn't begin with words. We started to kiss right away. Then we had sex right in her office. During intercourse, she told me this proved that I was a man, because only a real man could do this to her. She said she had never felt this way with any other guy; that not even her husband could make her feel like this. After that, we became involved, having sex regularly. Now she's officially my girlfriend".

At this point, Giuseppe did not know what to say. He was not a professional. Apparently, neither was Helena. He felt fear flair within him. This was a new experience for him. Usually he only cared about himself. But here Giuseppe discovered something he had never known--a genuine concern for someone else. He was really afraid for his friend. He knew that Jackson needed to talk, and might shut down if he overreacted. Hiding his feelings from Jackson was not easy, so he hoped his expression did not reflect his inner thoughts. He looked at Jackson and asked, calmly,

"What about her husband"?

"Well, he doesn't know what's going on. I've been lying to him. But, I decided he's not going to be my doctor anymore. That's too risky. Listen, Sep. Helena's unhappy in her marriage and wants out. Her husband has mistreated her and we have discovered that we have so much in common. She said she only wants to be with me, and that she will try to find a way to make that happen.

"She knows more about me than anyone, even more than you. She knows every single thing that ever happened to me, and I know everything that has happened to her. I feel safe with her. And the sex is great"!

Giuseppe tried to pay attention, yet his mind wandered back to the psychology classes he took at Stanford. The ethical boundaries established between therapist and patient are not only inviolable, they are supposed to be fully impregnable.

"Do you want to see her picture"? Jackson asked.

Giuseppe quickly caught himself and returned to the present.

"Sure". He did not really care what she looked like, but he wanted to keep the conversation going.

Jackson took out the photo and held it up with a smile.

"She's pretty", Giuseppe said. That was, indeed, the truth.

"She's very pretty", Jackson replied.

"Do you two get along or do you fight like you did with your last girlfriend?

"No. We never fight. We only argue about a couple of things".

"Like what"? Giuseppe asked.

"Well, one thing is my friend, Ricardo".

Ricardo had returned to Barcelona after graduating, but he and Jackson continued to correspond and speak on the phone.

"How is he"?

"He's fine. But there's a problem. Remember I told you that he was coming to visit this year"?

"Oh yeah. In a couple of months, right"?

"Yup. Helena doesn't think I should invite him".

"Why not"?

"Because he's gay. And because of what happened between us. She thinks he might put me in a compromising situation or try to do something. She's says I'm still too vulnerable".

Giuseppe thought to himself, "That's rich"! Here was a woman who had breached every conceivable ethical boundary in her own attempts to prey upon Jackson's vulnerability. She saw him as an easy conquest and had fostered and reinforced his transference, adding lies and her own sexual desires to the mix. She played off his personal tragedies by encouraging him to identify with her experiences, that is, if they were even real.

That night Jackson shared something else about Helena. She had played the death card. According to him, she revealed that she had only a short time left to live and that her doctor told her she should do whatever she wanted or needed to do in order to be happy these last years! This woman was amazing, and not for the reasons Jackson thought. Her capacity to manipulate was boundless. The whole thing with her doctor was almost certainly a lie. Jackson simply accepted it because he was so totally naive and hopelessly in love. Or thought he was in love.

Too bad Giovanni and I did not know about Helena before. She could have been a part of our discussions about evil. Giovanni would never call anyone evil, choosing instead to say that very sick people do evil things. Maybe it's the cop in me, but I disagreed.

I think some people are evil, or clearly possessed by it. In my mind, Helena could single-handedly dispel any doubts about Satan. To me she was the perfect incarnation. I have always found it difficult to establish reliable levels of evil, but I wonder if such emotional and psychological control does not qualify as the highest degree. People usually think of rape as being physically overpowered by another. That is too narrow a definition. Helena was raping Jackson. Emotionally, psychologically and sexually. He was not truly free, so he could not be a willing partner. That's rape.

If there was one absolute about Giuseppe, it was that he knew selfishness when he saw it. He was honest enough with himself to admit that he was the center of his own world. So even if Helena told the truth about dying, it only magnified her manipulation of Jackson. A person who really believed she was dying, who was really in love, would never do to Jackson what Helena was doing. The number of years does not matter. How can someone who has four, or six, or even ten years to live, entrap and envelope the emotions of any other person, let alone someone so much younger? What kind of trauma would Helena be subjecting Jackson to when her death came? Not even a warped mind can call that love. No. This was the most perverse of deceptions.

As for Ricardo, Jackson expressed no fears. They had resolved the issue between them months before, agreeing that there could be no future in such a relationship, and they reestablished the necessary boundaries. Besides, Ricardo now had a boyfriend in Spain. Even though Giuseppe had only just found about what happened with Ricardo, he, too, saw no reason for concern. He also found it interesting that Ricardo's visit was one of the main things Jackson and Helena argued about. He doubted they would have have argued if a girl was coming to visit Jackson. This caused him to wonder.

Perhaps Helena also believed that Jackson was gay. After all, she may be narcissistic, but as a therapist, she must be able to identify some of her patients' issues. Compared to girls his own age, Helena could show him much more about sex. Her manipulation could also make him believe he satisfied her more than he actually did.

No. Jackson's possible homosexuality would be her only real competition. Giuseppe suspected that Helena was employing Jackson's fear of being gay to build and strengthen her arsenal. In her scheming, it would be so easy to use that fear. If she could keep him away from any male temptation, she could continue to control him.

Giuseppe recognized what Jackson could not, namely, the depth of Helena's own emotional instability. As evil as her actions were, Giuseppe actually felt a little sorry for her. That must have been Jackson's influence in his life, because Giuseppe saw nothing remotely redemptive about Helena, at least not about what she was doing to his friend. Jackson kept speaking.

"Helena said she is not happy with her husband, but would be with me".

'Jesus Christ', Giuseppe thought to himself! 'This was awful'.

For Giuseppe, the over-the-top violation was the unprincipled use of hypnotherapy. Contrary to popular opinion, a person does not slip into unconsciousness through this procedure. It is more of a very deep relaxation. As such, a therapist cannot implant post-hypnotic suggestions. However, in this deep relaxation, one might easily be open to manipulation. In this case, a very creepy deception. Given Jackson's emotional make up and state of mind, he would have been more than susceptible and willing to believe anything. Giuseppe could feel chills course through his body. This woman played every cunning card in the deck. She was devious and Machiavellian to the extreme.

Jackson's therapy sessions were not just suspect. They were morally and therapeutically diabolical. Whatever Helena's background, she clearly was not a true analyst. But she was a perfect example of why we have laws to protect patients. If it became publicly known what Helena had done, she would lose her license to practice. Not just in Louisiana, but in any state. Giuseppe did not care about that. His concern was for his friend. The fact that she continued to manipulate Jackson in an ongoing relationship was additionally despicable and disturbing.

Along with Helena being an emotionally very sick woman, it became increasingly obvious to Giuseppe that much of what she shared about her life with Jackson was untrue. At the very least, the illnesses and impending death were lies. Chances are that much of the rest of her story was false, too. It was all just a tactic to get Jackson into bed. He needed real help. But what could Giuseppe do?

Jackson was completely unaware that he was being manipulated. Giuseppe wanted to tell him right then and there that he was Helena's little Pinocchio. Giuseppe was torn. He discovered that friends in Louisiana also knew that Jackson was dating his therapist, although they did not know the details that Giuseppe did. Unfortunately, when they voiced their concerns and pointed out that this was very unhealthy, and that Helena was just using him, Jackson could not or would not hear it. In his delusions, he simply ignored them. Giuseppe's mind was wandering again. Once more he put all his effort into refocusing as Jackson spoke.

"Helena wants to meet you, Sep. She also wants to meet Ricardo. She knows that you are both close friends. She said she wants to meet everyone who is important in my life".

More manipulation. She even wanted to meet Ricardo? There was only one reason for that, she wanted to turn Jackson against him. The guys were only friends and nothing was going to happen between them. But Ricardo still represented competition, and Helena did not want to take the risk. She did not really want to share Jackson with anyone. She was also probably afraid that Ricardo would see through her and tell Jackson the truth.

"I want to meet her, too", was Giuseppe's simple reply.

In a way it was true. His primary concern was Jackson. Giuseppe wanted to stand by him, to support him and let him know that he would always be there for him. So he had to keep his own fears and reservations about Helena in check. At least for now. She was incredibly sick and deeply in need of therapy herself, but Giuseppe wanted to see what he was dealing with.

*　　*　　*

Giuseppe turned to various advisors he knew from Harvard and told them the story, being careful to keep the names anonymous and unidentifiable. Without exception they pointed out the risks. On the one hand he could tell Jackson that he was being manipulated and point out the ethical issues. But since Jackson thought he was in love with Helena, he was unlikely to hear what Giuseppe had to say. He would probably respond with anger, and Giuseppe risked losing a friend, his best friend. On the other hand, he could say nothing. But when Helena tired of Jackson, or when Jackson finally discovered for himself what was going on, he might sink into another, even deeper depression. He had already been betrayed by some of his friends. Realizing that he had also been betrayed by his therapist, might prevent him from ever trusting someone again. That result could be catastrophic. That is where Giovanni and I came in.

It was in the spring of 1979, and Giuseppe had not been home since Christmas. In the meantime, Giovanni was about to be ordained a deacon, and my wedding was only a few months away. Giuseppe called us and asked us to spend a weekend with him. We each thought we could use the break, so we willingly flew to Boston. It was a transformational experience. My judgments were shattered by a Giuseppe I really did not, or had unconsciously chosen not, to know. I discovered a far more complex person than the egocentric friend from my youth.

I was amazed by and somewhat in awe of the man he had become. I discovered that for all his self-centeredness, he could be a deeply caring person. As Giovanni's identical twin, some concern for others was inescapable. But what I saw was a profound display of compassion. I did not know that Giuseppe could care so deeply for a friend. I never knew he could place someone else and someone else's concerns before his own. That was not our experience as children, nor even while we were in college. It was not even the way he treated Yolanda.

The weekend Giovanni and I visited, Giuseppe decided to take a phenomenally personal risk. Looking back, I believe he chose that weekend precisely because we would be there, and, if need be, he could fall back on us for strength, comfort and support. He had given a lot of thought to what he was about to do, and for someone surrounded mostly by casual companions, the cost could be palpable. He might lose the only real friend he ever knew.

# Chapter 9

We arrived at Boston's Logan Airport at 4:35 on Friday afternoon. Giuseppe was waiting for us at the gate, and seemed very relieved to see us. He said he needed to talk to us and asked if picking up a fast food meal would be OK. We both agreed. That night the three of us sat in Sep's room and talked. It had been a long time since we had done that. It was like revisiting our high school days. Except that back then our conversations were somewhat superficial. Of course, at the time they seemed important--bitching about our parents; mocking our teachers; ridiculing the students we didn't like; dreaming of our future careers. And, of course, bragging about the girls we were dating. But nothing in our past compared to the conversation we were about to have.

"I'm really glad you guys are here", Giuseppe said.

His expression was filled with consternation and there was trepidation in his voice. Who was this person? I had never seen him like this. Obviously, something was terribly wrong.

"You guys know my friend, Jackson".

Actually, we had never met, but we had hear about him. We both said,

"Yeah".

"Something has happened to him".

Come to think of it, it was odd that he did not come with Giuseppe to the airport, or stop by his apartment after we arrived.

"Where is he", Giovanni asked?

"I don't know right now, but that's not important. I've told you guys about him. Not everything, but enough for you to realize he's a great guy and an even better friend".

I was becoming uneasy.

"What's wrong"?, I asked.

"There's a lot I can't tell you. But I can tell you this much. Jackson occasionally experiences serious depression".

Both of us jumped to conclusions and thought the worst. I guess Giuseppe could see it on our faces, because he immediately continued,

"He's not suicidal or anything like that".

"Then, what", Giovanni asked?

Giuseppe once again refused to share the details of what his friend had told him. What he did share, though, was done to seek our advice and to garner our support.

"Well, there are still things I only know in confidence. But here's the problem. Last winter he had another very serious depression. He went to therapy, and while there he fell in love with his therapist. She's a married woman. In fact, she's married to his family doctor".

Giovanni was still in his third year of graduate school at the seminary and they were taking courses in counseling. So he responded.

"That's a common occurrence, Sep. It's no reason to be overly concerned".

"It's more complicated than that, Gio", he responded. "She's in love with him, too".

OK. We definitely never had a conversation like this before.

"They're in a relationship now. And",

He emphasized his next words by speaking very deliberately and slowly,

"It gets...even...worse".

"How much worse can it get"?, I asked.

"First of all, I don't believe that she really loves him".

For a moment I thought I saw a flash of anger in his eyes. He continued.

"I can't share the details of his sessions. I promised him secrecy. I can tell you this. She has manipulated him. Maybe not from the beginning. But early on she decided to twist his vulnerabilities to her own ends".

"How can you know that"?, I asked.

"Some of it's in the details of the sessions. What she did and the things she told him. After he told her about the experiences of his past, she began to tell him about her own past. Horrific things designed to play upon his sensitivity. Not coincidentally, she claimed that the same kinds of things that happened to him had happened to her. This is not normal for a therapist. Or ethical. She wanted him to identify with her, so that she could direct his transference in a way that would achieve her own personal desires".

Well, now we both knew there was genuine reason to worry. But why him? This was not the Giuseppe I thought I knew. Even Giovanni wondered if we had all slipped into an alternate universe.

He said, "Sep, I know he's your friend, but this is not like you. Since when do you care about someone this much"?

I don't think he intended that comment to sound so callous. After all, Giovanni was supposed to be the most understanding of the three of us. The one cut out not just for priesthood, but for sensitivity. I was already a heartless cop. I was the one who should have asked that question.

Surprisingly, Giuseppe did not seem to take offense.

"You have to know Jackson. I've never met anybody like him. Look. You guys know me. I don't warm to people very easily. I like being popular and I thrive on being the center of attention. But it's all surface. I prefer to keep everyone at arm's length. To stay in control. I don't let people in".

Neither of us had ever heard such openness from Giuseppe. I never thought he was that self-aware, and I did not think he could feel on this level.

"When I first met Jackson, he was just another guy on campus. Then one day we went for a walk along the river. We stopped for awhile and talked. As I looked in his eyes, I felt uneasy. At first. He peered right through me as though I were merely a mirage. That was uncomfortable enough. After all, I wasn't looking for a close friend. He just seemed like a nice guy and I wanted to talk to him and get to know him better. But at the same time, that look captivated me and I could not avert my eyes. His gaze was so paradoxical. It conveyed a mixture of joy and sadness, of admiration and disapproval, of innocence and guilt, of fear and tranquility, of intimacy and distance".

"All that from one look", I asked incredulously?

Giovanni shot me a sharply disapproving glance. He was afraid I would screw up the mood of the evening, and if Giuseppe clammed up now, we might never see this side of him again. However, that was not about to happen. He did not even see the wordless exchange between us. There was something ethereal about Giuseppe's demeanor. He just continued.

"Yeah. It was incredible. I've never met anybody like him before. I felt that without my saying anything, he already knew me, that he knew all about me. I think he would have known if I had tried to hide anything or to be dishonest. And his smile was completely disarming. It was bright enough to dim the stars and wide enough to bridge the oceans. That was how our friendship began. Over the next couple of years we became very close. You know, he actually knows me better than the two of you. So you can see why I'm concerned".

As Giuseppe reached for his glass, I thought 'Thank God for scotch'. It takes time to reach for the glass and take a drink. It therefore provides a brief respite from conversation, and I was not prepared for the heaviness of this one.

"Sep, what are you going to do", Giovanni asked?

This was no idle question. Giovanni sensed something ominous surfacing in Giuseppe.

"I want to talk to Jackson. First, I want to point out the obvious, that this is an unhealthy relationship, and ethically wrong. I want to tell him that Helena has lied to him, manipulated him, and is just plain using him".

As usual, my reaction was not as tempered or refined as Giovanni's.

"Are you crazy"?, I asked.

"Sep", replied Giovanni. "You can't do that. You'll be like his other friends. He won't hear what you have to say. In fact, because the two of you are so close, for you it will probably be worse. Clearly, he's being manipulated, but he thinks he's in love. He'll turn against you. You may lose a friend. Maybe forever".

"But I've never lied to Jackson. If I pretend that everything is OK, he'll see through me".

Giovanni continued, "Better for him to think you object than for you to voice it".

I nodded in agreement. "Gio's right, Sep".

"You guys don't understand. It's not just what he'll think. I don't know if you've ever had anyone look at you the way he looks at me. It's like he knows everything. What I think and what I feel. If I don't say anything, he's still going to know".

Giovanni replied, "It's still not the same as you speaking, Sep".

I interjected what I thought was a practical and down to earth question.

"Do you really want to risk losing Jackson as a friend"?

"Of course not. But I want to tell him the truth. I feel I owe him that. He's not just a casual acquaintance. He really is my best friend. Besides, there's something decidedly different about him. I don't like the person he is becoming.

"He's beginning to lose some of that incredible depth that made him care so much about others. He's more distant now, even a little cold to his friends. He tells people they can call him anytime they want, especially if they need him. That used to be true. It's not anymore. Most of the time he doesn't answer or return calls. He's becoming ever more isolated. Even from me. I think it's Helena's hold over him".

Giovanni leaned forward and said, "Listen, Sep. I'm going to be a priest and I think I see the world differently than you". Looking at me he continued, "Than both of you. I want to believe that the deepest of love is not sexual. It's much richer. It's what the Scripture means when it talks about God being love".

It was so hard for me not to roll my eyes. The last thing that either Giuseppe or I needed now was a sermon from a wanna be priest! Still, I thought that maybe Giovanni's ideas could help. So I kept quiet. He continued.

"Every friendship is an affair of the heart. That's where our friends dwell. The problem is that the heart is a messy place to be. The feelings that reside there seek expression. And since every real friendship is about love, sometimes those feelings are confused with sex. The deepest of friendships is more encompassing than sex. But sex is more powerful. As close as you and Jackson are, Sep, you cannot compete with the bedroom".

Maybe Giovanni would make a better priest than I thought. His argument certainly convinced me. I, too, cautioned Giuseppe.

"I think I understand how you feel, Sep", I said. "But have you thought about the pain you could unleash if you say those things to Jackson? I don't just mean his pain, I mean yours, too. If he means as much as you say, and you lose his friendship, can you handle that hurt"?

Again, Giuseppe amazed me with his concern.

"I don't care about my hurt or my pain. Jackson is on a train with no breaks and it's speeding up. He'll be hurt much more by Helena. I know what I stand to lose, and I know it may all be for nothing. He might end the friendship and stay with Helena, anyway.

"I asked you guys to come visit this weekend because I'm afraid. The three of us are not as close as when we were kids. But if this goes wrong, you are the only ones I can turn to. Maybe I can't prevent the disaster Jackson is headed for, but I'm going to try".

Our days of competition had ended many years before. But that night I found myself envious of Giuseppe. He had achieved, almost by accident, something I never even aspired to--a truly selfless love. I also found myself in the unusual position of really caring for him and worrying about his wellbeing. The next day we would know the outcome.

*     *     *

Saturday morning, I volunteered to fix breakfast. I am not a particularly good cook, but how can anyone screw up bacon and eggs? Giovanni suggested making a country-style skillet, but Giuseppe was not well stocked with food items. There were no potatoes, onions, bell peppers, tomatoes, sausages or mushrooms.

"Sep", I called out. "How often do you cook around here"?

"I almost always cook. I just didn't have time to get supplies before you guys arrived. We can go to the market later today. But I figured we'd be sightseeing and mostly eating out anyway".

He walked into the kitchen, looking very tired. He continued,

"Don't fix anything for me. I'm not hungry. I had a fitful sleep last night. In fact, I didn't really sleep at all. I'll just have some coffee. Besides, I told Jackson I would come by early. If you guys want, you can go out for breakfast and wander around town".

"What time do you think you'll be back"?, asked Giovanni.

"I don't really know. I can't predict how this thing is going to go".

"Sep", I said. "I think I can predict how Jackson will react".

"You don't know him, Tom".

"No, but if you go through with this, you're going to try discredit his therapist, who now is also his girlfriend. It doesn't take a genius to figure out how he'll respond".

"I thought about that all night, Tom, when I couldn't sleep. I'm not changing my mind. I'd better get going".

Giovanni spoke up.

"Sep, why don't we plan on meeting back here around noon. We can go out to lunch after, if you're feeling up to it".

"OK". And he was out the door.

Giovanni and I did not wait for breakfast. He grabbed a cup of coffee and we began to talk.

"Well, Tom, I guess this is not the trip we planned, huh"?

"Not at all. I was wondering, Gio. Why couldn't we get through to him last night"?

"Your guess is as good as mine. I know he's my twin brother, and that the three of us were close growing up. But he's different now. I'm not sure I really know him. I certainly didn't know he could be this close to anybody. I think he had his mind made up before we got here, and nothing we said would change it".

"Yeah", I sighed. "And that's what's going to happen when he talks to Jackson".

Giovanni looked out the window and simply said, "I know. He scripted his side of the conversation, but he can't control Jackson's ability to hear or how he responds".

We sat there for awhile in silence. Then I asked,

"If we're right, he's going to be very hurt when he gets back. What are we going to do"?

"I don't have any idea, Tom".

# Chapter 10

Giuseppe rang the bell. Jackson opened the door and invited him in.

"Do you want some coffee"?, Jackson asked.

Giuseppe usually only drank one cup a day. But he thought it might steady his nerves, so he said,

"Yeah. Thanks".

Giuseppe forgot that Jackson liked to brew Louisiana style. Traditionally, people have joked that this coffee is so strong you can stand a spoon in it. It's an odd thing being nervous. Even on a warm day, the body shakes inside, the same as on the coldest and darkest days of winter. So he was glad for this cup. It was fresh, and hot, and warmed him nicely. It also gave him a shot of courage.

This was not going to be a conversation where he could get right to the point. Giuseppe thought he figured a roundabout way to address the topic. So, he began with what he supposed would be an innocuous question.

"When is Ricardo, coming from Spain"?

"He's not". Short, simple response, revealing no other information.

"What happened"?

"I called him and told him that the timing wasn't right. I just said that I'm caught up in a lot of activities and would not have any free time".

"Is this because of Helena"?, I asked.

"Yes. She doesn't think he's a good friend for me. And she's convinced me, too".

"So you lied to him".

"Well", he started to say.

"And now you're letting her decide your friends for you"?

"It's not that so much".

"Of course, it is, Jacks. You know Ricardo is not interested in you as a sexual partner. And in the time we've known each other, you have always spoken of the importance of friends. Of wanting to meet good and true friends. That's what Ricardo is. At least that's what you told me".

"I thought he was. But now I think I might have been wrong. Sometimes he bothers me".

"All friends bother each other at times, Jacks. But I remember when you were trying to plan a visit from Ricardo several months ago. Diana was your girlfriend then and she demanded a lot of your time, remember? When I asked how Ricardo's visit would fit in, you told me 'my friends come first in my life'. It looks like that has changed".

"No. It's just that Helena is my therapist. And my girlfriend. She knows me better than anyone and she thinks his visit is a bad idea. She's probably right".

Maybe this was not such a roundabout way, after all. It seems like they got to the point rather quickly. The initial question proved to have been only a slight detour. They had already arrived at the juncture where Giuseppe would have to challenge Jackson's relationship with Helena. Now what? This was a delicate moment. There would be more of them in this conversation, but he needed to try to keep Jackson in dialogue with him. Certainly at the beginning. He choked down the tension in his voice and tried to ask, offhandedly,

"Jacks, can I tell you something about you and Helena"?

"Of course, Sep. You're my best friend. You can tell me anything".

Was it his imagination or did Jackson sound a little wary? God knows he had reason to be. And he could always read Giuseppe so well. Not that this conversation required particular skill in that regard! Jackson's voice didn't reveal anything, though. Neither did his look.

Giuseppe hesitated. He seemed lost in his own thoughts. 'Maybe everybody was right. Maybe he should just let it be. Not one person, not the counselors on campus, not Giovanni, not Tom, agreed with his decision to confront Jackson'.

He could almost feel the friendship slipping away. But Jackson's wellbeing and happiness were more important than the friendship itself. Besides, he was committed now. His mind and heart had probably already been probed by Jackson's damned insightfulness, anyway. Even if he tried to completely shift direction, he had already been exposed. Still, he hesitated.

"Sep. Just say it. Whatever it is".

"Jacks. Every relationship, every friendship must be predicated on honesty and truth. Otherwise, it may last for a while, but it is doomed to failure. Our friendship has always been like that, so I can't sugar coat this for you. I don't think your relationship with Helena is based on honesty or truth, and I think it's unhealthy".

"How can you say that? You've never even met her. She's wonderful, Sep".

The tone in his voice was defensive. That was a natural response. Jackson thought he was in love and was staking his claim for this relationship. He was taking the same position he had with others. So far, he did not seem angry. But Giuseppe was going to say more than any of Jackson's other friends had dared to say.

"Yeah. She's so wonderful, she's carrying on this affair with you behind her husband's back. And that's what it is. No matter what she says to you, to her this is an affair. But she lets you think it's so much more. Listen, Jacks. She's using you, and what she's done is morally and ethically wrong". The first big bomb.

"What the fuck do you mean"?

Now there was anger. If it got out of control, he would never hear the rest of what Giuseppe had to say. And he had to hear the rest of it, even if he didn't listen right now. Maybe it would germinate in Jackson's mind and he would be able to reflect on it later. Although that was doubtful.

For the first time Giuseppe realized the trap he had set for himself. Jackson wasn't going to think about this alone. How did he not see this? Jackson was going to tell Helena about it, too. It was as if he was still hypnotized by her. He was so deeply under her control, that she would destroy Giuseppe in his mind and drive him out of Jackson's life for good.

Giuseppe recalled one of his psychology classes. The professor talked about an inner saboteur. Something inside that won't let us succeed, that sets about to destroy what we hold most dear. Giuseppe held this friendship most dear, and yet, here he was on the verge of destroying it, or letting it be destroyed. He had been advised not to proceed with this confrontation. Was this his inner saboteur moving him forward? It couldn't be. After all, he was trying to rescue his best friend, not destroy the friendship, itself. But that's the point of the inner saboteur. It is seductive and deceives our reason. Most of us are not even aware of its activity at the time. It didn't matter now. Giuseppe had already crossed the threshold. Saboteur or not, it was too late. He continued.

"It's wrong for a therapist to get involved in a relationship with a client. Period. That is one of the cardinal rules of therapy. For one thing, there is no equality of power. The therapist will always dominate the patient".

"That doesn't apply here. She's in love with me, too".

"That does not make it an equal relationship. And while you mention it, here's another thing, Jacks. I don't believe she's in love with you". Bomb number two.

"She's merely taking advantage of your past. Your hurts, your weaknesses, and your vulnerabilities. You have always been naive and too willing to trust. That's why you've been betrayed over and over in your life. She knew all this. She knew you were easy prey. And because she's your therapist, she knew how to control every session to lead you right where you are today. Now you're being betrayed again. Only this time it's Helena".

"That's not true. I fell in love with her first".

"And she let you pursue it. Actually, she pursued you. Don't you see?

"Helena was supposed to help you. Instead, she's exploiting your trust and abusing her power. It's just as despicable as every other abuse you've experienced in your life. In fact, it's even worse, because she helped you acknowledge the pain of your past. Then she took that pain, twisted it, and used it only to abuse you again.

"You used to use the term 'emotional blackmail' to describe what people did to you. I don't know why you can't see it, but this goes way beyond that. This is truly pernicious. You're really being betrayed by her, Jacks. And this betrayal is the worst one of all. Jacks, Helena's raping you. And what makes it so bad is that she's making you think you want it". Bomb three.

"Shut up, Sep". But Giuseppe continued.

"She's manipulated you into a trauma bonding, from which you will not easily break free. At least not on your own".

"None of this is true. I'm telling you, I fell in love with her first".

"You keep talking about love as if she really loved you. That's simply not possible. If she did love you, she would never have engaged in this relationship. She knew what you had been through. Instead of helping you to heal, she took that information and used it for her own ends. Even if you fell in love with her, she was supposed to remain objective and preserve professional distance. Just one passionate kiss or one fuck would have been a violation of her oath and a betrayal of your therapy. To keep it going is deceitful, manipulative and despicable".

"You're the one who doesn't understand, Sep. She went through the same things I did. The things that happened in her childhood, even things in her marriage, are so similar to mine. We have a natural bond. We share the same kind of history, the same hurts, the same betrayals. Both of us have been afraid to trust anyone, but we can trust each other. We know each other inside out. Our love can help heal us both".

"Listen to yourself, Jacks. You're like a fucking robot repeating ideas she put into your head. And every one of them is a violation of her oath as a therapist. Even your own words prove that this is an unhealthy bond. She has maneuvered you into a sick symbiotic relationship. Besides, how can you know that what she told you is even true"?

"Because I love her and I trust her".

"You're so naive, Jacks. More than that, you're a fool".

That was a slip of the tongue. Giuseppe so wanted to recall those last three words. The anger rising between them now was not going to be contained much longer. There would be no physical violence. But they both knew the power of words to hurt. Right now, Giuseppe was hurting Jackson with what he said. But he was not lashing out at him, or trying to hurt him deliberately. He was trying to get Jackson to face the truth. For his own good.

Giuseppe realized that Jackson's only response today would be to strike back. He would use words far more hurtful, because they would be driven by an attempt to intentionally inflict pain. To hurt Giuseppe, as much as Giuseppe was hurting him. That was part of the risk. He continued.

"Jacks. I'm not trying to cause you pain. But I don't think you realize what is really going on".

It was time for another bomb.

"Helena is not dying from those illnesses she talked about".

"Fuck you, Giuseppe"!

It had been a long time since Jackson called him by his full name.

"Are you some fucking doctor now? Or do you have some fucking crystal ball?", he asked.

"No", Giuseppe replied. "But I know that this is just more of her manipulation. She said her doctor told her to do whatever she needed to do in order to be happy during her remaining years. Really? That's fucking nonsense. No doctor would say that. And even if he did, no therapist would repeat it to a patient. The whole concept is so incredibly selfish, that it can only be a lie. I mean, shit! Helena's a therapist for god's sake. She knows what she's doing, Jacks. It's a deliberate attempt to deceive and control you. And you're probably the only person I know who could fall for that".

"You really are a son of a bitch, Giuseppe".

Jackson's vocabulary was not particularly creative at this point. But when you can't think of anything else to say, "fucker" and "son of a bitch" work just fine. He was getting more vehement. That was to be expected. But his anger was not the real problem. Jackson needed to face the truth. But how could Giuseppe get him to hear and sense that this was, indeed, truth?

A bolt shot through Giuseppe's head. He would try to diffuse this by appealing to the best in Jackson.

"Jacks. You are one of the most sensitive and beautiful people I have ever known. And I'm not the only one who sees it. Everyone does. That's why people are drawn to you. It's probably the reason Helena was drawn to you, too. There certainly is no way Helena didn't see what the rest of us see.

"She may be unhappy in her marriage. I can believe that much. But she recognized your inner beauty, your tenderness, your compassion and your desire to help people in need. Then she used all that, the best parts of you, to achieve her own selfish ends.

"Think about it, Jacks. If you found out you were dying, would you turn around and use another person this way? Would you tie another's emotions into knots for your own personal pleasure, knowing that you would leave that person in shambles when you died? No. If you really love somebody, you don't use that person just because you're dying. In fact, it's exactly the opposite. Instinctively, you know I'm right.

"I think Helena lied to you to get you into bed. That way you would continue to be dependent on her. But Jacks, whether she lied or told you the truth, Helena is emotionally a very disturbed woman. And every goddam psychologist in the world will agree. And they will tell you that this is a dangerous situation".

"I think you've said enough, Giuseppe".

"Listen, Jacks". Giuseppe continued to reaffirm Jackson's goodness. "The reason you would not play the death card to get some temporary pleasure out of someone, is that you are too good a person. You care about other people. That's what therapists are supposed to do, too. So if Helena was really dying, and if she really cared about you, about what was good for you, she would not have let this happen. The truth is, she's only focusing on herself. She's incredibly selfish".

"It's not selfish. She does love me".

"Jacks".

"Don't call me that", he replied. "Only my friends can call me Jacks. You don't fit that category anymore".

"Fine, Jackson. No matter what you say, I'm still your friend, even if you're angry with me right now and don't see it".

"No, you aren't. If you were really my friend you would support me. And I'm not just angry now. You have attacked the woman I love, and you have attacked me. I don't think things are going to get better between us after this. I think I'm going to stay angry for a long time to come".

"You're saying that because you like having a girlfriend. You like the sex".

"You're such a fucker, Giuseppe. It's not just the sex. We like spending time together. Going places and talking, like you and I used to do along the Charles River. We just like being together. It's all therapy for me".

Wow! Giuseppe was almost ready to give up. Jackson wasn't hearing him.

They had both been raising their voices as if that would win the argument. Jackson had been shouting for awhile now. Maybe they both had. It sounded as if Jackson had already turned a deaf ear to what Giuseppe was saying. But it wasn't over yet. However, if Giuseppe wanted Jackson to be able to remember and think about what he said, he was going to have to lower the volume. He took a deep breath and said, somewhat calmly,

"That's all part of the manipulation, Jackson. Helena wants to possess you. Only a pathologically selfish person would do what she's doing under the pretense of death. That makes it all about her. Not you. So, whether she's dying or not dying, Helena has already betrayed you and now she's continuing to manipulate you".

He couldn't tell if he was making progress. Jackson was not looking at him. Giuseppe continued,

"Part of the problem is that you don't really know what love is, Jackson. Helena is much older than you. That's already a complicating factor. On top of that, emotionally, you are a very young twenty-four. You have always been extremely naive and too trusting. I'm not your therapist. I'm not even a psychologist. But maybe you are easily manipulated because you want so much to be accepted and loved for who you are. Well, this much is clear. Helena is not accepting you for who you are, and what she's doing is not love".

For a moment Giuseppe thought he was getting through. Jackson look at him with tears in his eyes. But deep down Giuseppe knew he was not winning the argument. The tears were springing from anger, not realization.

"I thought we were friends, Giuseppe. You just said that you're still my friend. Then you should want me to be happy".

"That's the point. I do want you to be happy. Truly happy. But that can only happen in an equal relationship. You can't find happiness by being someone's puppet".

Another emotional shift occurred. Jackson's hurt and anger turned nasty. He didn't yell, but his vicious tenor was unmistakable. He squinted his eyes, casting a cold chill Giuseppe had never seen before.

"You're just jealous, Giuseppe".

"That's ridiculous, Jackson. You've had other girlfriends, and I never objected to those relationships. Even the last one, Isabel. She was crazy. In fact, she was loony. But at least she was your own age. In spite of all her personal problems, the power dynamic was equal, and she was not manipulating you. Come to think of it, have you ever noticed that the girls you are attracted to are all fucking nuts"?

True or not, that did not help. Jackson responded angrily,

"You claim Helena is selfish. Then what about you? You've always been a user. And you don't care who you hurt. You don't even have a girlfriend. Not really. I don't think you really care about Yolanda, or anyone else, for that matter. You despise Helena and you're jealous because I have found love and you're still alone".

"You don't mean that", Giuseppe replied.

"The hell I don't. I don't know why I ever bothered with you or wanted to be your friend. You were like a lot of other people I've met. I guess I felt sorry for you. Right from the start. You seemed so alone. Popular, yeah. But lonely inside. You had no one to care for and no one who cared for you. Back then, I didn't know why. Not even as we shared our personal stories. Now I do.

"You're empty inside, Giuseppe. All your relationships are hollow. You don't even get along with your twin brother. It's really sad that you can't be happy for me. There's one thing you're right about, though. I am a fool. Or at least I was a fool to ever think we could be friends.

"I don't know why I trusted you with my life, my history. I wish I could take it all back, but I know I can't change the past. Helena taught me that. However, I do have control over my future. I don't want to be your friend, anymore, Giuseppe. In fact, I don't even want you in my life anymore".

Giuseppe had been warned about this. As he listened to Jackson, he knew he was not hearing anger, so much as determination. He knew now that he lost more than an argument.

If Jackson wanted to hurt Giuseppe, he succeeded. There were just enough traces of truth in what he said. He was wrong about Yolanda, but he was right about Giuseppe being a user. And being hollow. That had haunted him since he was a teenager. Ironically, it was Jackson who had taught him depth of character and how to care for others. He was no longer an empty image of himself. And now it was Jackson who laid bare the festering wounds of the past. Giuseppe was not about to let his feelings become the issue here.

"Fine, Jackson. I'll leave, and I'll leave you alone, if that's what you want. But when I walk out the door, try to be honest with yourself for the first time since Helena entered your life. She's driving a wedge between you and your friends. First, you rejected Ricardo as a friend, and now me. How many more friends will you have to lose so that Helena can have you all to herself? Then ask yourself which are the real relationships. Who are the good and true friends, the one's worth having? Who's going to be there for you when you need a friend?

"I'll be honest, Jackson. You've always been able to see through me, so you know what I'm saying now is true. I was empty inside. That changed when I met you. I discovered what real friendship is. And it is something I have come to treasure deeply. Even after I leave today, I will still care for you. Not the way Helena pretends to care. Not for anything I can get out of you. Just simply for you. For who you are and for what you have given me.

"Remember this. If you ever need me for anything, whether you want me fly to Louisiana or wherever else you happen to be, or even if you only want to talk on the phone, you will always be able to find me. And I will not let you down. I will always be there for you.

"Thanks for the last few years, Jackson. Thanks especially for your friendship. I truly am a better man because of you".

With that, Giuseppe walked out the door, and out of Jackson's life.

*    *    *

After breakfast, Giovanni and I had walked around for awhile. We were not really sightseeing. For the moment, we were not interested. Much of the time we just sauntered aimlessly and in quietude. We may not have been thinking the same thoughts, but we were both engaged by the same problem. Occasionally, one of us would break the silence with a comment or question. Always about Giuseppe. Since this was such a different personality, neither of us knew what he would be like when he got home. The one thing of which we were both quite certain, was that the conversation with Jackson was going to prove a disaster.

We made sure that we arrived back at the apartment before Giuseppe. Whatever condition he was in, we did not want him walking into an empty room. The door opened, and there was no need for words. Giuseppe's expression was more revealing than an entire lexicon.

I started to speak, and Giuseppe raised his hand.

"Don't. Please don't say anything just yet".

We all sat down. It was awkward. We knew someone had to say something, and it should not matter who started. Neither Giovanni nor I would ever say 'I told you so'. Certainly not right now. But I don't think Giuseppe was worried about what we would say. I don't think he knew what he wanted to say, himself. Since he was sure we could read his expression, no words were necessary, anyway. So we waited.

I went to the kitchen to make another pot of coffee. When I returned, I asked if either of them wanted any. Only Giovanni did. I sat back down, took a sip and looked at the floor. Finally, Giuseppe spoke.

"You were both right. About everything. Jackson wouldn't listen to what I had to say. I mean he heard the words, and I think he heard the points I was trying to make, but he wouldn't listen. Or maybe he couldn't".

Giovanni was first to respond.

"You don't have to tell us anything you don't want to, Sep".

"Yes. I do".

Once again I found myself stunned by this person in front of me. I had never seen Giuseppe cry. Not since we were little kids. He wasn't actually crying now, either. But his eyes filled with moisture, threatening to brim over. It was obvious that he was engaging all his strength to hold back tears. As if he feared unleashing a flood he could not control. And one thing about Giuseppe, even this new version, was that he would maintain control. Displays of weakness were not in him. Another thing that was obvious was that the tears sprung from a well of intense hurt. But was this hurt due to the words he and Jackson exchanged, or something that Jackson did, or both? Giovanni and I wanted to respect Giuseppe's feelings right now, so we waited. After a few minutes he continued.

"How can good intentions go so fucking wrong"?

It was not a question to be answered. It was rhetorical.

"I went there to try to help Jackson. I told you guys last night that I know things about him that I can't repeat. Not even to the two of you. They tie into what evolved from his therapy. I'm telling you, this therapist is astonishingly manipulative and profoundly evil".

"You didn't say that, did you"?, asked Giovanni.

"Not exactly. At least I don't think so. I did tell him that she lied to him, probably about the things that supposedly happened in her past, and certainly when she told him she was dying".

"Whoa", I said. "You didn't tell us that last night".

"I didn't mean to say it now, either. It just slipped out. Maybe I did say things to him that I didn't intend. I thought I kept close to my script. Anyway, the thing about her dying is not really confidential. Only the details about it.

"I told him everything I wanted to say. That the relationship was unhealthy. That she was abusing, even raping him. I pointed out that she is manipulating him and trying to decide his friends for him. She's trying to destroy his friendship with Ricardo. I think she wants to destroy his friendship with me, too".

As an after thought he tagged on, "But I don't think she has to worry about that anymore".

"What do you mean"?, asked Giovanni.

"First, let me tell you the rest. I told him that the relationship is not based on truth, that she is using him. I pointed out that no therapist should get involved with a patient. That it is a breach of ethics, and that no such relationship was ever equal. That a good counselor would never tell a client the kinds of things Helena told him. I pointed out that she doesn't really love him. She can't, because if it were real love, they would not be in this situation. That everything she did and said was just to get him into bed. Not only did she not love him, I told Jackson that he was too immature to know what real love is. I emphasized that she is continuing to manipulate him and trying to keep him dependent on her".

"Does it really surprise you, then, if he was upset"?, I asked. "Did you really expect him accept all that? That's a shit load of stuff to lay on anyone, Sep"!

Giovanni brushed aside my comment and asked,

"How did he respond"?

"At first he denied everything I was saying. He said she really does love him. Then he got angry and started yelling. At one point I actually thought I was getting through to him. It was like he knew there was some truth to what I was saying, even if he couldn't admit it. But what really hurt was what he said about me".

Giuseppe paused here, almost like he did not want to continue. He looked exhausted. He got no sleep the previous night and had been run through an emotional grinder that morning. I was surprised to see him hold up as well as he did.

"I told you guys how insightful Jackson is. Between what he can read of me and what I have told him over the years, he knows me too well. He took dead aim and struck right at my heart, pointing out how hollow and empty I am. How alone and lonely I have always been".

"That's not true, Sep", Giovanni objected. "If you were hollow, you would never have gone to see him and would have never challenged him. You would never have risked a friendship so important to you".

"I agree, Sep", I replied. "I mean, I was against you going over there this morning. But you put a lot on the line. You were willing to risk everything to help him and to rescue him. That's not the work of an empty person".

"Yeah. You guys would see it that way. Toward the end he said he did not want to be friends anymore or even want me in his life".

"He didn't mean it", Giovanni responded.

"Yes. He did. You had to be there. To see him. Don't forget. I know him only too well. And those were not idle words. They accompanied an icy glare that I've never seen before. He meant everything he said.

"It was even more evident to me this morning that he is completely under Helena's control. I really didn't have a chance today. I had only a flicker of hope. Now I don't have either".

"Then fuck him", I said. "Just pretend he's dead".

Giovanni started to respond to me, and his comment would not have been pleasant. But Giuseppe beat him to it.

"I can't, Tom. The reality is he's not dead and I can't just make him dead to me. I told him I'd leave him alone, but that I was still his friend. And if he ever needed anything, all he had to do was ask".

He paused for a moment, as if searching for the right words, then continued,

"I'm a bit torn, because a part of me agrees with you, Tom. The Jackson I knew and grew to love is dead. He died in those therapy sessions. And the new one is not only a stranger, he is not as good a person. He is not as kind, or loving. He does not care as much about his friends. Regardless of what he may think about himself, now, Helena did not help him".

"Then he isn't worth it, Sep", I said. "And you can't waste your time".

"It's not that easy. You still don't know him. You guys have never even met him. Or anyone like him".

"Now you sound like Jackson", I said. "He objected to what you said about Helena because you had never met her".

"It's not the same. I'm not trying to defend something evil, or someone who is a manipulator. Besides, I believe, or at least I want to believe, that the old Jackson can return. Deep inside, I can't accept that he's dead. I believe that he can be emotionally healthy and be the gentle person he was before. And also, I still care about him".

"But", I persisted. "Friendship has to be two-sided, Sep. You can't force him to be your friend. You gave it your best shot. You have proved yourself a friend over and over. Even this morning. You just couldn't win. Let him go".

"You're both right", Giovanni interjected. "Friendships have to be two-sided. Love does not. At least not true, altruistic love. Parents don't stop loving their kids because they turn out to be assholes or turn their backs on the family. And", here he glanced at both me and Giuseppe, "I know you guys don't want to hear anything religious, but God doesn't stop loving us because we sin or turn away from him".

"Well", Giuseppe said with a sense of finality, "I don't think he'll be calling me for help".

"You never know", Giovanni replied.

"Listen, you guys. I think I've fucked up this weekend enough. Let me take a short nap, and we can go out and see the sights. Besides, I think that I could use a good, stiff drink tonight".

Giuseppe got up and headed for the bedroom. Then he turned and said, "Maybe two or three".

Giovanni and I realized there was not much more to say. I lit a cigarette and poured another cup of coffee.

The rest of the weekend was uneventful. We saw a good part of

Boston's downtown, and had a couple of good meals, but we needed to take an early afternoon flight back to Los Angeles.

The three of us never spoke of Jackson again. I think Giuseppe was trying to test his theory. If Jackson needed him for something and contacted him, there would be reason to speak to him and about him. Otherwise, it was a lost friendship that Giuseppe would bury in his heart.

The whole experience had a profound impact on Giuseppe. His personality would undergo another transformation. Giuseppe had been concerned that Jackson would never trust anyone again. That was yet to be learned. Ironically, it was Giuseppe, himself, who would remove trust from his vocabulary. From both his personal and business relationships. He reached the conclusion that he would only be able to rely on himself.

# Chapter 11

Giuseppe returned to Los Angeles that May, but he did not travel alone. Personal tragedy trailed him. Although of an emotional and psychic nature, it was nonetheless real. It is doubtful that even he knew the strength of its hold. His lost friendship weighed on him as nothing else ever had, and it would alter his personality as negatively in the end as it had positively in the beginning. Unlike Jackson, Giuseppe was not inclined to seek counseling. He felt sad, of course, but life goes on. He made a commitment to himself: no one else would ever again get that close to him. In the end, it was only a friendship. Except it wasn't. He buried the loss and the hurt as deeply as possible, but the entire experience had already changed him.

Giuseppe did not waste his business degree. He quickly began building his new career. He had been quite frugal over the years, saving almost every dollar he earned. Still, it was not enough to start a business. So he applied for and received a managerial position at Pacific Stereo, a large hi-fidelity, stereo and electronics chain headquartered in Northern California. Eventually it would expand to 56 stores in California, and a number of other locations in Washington, Texas, Wisconsin, Illinois, Georgia and Missouri.

Giuseppe was hired for the Torrance store about twenty minutes from Los Angeles. While at Pacific Stereo, Giuseppe learned as much as he could about the burgeoning home stereo business and the major brands that were saturating the lower to mid-priced market such as Kenwood, Pioneer, JVC and Sherwood. It was during this employment that he met his future business partners. Jonathan Williams managed the North Hollywood store, and Andreas Mertz was stationed in Santa Monica.

Pacific Stereo had its own review and evaluation team that put all new products from every manufacturer through a rigorous testing program. They evaluated not just the technical specifications, but also the practical elements, such as ease of use, and what might today be called user-friendliness. These reviews and critiques were widely respected throughout the industry. Over the years, Pacific Stereo introduced a number of house brands to market. Some were fairly decent, others never lived up to expectations.

Andreas Mertz had already worked at Pacific Stereo for several years. One day he suggested a clever idea to upper management. Why not use the reviews and evaluations of competitors' products to their own advantage? The idea was to take the best elements of the other products and create a new house brand for Pacific Stereo that would be better than anything else available. From this proposal a new modular stereo system was born. It was appropriately called "Concept", and it received stellar reviews.

Andreas did not know how to sell himself. Pacific Stereo embraced his idea, but he never received proper recognition or compensation. Additionally, despite his prodding, management never marketed the system outside of the Pacific Stereo stores. As a result, many salesmen encountered resistance from consumers. After all, most customers were disinclined to put out a significant amount of money for a product they had never heard of. That was unfortunate, because Concept was equal to if not better than almost anything else on the market.

Pacific Stereo filed for bankruptcy and dissolved in 1986. But by about 1982, Giuseppe had already learned everything he needed to know. He could see where the company was headed and he had his own vision of the future of the electronics industry. He wanted to start his own company, but lacked sufficient resources. He also lacked a foundation for launching his own career. What he really needed were a couple of partners he could control. He had become friendly with both Jonathan Williams and Andreas Mertz and decided to set up a meeting one Sunday afternoon.

They met for lunch at the Hamburger Hamlet on Hollywood Blvd, across from Grauman's Chinese Theater. They requested a table in the far corner where they would not be disturbed by the throngs of tourists crowding Hollywood Boulevard as they searched for their favorite stars on the "Walk of Fame". After settling in and ordering their food, Giuseppe began.

"How much do the two of you know about the finances of Pacific Stereo", he asked?

Andreas responded first.

"Well, I follow the stock reports, and I have noticed a few store closures, but I don't know anything definitive".

"I don't know anything at all", Jonathan chimed in.

"Well", Giuseppe continued, "Those store closures are touted as a response to low volume sales in depressed areas. That's just bullshit. The company over-expanded. I mean, really. Texas, Georgia, Wisconsin and Missouri? Give me a fucking break. They should have stuck to the West Coast".

"So, what's the point"?, asked Jonathan.

"The point", Giuseppe replied, "is that Pacific Stereo is going bankrupt. I give them five years, ten at the most. But no matter what, the company is history".

"And"?, queried Andreas.

"I want to break out on my own", Giuseppe said. "I have some ideas, but I can't do this alone. I need some seasoned people who can help me manage a new venture. Between the three of us, we have all the experience we need. I think we can open our own, independent store".

With some concern, Jonathan asked, "But if Pacific is going bankrupt, how do we know we can make a go of this"?

"My strategy is to leave the mass market behind. I want to focus on the wealthy. Sell high-end products that we could never have carried at Pacific".

Giuseppe could see that they were intrigued. And, of course, he did not tell them that his vision went way beyond stereos. For the time being, all he wanted was someone to buy into his idea.

Andreas tended to be a practical person. He asked,

"What about funding? Even if we pool our resources, the three of us do not have the money".

"No", replied Giuseppe. "But when I was at Harvard, I did my Master's thesis on business plans. I have one that I think will work. We won't have any problem getting a loan, and once we get set up, I know we'll succeed. Look, the three of us have a lot of collected experience".

"So, tell us more", Jonathan said.

"Well, look". Giuseppe put his arms fully on the table, leaned forward and continued, "There are some superb systems out there that Pacific would never be able to touch. I propose we open a store in the Beverly Hills area and carry primarily high-end equipment. We would draw our clientele from Beverly Hills and Bel-Air. The rich. We don't need a chain of stores. If we market well, people will come to us".

Andreas interjected, "It's an interesting idea. Especially if you're right about Pacific Stereo going bankrupt".

"I am right. And, regardless of when it happens, we'll each be out of a job. Look I don't expect you guys to jump at the idea today, and I'm not putting a contract in front of you. Just an idea. But I want you to think about it seriously. With my business plan and our experience, we're bound to succeed. Just give it some thought. If you want in, we can work out the details later. But I don't want to wait too long. If you're not interested, I'll find someone else".

Giuseppe did not just have a valuable degree from Harvard, he also possessed an innate business acumen and the ability to sell almost anyone on any idea. At least if he really believed in it. He was simply skilled at selling himself, and communicated only as much of his thought as he needed to succeed. And that Sunday he succeeded. He put over his idea and managed to hook his soon-to-be partners.

They did not see the future the way Giuseppe did, but then he never disclosed his ultimate goals. He had a vision he would not share with anyone, partner or not. Giuseppe engendered trust. He always did. But he no longer extended it others. That ended with Jackson. He had no intention of allowing either Jonathan or Andreas the comfort of real friendship. In a way, this enabled him to keep his business deals coldly professional.

In this case, he convinced both of them to join him, to set out on their own and open a new kind of stereo store. The three of them continued to discuss the idea over the next couple of months. The more they talked, the easier it was for Giuseppe to convince them that the real profit in stereos was to be made by courting the rich and grooming lifelong clients.

Giuseppe had a grander pursuit in mind. This enterprise would prove a solid foundation for initiating a research and development program. That is where his dream really lay and it was all his. He had no intentions of sharing it.

They opened their first location on Santa Monica Blvd just east of La Cienega Blvd. They originally looked for a location in Beverly Hills, but the leases were too expensive. This store was close enough, however, to draw clients from Beverly Hills, Bel-Air, even Brentwood and the Pacific Palisades.

Naming the store was tricky business, but it would ultimately be whatever Giuseppe wanted. He managed to forge a partnership where he controlled fifty-two percent, leaving Williams and Mertz to equally divide the other forty-eight. Finally, they settled on:

Living Stereo
*Where Sound Meets Sight*

Giuseppe hoped that the slogan 'Where sound meets sight', would have a double entendre. On the conscious level, the equipment simply looked great. But he also wanted it to play on a subconscious level. He wanted to convince customers that the best reproductive sound was something that be could be seen. It was not just hearing an orchestra, it was being able to visualize them. It was not just hearing Joni Mitchell, James Taylor, Elton John, or Carly Simon performing at The Troubadour on Santa Monica Blvd. It was to "see" them on stage through the finest stereo equipment of the day.

The new partners decided to stay clear of most inexpensive products, focusing their attention on high-end components such as Halcro, Quad, Nagra, and Arcam. For good measure and brand name recognition, they also carried Marantz, Harman-Kardon, Denon, and Onkyo. Of course, anyone was welcome to spend money in their store, but it was the rich they wanted to target.

*    *    *

Giuseppe and Yolanda continued to date after his return to Los Angeles. They were were both attendants at my wedding with Giuseppe being best man and Yolanda a bridesmaid. It was a grand affair, but did not motivate them to follow suit.

I managed a few moments at the reception to speak with Giuseppe.

"Doesn't this give you any ideas"?, I asked.

"Oh, plenty. But the timing isn't right. Yolanda wants to finish her degree and get established as an educator".

"Well, don't wait too long", I replied. "You're not the only one with your eye on her".

"No, but she's not interested in anybody else. I know that for sure. Besides, you should know better than I that you can't have everything you want right away. I have plans for the future, and sometimes you have to sacrifice in order to get ahead".

"Well, Sep. I'd sure like to see you two get married. I think Giovanni would, too".

"You two worry too much about me. I promise I'll be fine. I'm already over that stuff with Jackson".

Now, there was a classic example of denial. And yet, it was vintage Giuseppe. The same Giuseppe I thought I knew before the Boston trip. He had this uncanny ability to compartmentalize, pushing back and isolating anything he did not want to face. The problem is, that is not the same thing as dealing with a problem and resolving it. He only succeeded in driving down and burying his emotions. He emerged with the steely determination that he would never be hurt again. It left him with the dangerous illusion that he could control himself and everyone else.

On the other hand, there really was no reason to rush into marriage. Yolanda had already begun to free herself of doubts about Giuseppe. Still, she would not graduate from the USC School of Education for another year and wanted to establish herself as an educator. As a result, they would not marry for another five years. This enabled Giuseppe to pour himself into his new company and lay the foundation for an even more ambitious future.

# Chapter 12

Giovanni had been my best friend since we were kids. Even before his ordination I began to worry about him. I don't know if it was his arrogance, or naiveté or both, but he was going to have trouble with the institution. We were raised in a church that was changing, if not disappearing. Except, of course, within the hierarchy of the church, itself. Giovanni wanted to embrace the change. But how would he fit in?

When we were kids, every nun wore a habit. They were taught in the convent to walk on the balls of their feet so that they appeared to float on air. Only their faces and hands were visible. Even the most congenial of them were something less than real. The closest they came to being human was the competition between different communities for the most outlandish outfits. This had the unintentional consequence of birthing a popular television series, "The Flying Nun" about a very petite sister, who was frequently whisked away by gusts of wind.

As for the priests, they did not float on air, they walked on water. They had the answer to every question, even questions that had never been asked. Not unlike the sisters, the priests also had a costume. For them it was the Roman collar. Most of them would never even think of being seen in normal clothes. This both distanced them from reality and led the priests, themselves, to think they were a cut above. Many tried to pass this off as professionalism. It was not. It was clericalism. And Giovanni wanted no part of it.

The truth is, these facades created a false persona for priest and nun alike. They also masked the reality that priests and nuns are just like everyone else with the same strengths, weaknesses and limitations. Giovanni, like some other younger priests, wanted to be more human, not less.

When I think back on it, I believe that Giovanni felt constrained. Not only unfree, but unable to be real or to be his own person. His early attempts to define himself were met with rigid resistance. He felt that he was confronted with two choices: He could sell his soul and principles and move up the clerical ladder, or he could live in constant tension with the powers of the church and run the risk of languishing in a Catholic vacuum.

In his first year as a priest, all clergy were required to attend a workshop explaining changes within sacramental practice. For convenience, it was offered several times in various locations throughout the archdiocese. The presentation Giovanni attended, happened to be the same one at which Cardinal Manning was present. Giovanni did not wear a collar. It was not his custom. Besides, the meeting was only for priests.

He was unable to avoid the Cardinal over the course of the evening, and when they met, Manning was not pleased with Giovanni's choice of clothing. Manning, though, was notoriously passive aggressive. He exchanged pleasantries with Giovanni, even managing a less-than-authentic smile. The next day he directed Msgr. Rawden to call Giovanni into the office and reprimand him for not wearing the Roman collar at the workshop. Giovanni found this both discouraging and disheartening. If the Cardinal thought this exercise in power would control him, it backfired. All it accomplished was to strengthen his resolve to be a different kind of priest.

Giovanni's assignment as associate pastor at St. Hildegarde Parish lasted four years. How, I do not know. It seemed as though everything he did irritated his pastor. Giovanni was a tennis enthusiast. One day a friend gave him a bumper sticker for his car that read: "Tennis is for swingers". Like many bumper stickers it deliberately carried a dual meaning. Giovanni affixed it to the back of his car. Fr. Hansen was not pleased.

He called Giovanni into his office.

"Father", there was that word again. "I think it is inappropriate for you to have that bumper sticker on your car".

Giovanni was not coy, but he thought he'd have a little fun, and maybe even cause Hansen to raise his voice or lose his temper.

"Which bumper sticker"? There was only one.

"About tennis being for swingers. It sends the wrong message".

"It's just a bumper sticker, for God's sake. It's all in good fun. Tennis is about swinging a racket. No one is going to think that I'm a swinger the way you mean it".

"I still think you should remove it".

"I'll think about it, but I doubt if I'll change my mind. I think it's your problem".

That should at least have gotten him angry. Instead, Hansen just stayed cool and looked down at his desk.

Hansen was a curious study and a perfect example of the delusion created by the priestly facade. He could be seething inside, but he never lost his temper. He could not be seen as a real human being, not even to another priest. Sadly, he was a psychological mess, giving new meaning to the term "anal retentive".

He would count the cookies in the cookie jar to make sure no one on staff was eating them. He was concerned about the physical condition of the church buildings and grounds, and frequently crossed the parking lot to pick up a piece of paper no one else even noticed. At the same time he cared little about the spiritual wellbeing of the parishioners. He rarely looked an adversary in the eye, and he never lifted his eyes above a woman's feet.

Hansen continued.

"Father, there's something else. I don't think you should wear your tennis shorts around the house, even if you're on your way to the car. It is immodest and could give scandal".

"You've got to be kidding me", was Giovanni's reply!

"No. I'm not. You should wear a cassock. Then when you get to the court, you can take off the cassock, and you'll be in your tennis shorts and ready for the game".

"Do you really think the people don't already know I have legs"? Sarcasm always came easily to Giovanni. "Or are you jealous because I have better looking legs than you do? You don't really think someone will actually get excited because I'm wearing shorts, do you"?

"Father, I don't find you amusing".

"Maybe not, but you don't have the authority to tell me not to wear tennis shorts when I'm heading off to the courts. If that's all, I have more important things to do right now".

Giovanni stood up and walked out of Hansen's office. There was always a bit of the devil in Giovanni. As time went on, instead of giving into Hansen, he began deliberately walking through the office in his tennis shorts to prove his point. That point being twofold: priests do have legs, and Hansen would not tell him what to do.

In terms of interacting with parishioners, Giovanni's warm personality, his skillful preaching and genuine care for people created a stark contrast to the shy and retiring, but controlling, Hansen.

It became clear that Hansen appealed to those parishioners who viewed the Church merely as a means to salvation, those who were content to go to Mass on Sunday and be done with religion. For them, keeping the buildings and grounds clean and trimmed was all they wanted. It gave them a sense of pride in their parish, however superficial.

For those who needed counseling, or guidance, especially in times of crisis, it was Giovanni they called for. Hansen had no skills in this regard. As time progressed, it was obvious that more people were calling to set up appointments with Giovanni, than they were with the pastor. Hansen took notice. He wanted Giovanni out. Transferred. Anywhere.

Giovanni complicated matters by his indiscretion. At gatherings of priests, he enjoyed engaging older priests in theological discussions. Since many of them had not read a book since ordination, this allowed Giovanni to expound on some newly-minted theory about which they knew nothing.

In one particular discussion, Giovanni went after an amiable, older priest with limited intellectual and argumentative skills. Interpreting a line out of the Gospel of John, Giovanni reasoned that God was a being in process. While the Christian Faith proclaims that there are three persons in one God, Giovanni suggested that in the future there might be four. The older priest lacked the ability to grasp the concept, and certainly had no competence to argue how Giovanni might be wrong. He just threw his hands up in the air, saying, "No. No".

Giovanni took a nefarious delight in these encounters. As his friend, I became concerned about the direction this was taking him. He had a circle of close friends, but was quickly becoming persona non grata among the rest of the clergy. The only thing that saved him was his quick wit and delightful sense of humor. It was not, however, enough. No one wanted to work with him, which made assigning him to a new parish a difficult task.

He had seen too many priests turn priestly ministry into a sinecure. He vowed not to follow suit. So it was with some dismay that he discovered a most unlikely advocate, Msgr. Benjamin Hawkes. Although they were poles apart theologically and politically, he actually liked Giovanni.

Hawkes was unbending in his authoritarianism and deliberately set about to intimidate other priests, demonstrating in every conceivable way that he was the power behind the throne. It worked with most of them, and the result was that the average priest would cower before him, or avoid him altogether. Not Giovanni. This was the one time his arrogance served him well.

At various functions, Hawkes would seek out Giovanni and attempt to bluster his way through a conversation. Giovanni always stood his ground. On one occasion, Hawkes tried to browbeat Giovanni by saying,

"Fr. Lozano, don't you realize that I have power over you"?

"Listen, Ben". As a matter of principle, Giovanni always called Hawkes by his first name. He wanted to level the playing field.

"I recognize the authority you have in Church affairs. I also realize that you control the money in the Archdiocese. Now to some people that is the same as power. But the truth is, the only power you have over me is what I give you. And I do not give you any".

Such exchanges were uncommon for Hawkes. I think he respected Giovanni for standing up to him, as much as he despised the majority of priests who did not. Regardless, it made for an unusual relationship. At any gathering of priests, Hawkes went out of his way to greet Giovanni, and spend time in useless conversation. This did not go unnoticed by the rest of the clergy, though no one could quite figure it out. Other than a possible faith in Jesus, Hawkes and Giovanni had nothing in common, and these friendly encounters did nothing to help Giovanni in his other struggles with the Church.

*     *     *

As he became more liberal, Giovanni also became more outspoken. For whatever reason, he zeroed in on the most contentious and controversial issues of the day. Although not accurate, he made a name for himself as someone opposed to everything the Church taught. It was not long before FKIA was appended to his name by more than just his friends.

The existence of hell became a particular case in point. To be fair, Giovanni took a two-pronged approach to damnation. First, he emphasized the love of God, demonstrating how God never turned his back on the ancient Israelites. He also noted the emphasis in the New Testament on the gratuity of God's love. For example, Paul's declaration that God sent his only son while we were still sinners. He skillfully demonstrated that salvation is God's free gift, and not merited by anything that people do. His conclusion was that if God is truly all-loving, there could not possibly be a place of eternal punishment.

As he continued to preach these ideas, he created an ongoing dialogue with parishioners. It became obvious to Giovanni that most people believe in hell not for any theological reasons, but because it serves as a means of retribution. They take comfort in the idea that bad people go to hell and that there is a reward for living a good life. It was fairly simple to identify the self-serving element in this approach. In a very practical way, believing in hell gives people leeway to be unforgiving in their own lives. If God sends even one person to hell, then maybe our own enemies will be there, too. That was the position Giovanni's sister, Bianca, took. She despised her ex-husband and needed to believe that he was going to hell. But that was pure vengeance on her part. Somehow she missed the whole thing of forgiveness.

In one conversation with Giovanni, I took Bianca's side.

"Gio, when we were growing up, we were told that God is all-just. So if someone commits a mortal sin, they sever their relationship with God. That happens all the time in the way that people treat each other. And if they die before asking forgiveness, they go to hell".

"Ah, but Tom, you don't really believe that".

"I don't believe in God, but I believe in hell".

"That doesn't even make sense", Giovanni replied. "But let's leave that aside for the moment.

"Here's the problem with hell. It all comes down to what kind of God you believe in. If you believe in a God who seeks to punish and destroy, and many people do, then hell is a part of your faith. But if you believe in a God who loves and forgives, then there is no room for hell".

"That's sophistry", I said.

"No. It's not". Giovanni continued.

"If there is one thing that encapsulates God, that sums up everything God is, it was written in the First Letter of John: 'God is Love'. As such it is in the very nature of God to forgive. The moment God stops forgiving, he stops being God".

"But", I countered, "what if someone doesn't want to be forgiven? What about someone like me who doesn't even believe in God? I'm certainly not going to ask forgiveness".

"The point is, that forgiveness resides not in the sinner, but in God. People have trouble with this whole concept, because forgiveness is not the norm in human life. We try to get even with people who hurt us.

God, however, has to forgive in order to be God. Otherwise, at best, he is some super human being. In the Christian faith, we are called to be like God. That means we, also, are called to forgive".

Although there was a practical dimension to preaching about forgiveness and reconciliation, the idea of universal salvation was still somewhat academic, and stirred no real concern among Church authorities. It was when Giovanni tackled more direct and practical issues of Church teaching and power, that he sealed his fate.

*   *   *

The Pope holds general audiences on Wednesday afternoons. This gives him the opportunity to expound on some matter of importance knowing that people from all over the world are listening. At one such audience, Pope John Paul II addressed the contentious question of women's ordinations. He asserted that women could not be ordained priests, and declared that the discussion was over and people were not to continue talking about it.

That was too much for Giovanni. To begin with, the teaching on women's ordination is not infallible, and, in reality, it can be changed. Giovanni has certainly always believed that it will be. He has never been able to abide authoritarianism. So, the following Sunday he acknowledged in his homily that only the Pope could change the teaching on women's ordination. At the same time he stated in no uncertain terms that the Pope did not have the authority to tell people what they could or could not talk about. Then he proceeded to advance a theological argument in favor of ordaining women to the priesthood.

I had often wished that Giovanni would stop sharing these stories with me. It's not that I disagreed with his ideas. I didn't. But his methods were not helpful. I grew tired of always having his back, of being his apologist. And I was really tired of challenging his style and approach. He would not listen to me. He was my friend, and I really wanted him to succeed. But there I was, a non-believer, and I apparently understood the church better than he did.

Giovanni had one thing in common with Pope John Paul II, namely, the application of Gospel principles to social and political life. They did not agree about all those principles, or how they played out in practice, but neither of them shied away from addressing the realities of modern life through the lens of the Gospel.

Given Giovanni's liberal foundation, he found himself ever more frequently condemning the policies of the U.S. government. Although he challenged both Democrats and Republicans, and never endorsed any person for office, it was obvious that he found the Democratic party much closer to the values of the Gospel. As one bishop told him, "Other than the issue of abortion, the Republicans have nothing in common with the Catholic Faith or the Gospel of Jesus Christ".

The Archdiocese of Los Angeles is the largest in the nation. So, given the increasing Catholic population and the declining number of priests, even Giovanni was given his chance to be a pastor. Needless to say, he was not given one of the wealthy parishes, what some priests referred to as "plums". But he finally was his own boss. Officially, so to speak. He was appointed pastor of St. Catherine Parish on Vermont and Adams in Los Angeles.

To some extent, he disappeared from the Archdiocesan radar screen. He focused his energies on building his new parish into a genuine community where people knew each other, cared for one another, and grew together in their faith. Even if it was a more liberal faith than the next parish over.

# Chapter 13

Although I did not know it at the time, my marriage with Emily was coming to an end. It wasn't as painful as I thought it would be. We had been drifting apart for so long, that splitting up seemed natural. I had decided to follow the chief's advice and take the detective exam. She actually encouraged me. I think it was because she also wanted me out of the C.R.A.S.H. unit. She didn't trust Gates' motivation, but she appreciated the fact that I would be in a less dangerous, and, hopefully, less corrupting environment. So I began preparing. The written test was comprehensive and intense. Still, in the fall of 1983 I passed it along with the oral examination, and made detective, grade D1.

I had a good relationship with my captain, and he encouraged me to remain at the Southwest Division, even offering to intervene on my behalf if I chose to stay. It was a tremendous vote of confidence, and I was appreciative of his support. But I needed more than this promotion. I needed a change of venue. So after making detective, I found myself transferred to the Hollywood Division, part of the West Bureau.

The Hollywood Division was more than just a change. People have always had a fascination with the rich and famous, even before the phrase existed. But I discovered first hand the obsession that consumed the public when it came to movie stars. To be sure, the division covers a broader area than the residences of actors. But the very fact that the film industry demands such great attention, magnifies every crime. From assault to burglary to homicide. As such, the detectives in Hollywood are actually under even more pressure and scrutiny. Still, it was a relief from the world of street gangs.

My academy class did not designate me "the man most likely to be chief". That would have been laughable. Not only did I consider it out of reach, it was not even a dream. However, following my meeting with the chief back in 1982, I discovered that I did have a decent amount of ambition. I was not going to remain a beat cop forever. Nor for that matter, just a detective. I was dedicated to my job, and I made sure that I was noticed.

In the summer of 1984, the Games of the XXIII Olympiad came to Los Angeles. In one sense, it was déjà vu since the city first hosted the Games of the X Olympiad in the summer of 1932. Things were different this time around, though. Los Angeles had grown much larger with a population of 3 million in the city proper, and nearly 8 million in the metropolitan area.

As in 1932, there was significant turmoil in the world. This time it was not the depression. Nor were the world's powers twisting themselves toward world war. Instead, terrorism had surfaced as an international danger. From Belgium to Turkey, from Austria to Canada, from Colombia to Yugoslavia, no country was immune. Only months before the Olympics, truck bombs in Beirut, Lebanon, struck United States and French military barracks, killing 299 American and French servicemen. Los Angeles was on heightened alert for the games.

The Los Angeles Police Department was prepared to provide ample security for the games, at least within the city proper. But the venues for the various competitions were spread over a vast area of Southern California, thereby requiring the involvement of police departments from three counties and multiple cities. With the rising threat of a possible terror attack, Federal agencies set up a joint task force with the LAPD. I successfully lobbied to get myself assigned to this interagency team. As it turned out, the Olympics proceeded without incident, and once again, I was recognized for my commitment.

I moved up the detective ladder as quickly as possible, seeking a promotion after putting in the minimum required time for each grade. In 1985 I successfully sat for the next oral exam, becoming detective, D2. I followed that one year later with the oral exam for D3, the highest level of detective. Both D2 and D3 are supervisory positions over D1. The difference between them is primarily pay scale. But it was not the money that drove me. It was my desire for recognition and advancement. I still was not sure how far I wanted to go. But at least lieutenant was now within reach.

*     *     *

As a detective, I found myself being the cop I always wanted to be. Instead of planting evidence, I was discovering it. The hours were a challenge, and certainly not kind to a married man. I realized then that I was correct in my arguments with Emily over kids. Emily and motherhood were almost synonymous, or would be if she met the right guy. As for me, I was not cut out to be a father. Emily and I stayed together through the fall of 1984.

Although she was not a sports reporter, she covered many elements of the Olympics for her newspaper, once again focusing her reflections on the world of Great Britain. She was to provide her readers with unique insight into the importance of sports among the Commonwealth nations, especially her own home, England.

During the games, it would have been impractical for us to separate. Besides, given my involvement with the task force, we rarely had time for each other. It was sometime in early October that we made it official. I know I should remember the actual date, but I don't. I do remember that it was my first personal experience with divorce. My parents and the Lozanos had stayed together, as did the parents of most of my other childhood friends. The few divorces we heard about as kids, were distant and did not affect us.

I arrived home at about 11:30 PM, and Emily had all her personal belongings packed. She did me the courtesy of not walking out while

I was at work, and leaving behind only a note. That was more the stuff of movies. She was also kind enough to wait up for me.

"Tom", she began, "I'm leaving".

I look around at the suitcases and said somewhat slyly,

"Oh. Silly me. Here I was thinking you had been out shopping".

Emily was not ruffled. She even smiled as she said,

"Tom, I've grown used to your humor. Even your sarcasm has a certain charm to it. But don't forget, I know you. You resort to mockery when you're at a loss for words, or when you want to hide your true feelings. You can't put that past me. Besides, we both knew this was coming. Now just seems like the right time".

A surreal silence ensued for a few moments. There was no animosity, no yelling, not even a good argument. I suppose we depleted those throughout the marriage, with Emily winning almost every fucking disagreement. This night was calm, almost peaceful. More like two friends who had just completed a lengthy vacation and were saying goodbye to each other.

"Are you leaving tonight"?, I asked.

"No. I'll sleep on the couch and leave early in the morning".

"That's not right. I'll take the couch", I replied. I was not trying to be chivalrous. It just seemed that she deserved the more comfortable place to sleep. Besides, I could already envision many nights of sleeping alone in an empty bedroom. This did not need to be the first.

"Emily, I'm going to have a scotch. Would you like one"?

"That sounds good. Thanks".

Even the time it took to pour the scotch did not inspire brilliance or uncover any words of wisdom on my part. I silently prepared our drinks, straight up for me, one ice cube and splash of water for Emily. I handed her the glass.

God, she was still beautiful. I've never quite understood the deeper emotions of the human heart. Emily and I had been married for five-and-a-half years. But for many months there had been no sex or moments of intimacy between us. We had more than a casual interest in each other's jobs, but nothing approaching the concern that binds husband and wife. I looked at her, and in that moment I wanted to reach out to hold her and kiss her. I wanted to reignite the flames of passion that had become mere embers inside us. To unloose the ecstasy we had both so carefully and deeply buried. The thought of sleeping together and making love one last time was almost unbearable. But this was fancy, the illusions of an imagination untethered to reality. Emily reached for the glass. It was automatic, unthinking, as if I were only the local bartender. No. Tonight, there would be no last outburst of love.

Emily left the next morning. I forced myself to rise early. I said goodbye leaving only a final, gentle kiss on her cheek. With no animosity between us, the divorce would prove to be what is euphemistically called "amicable". What is so friendly about two people severing the bonds of marriage? At least we would not be fighting over money or possessions.

After Emily and I split, I regretted going home to an empty house. As distant as the two of us had become, at least there was another person there. Many a night I left the station and headed to the nearest bar, just to have some company. Frequently enough, I did not spend the night alone. I think I liked the idea of no commitments. I certainly had no desire to try marriage again. A steady girlfriend was as close as I wanted to get. And I didn't want that to last too long, either. I found serial monogamy less demanding. And probably less fulfilling.

*     *     *

Once I left C.R.A.S.H., my rise in the ranks of the LAPD was more methodical than meteoric, and I did not miss a beat. My evaluations from each assignment were exceptional. Of course, I have to admit some luck from my C.R.A.S.H. unit days. No one ever discovered my involvement in the planting of evidence. That could have ended my career, even if it did result in putting dangerous criminals behind bars. It was also something I had put behind me. So, by 1988 I was ready to take the oral and written exams for Lieutenant. I passed these with ease. Subsequently, an opening occurred for a lieutenant in the Wilshire Division. I applied for it, and with strong recommendations from my captain found myself transferred. Like the Hollywood Division, Wilshire is part of the West Bureau, but it is a very different job. There are more crimes requiring real detective work in Wilshire. I was clearly going to be kept busy over the next few years, until my next promotion.

That next advancement came in 1994. By this time, Gates was history, replaced as chief by Willie Williams. It was a time of upheaval and renewal in the department following Gates' disastrous handling of the 1992 riots. An intense effort ensued to restore public confidence in the LAPD. As various programs to upgrade the department were underway, I was ready for my next move.

Ever since becoming a detective, and setting my sights on the position of lieutenant, I knew that I wanted to be in the Robbery Homicide Division. RHD is an elite part of the LAPD. It has immediate authority over high-profile cases regardless of the division where the crime occurs. In one sense, it is where the action is. I had been a lieutenant for a little more than five years when a position opened in RHD. Following my application for this spot, my entire career was put under a microscope. Having received stellar reviews throughout my time with the LAPD, I was selected. It was my job in RHD, that caused me to receive the call about Giuseppe's family. It was the one night in my life that I wished I was anything but a cop.

# Chapter 14

Giuseppe's return from Boston, coincided with another period of emotional distance between us. This time, however, it was not difficult to peg the cause. From my perspective, Giuseppe never recovered from the loss of his friendship with Jackson. I wouldn't say that his personality turned on a dime, but there was a Jeckyll and Hyde quality to his relationships, at least with me, and, I think with Giovanni, too. Yolanda didn't seem to notice. By this time she had fallen in love with Giuseppe. She was under his spell and had no reason to suspect that he kept anything from her. In reality, she was not aware that he did not take her fully into his confidence. Neither in terms of his business plans, nor his emotions. He just allowed his outgoing personality to mask anything he wanted to keep hidden. And for the most part, it worked.

Giuseppe would not allow himself to trust anyone. Williams and Mertz were his business partners, but he kept them at bay as much as possible, never even hinting at his future goals. The one thing he was up front and honest about was his business proposal for the new stereo store. The success of their venture lived up to all Giuseppe's hype and promises. Living Stereo flourished almost from the day they opened its doors.

They had secured supply contracts for a wealth of high-end products. They shunned the mass media marketing that characterized their former employer, choosing instead to advertise in select and esoteric magazines and publications that targeted the rich. If their advertising program worked, they knew they would also be able to rely on word of mouth. And it worked.

Living Stereo opened its doors for business on Friday, March 16, 1984. Because the store was new, there were a few people who wandered in merely out of curiosity. More important, however, were the clients who arrived with the specific intent of laying out thousands of dollars for new equipment. Living Stereo had what they wanted. And these clients provided a leap into an unexpected area that even Giuseppe had not considered.

As the client base grew, it expanded from the homes of the wealthy into the boardrooms of L.A.'s largest and richest corporations. The United California Bank Building became First Interstate Tower the same year that Living Stereo opened its doors. One year later, First Interstate' CEO, Joe Pinola, contacted Giuseppe and asked him to install a state-of-the-art system in their corporate offices. He agreed and Pinola spared no expense. First Interstate quickly became the envy of every other corporate and legal office in Los Angeles. It was not long before Living Stereo was contracted to install high end equipment in the most luxurious complexes throughout the city.

Giuseppe and Yolanda were married that same summer, and he was left feeling that the sky was his only limit to success. The wedding took place at St. Andrew Parish in Pasadena, with Giovanni presiding. Giuseppe asked me to be best man, I'm sure a return compliment for my selecting him at my wedding. More cynically, though, he was not even remotely close to anyone else. The ceremony was even more moving than my own had been, and for awhile I was carried away by it all. I looked at Giovanni and Giuseppe and myself, and I thought how comfortable we all seemed together. Several times during the Mass and reception I also found myself missing Emily. Our marriage problems were not a secret from our close friends and she did not attend this ceremony. I privately wondered if Giuseppe and Yolanda would have a more successful marriage. I certainly hoped so.

While Giuseppe guided the direction and fortunes of Living Stereo, Yolanda taught English literature in high school. Three years running she was named teacher of the year at Blair High School in Pasadena. The awards, however, were not her greatest source of satisfaction. She was most pleased about teaching teenagers to love great literature. She expected her students to relate to and appreciate J.D. Salinger's "Catcher in the Rye". That was actually easy, given the angst of adolescence. Yolanda's assigned reading list included major works such as John Steinbeck's "The Grapes of Wrath", and "The Great Gatsby" by F. Scott Fitzgerald. But she also encouraged the reading of more obscure books such as Paul Wellman's "The Walls of Jericho", and one of her personal favorites, A.J. Cronin's "The Citadel". She would continue to teach at Blair until the birth of their third child.

*   *   *

For the first seven years, the newly-weds lived in Giuseppe's apartment on Olympic Boulevard in Los Angeles, between La Cienega Blvd. and Curson Ave. It was a comfortable two bedroom flat with room enough for the first baby. Carmen was born on September 11, 1985. She was nothing short of an adorable baby, every bit the image of her mother. Yolanda and Giuseppe asked me to be the godfather, and, of course, Giovanni would baptize her. I was honored, but I was sure Giovanni would object because of my agnosticism. I was wrong. He said as long as the godmother was a practicing Catholic, it did not matter what I believed. I honestly think he would have had no objection anyway. Friendship trumps the regulations even of the Catholic Church.

Giuseppe worked very hard during the next couple of years. Living Stereo was a bigger success than even he had expected. By 1986, he knew they needed to expand. He and his partners wanted to avoid the mistakes made by Pacific Stereo, but adding one store was not too big a gamble. And they wanted to maintain their core home business. After many hours of planning, and identifying the demographics, they decided to open their second location on Pacific Coast Highway in Redondo Beach, at the foot of Palos Verdes Peninsula and Estates. Like the Santa Monica store, this one was an instant success.

Meanwhile, Yolanda became pregnant with their second child, and on September 5, 1987, another beautiful baby girl, Gina, was added to the young Lozano family. Yolanda had her hands full with two girls two years apart, and she began to feel that their home was shrinking. But she loved every minute of it. Everyone, including myself, doted on the girls. They could not have been cuter, and for me it was an opportunity to be a parent, even if only vicariously. I remember pointing out to Giuseppe that if they were going to have any more children, they should aim for a different month. Otherwise, they would go broke celebrating birthdays in September.

One day in February of 1988, Giuseppe shared with Yolanda a part of his future goals. He was still capable of some affection which he mostly reserved for Yolanda. He had given her the silly nickname "Anda". He thought it had an elevated quality to it. "Yolie" was too hokey sounding, and "Lannie" was just ridiculous.

"Anda, I need to talk to you about something".

Minus the babies needing to be fed or changed, Yolanda was always ready to talk to Giuseppe. In fact, ever since Gina was born, Yolanda welcomed these opportunities all the more. She loved the girls, but craved adult conversation, especially with Giuseppe. It was such a welcome respite.

"I know that you are not very interested in electronics", he continued.

"Sep, you know how much I love music, and thanks to your job we have a wonderful Nagra with great sound. But, honestly, it's like the car. As long as it works when I turn it on, I don't care about anything else".

"To tell you the truth, Anda, I'm bored with stereo systems, with the Living Stereo stores and with corporate installations. That's not the real future of electronics. At least it's not the future for me".

"But, Sep. It's still a new business. What else would you do", Yolanda asked?

"I was thinking about computers. There will always be a demand for stereos, and people who want great sound will go to stores like Living Stereo. It's just not for me, anymore. I only opened Living Stereo to establish myself. With Williams and Mertz on board, it was an easy start. But it was never my goal to be in stereos".

"You're not seriously thinking of getting into computers, are you"?

Yolanda was a little leery, and there was a touch of frustration in her voice. Giuseppe had convinced her that they needed to sacrifice to get ahead and, so far, she was willing. At the same time, she wanted a more comfortable life. Not that they were hurting. They lived in a nice enough neighborhood, but she would have liked more room, and a yard for the girls to play in. She thought they could make a go of it through Living Stereo. The company was thriving and Giuseppe had to be making a small fortune. So why were they still living a parsimonious lifestyle? This new idea just seemed crazy.

"No, Anda. I don't want to get into computers per se. I want to manufacture the microchips inside the computer. There's a whole new world out there. And the future is exciting for anyone who has a vision. I have".

"But, Sep", Yolanda tried to interrupt. Giuseppe continued.

"Wait. You don't read the same journals I do. The Atari 2600 game system was revolutionary. It started something new".

"Yeah. And then the company went bust", she reminded him.

"But that was just the beginning. The Nintendo Entertainment System that was released last year is a huge step forward. Have you read anything about it"?

"I've been a little preoccupied with the girls". She hoped the understatement was clearly communicated.

"Listen, Anda. I don't think even Nintendo knows what they're onto. We're about to see another revolution. This one in the computer industry and everything connected to it. It won't be long before consoles will be obsolete. Kids will be playing computer games on handheld devices that fit in the palm of their hands".

"You're crazy, Sep".

"No, I'm not. It's coming. Nintendo's Game and Watch series was no fluke. And whoever corners the computer chip market is going to clean up big time".

"So we stay put on Olympic Blvd? When do we get ahead? When does our family actually benefit from all your grand plans"?

"I told you a long time ago, that we had to sacrifice. We're not going to live here forever, but each attempt to succeed will require more sacrifice. I promise you that within four years, we'll have a house of our own in a good neighborhood. In the meantime, we can move to another apartment, if you want".

"So besides sacrificing", Yolanda asked, "where do you get the money to start a new business"?

"I'm going to sell my share of Living Stereo. I already have a buyer".

"Wait a minute, Sep", Yolanda observed. "You're not asking me. You're telling me. Right"?

"Come on, Anda. You make it sound so unsavory".

"Well, just what is it that we share in this marriage? I'm the one left to deal with the kids while you're out conjuring up crazy schemes for getting rich".

"I have to sacrifice as much as you do. I would love to move into our own house. It just takes time. And this is not a crazy scheme. I know what I'm talking about with these computer chips. Just give me a couple of years, and I'll put you on easy street. I promise, Anda".

He put his arm around her, drew her close and gazed into her eyes. He gently kissed her lips and then began to glide cheek to cheek. Even without the music, it was a dance of sublime grace. God, she was such a sucker. He knew just how to make her melt. After a few minutes of bliss, she pulled back and asked,

"What about Jonathan and Andreas"?

"They can stay with the company, if they want. I'm not taking them along. This is going to be my business. With the profit I make from selling my share of Living Stereo, and my new business plan, I'll get a solid loan. I'll be fine. You and the girls, too".

"Do Mertz and Williams even know you plan to sell"?

"Not yet".

Yolanda cast him a glance that was more than quizzical. It was disconcerting.

"Sep, there's something wrong with this. Not starting a new business, but leaving them hanging. If it hadn't been for the two of them, you would never have been able to open Living Stereo".

Giuseppe responded with a rigid lack of compassion.

"They're big boys, Anda. There was a reason I set up the contract with fifty-two percent for myself. I didn't want to have to get their approval for what I did".

Yolanda wondered what had happened to Giuseppe. Actually, she wondered what had happened to herself. Was she just so absorbed with being a mother? Was she just blinded by her love for Giuseppe? Whatever, she did not see this change coming. For Giuseppe, this was not change so much as evolution. It was part of who he decided to become nine years earlier. He was keeping the promise he made to himself.

*    *    *

For several months, Giuseppe had been in secret negotiations with "The Good Guys", a west coast consumer electronics chain. It was not unlike the old Pacific Stereo, though it included modestly better products. The founder, Ronald Unkefer had taken the company public two years earlier, and then began to target a more upscale market. But he was still unable to attract the same class of consumer that Living Stereo did.

Giuseppe and Unkefer thought this was the perfect match. The Good Guys would purchase Living Stereo, and at least for several years continue to maintain the two names, operating the stores independently. At the same time, the merger would provide Unkefer and The Good Guys a nice foray into the true high end stereo market. On April 21, 1988, Living Stereo became a wholly owned subsidiary of The Good Guys.

Once again, Giuseppe was right. His partnership with Williams and Mertz, however, did not end well. I don't think he expected it to, but neither did he care. He got what he needed out of them, and was more than willing to cut them loose. The business world, like so much else in life, is cutthroat. With Giuseppe's share of Living Stereo, he held the knife firmly in hand. They'd have to find their way with a new partner, even if that new partner was a big corporation.

It really was not a bad venture for Williams and Mertz, either. They stood to gain a great deal, particularly if the sale and marketing went as planned. That really wasn't the point. They felt betrayed by the fact that Giuseppe never included them in the discussion. He didn't inform them until the deal was sealed. Giuseppe was unfazed. He was moving on, and Williams and Mertz were simply another necessary sacrifice.

# Chapter 15

Optimists want to believe that the human heart beats warm. Reality is a little less sanguine. Most people are driven by self-serving interests. If that sounds like the musings of a languorous cop, so be it. It's also the truth. Perhaps modern life, with all its distractions and allures is the culprit. Regardless, in spite of all the platitudinous preaching of religion, greed remains the driving force in life. It is, of course, masterfully masked in euphemistic terms. But it is greed, nonetheless. And when it takes hold, the individual becomes frigid and heartless, and all society suffers the consequences.

In the 1980's, an unadulterated avarice muscled its way to the forefront of American life. I don't mean to suggest that it was not already lurking in the shadows. But there is something shady about shadows, that keeps them far from center stage. All that changed when Ronald Reagan was elected President of the United States. In many ways he was no worse than most other politicians. But his affable personality and communication skills, enabled him to contort the values and principles of American life in a highly touted quest to enthrone the individual.

Arguably, Reagan's most famous campaign statement was not a

statement at all. It was a question: "Ask yourselves, are you better off than you were four years ago?". The tragedy lies in the fact that the question, itself, was deliberately deceptive. It was addressed not to the country as a whole, but to individuals. And it was designed to appeal to the worst in people. To the lowest common denominator. The insidious result was the crafting of a new American dream in which personal gain was the only virtue. Amazingly, people from all economic brackets ceased caring about their neighbors, choosing instead to advance only their own personal desires and interests.

Government was castigated for doing exactly what it was supposed to do, namely, protect and care for all its citizens, especially the most vulnerable. In order to succeed in that task, the wealthy must contribute from their surplus. Jesus set the foundation when he said, "Much will be required of the person entrusted with much, and still more will be demanded of the person entrusted with more". Jesus' words, however, would no longer sound in America.

Beginning with Reagan, the term "common good" vanished from the American social and political discourse. Those few--mostly clergy--who used the term were ignored, ridiculed or accused of being communists. No one in political life would take that risk. For in the United States, probably nothing is more detrimental to a politician than to be painted as a socialist. Never mind that most Americans claim the United States is a Christian nation. Never mind that Jesus, himself, was unabashedly socialist. It does not play in the U.S.

Giuseppe was well-positioned to take advantage of this shift from a community culture to the individual. Rather than use his intellectual and creative skills to benefit others, he bought into a perverted version of the American dream, one that was based entirely on greed. He was insightful enough to realize that this new vision of America had nothing to do with social or family values, even though it was framed in that language. He marveled at how Reagan and his ilk managed to dupe a large part of the nation. Giuseppe understood that the new America was all about wealth. Getting it, keeping it, and the poor be damned. He was amused by the language and illusion of fiscal responsibility. All this was a far cry from the social, religious and family values Giuseppe grew up with, but it was consistent with his own narcissism.

This was demonstrated in Giuseppe's misplaced admiration for fellow Southern Californian, Michael Milken, whose claim to fame was to make the trading of junk bonds a staple of the new Wall Street and the bilking of the poor the thoroughfare to wealth. Had Giuseppe's interests trended toward investments, they might have ended up cellmates in federal prison. Instead, he set about to become the computer chip wizard.

Giuseppe was intelligent. More than that, he had more than his share of business acuity. Once he clarified his goals, he cut a straight path toward success. Like other entrepreneurs, he deserved credit for honing this skill. Also, like other entrepreneurs, his success rested definitively on the backs of his workforce. This was even more so the case for Giuseppe since he was not a computer engineer. It was their genius in designing microchips that would make him a multi-millionaire. His brilliance lay in creating a vision and hiring the most highly skilled, creative engineers in the industry, and in cutting very shrewd deals for materials and production.

No one knew it at the time, but Giuseppe's new company, The Pegasus Group, would end up setting the industry standard in microchips. Its research and development division would rival the U.S. military in security and surveillance technology.

\*     \*     \*

Retail stores such as Living Stereo require carefully chosen locations to maximize traffic and sales. Such is not the case with research facilities. For a short time Giuseppe flirted with the prospect of situating The Pegasus Group in the Silicon Valley, just south of San Francisco. It was a natural choice, since dozens of technology companies were already located there. However, if Giuseppe learned anything in Boston, it was that no place offered the comfortable weather of Southern California, and he was staying put.

Even before the sale of Living Stereo, Giuseppe had scouted out possible locations for his new company. He found a spot in Mission Hills in the northern part of the San Fernando Valley. The real estate was still reasonable, and significantly cheaper than Silicon Valley. The junction of two major freeways, Interstates 5 and 405, made it a convenient commute from the heart of Los Angeles, where he planned to make his new home. In August of 1988, he set his research team to work.

For signage, Giuseppe simply chose the company's name "The Pegasus Group". It would mean nothing to passersby, at least not in the beginning. Never short on vision or confidence, however, he was certain that over time it would become a household name. Giuseppe's plans did not include attempting to unseat Intel. He had grander designs than merely home computers or game systems.

As Giuseppe had envisioned, the gaming industry was about to explode. Nintendo introduced the Game Boy handheld video system in Japan exactly one year to the day after he sold Living Stereo. It would take another four months to enter the U.S. market. Giuseppe was in no hurry. In fact, he welcomed the delayed domestic release. He was already looking past this device, and wanted to be ready for the next innovation.

The correlation between personal computers and handheld gaming was self-evident. As a result, The Pegasus Group initially focused its attention on improving the graphics processing unit, popularly referred to as the graphic chip. This was Giuseppe's nod to the personal computing industry. Intel had years of experience on Pegasus, but Giuseppe succeeded in hiring only the brightest engineers, even luring a few away from his competitors. Including Intel. As a result Pegasus chips quickly became equal to, if not better than anything else on the market.

Giuseppe's vision far surpassed the home computer and gaming industries. He wanted to develop the world's most sophisticated surveillance systems. His aim was as high as his ambition, and just as true. In October 1989 he was poised to conquer yet another market.

In his Living Stereo days he established a solid relationship with Joe Pinola, CEO of First Interstate Bank. So Giuseppe offered him first crack at his new security system. Overall security in the First Interstate Tower was good. Still, Giuseppe convinced Pinola that he had something to offer that could not be equalled or duplicated. The Pegasus Group was not only able to provide an unsurpassed security system, they could also install it in record time. First Interstate, was, after all, their first and, so far, only customer.

By Christmas, the new system was up and running, and once again, First Interstate Bank was the envy of every corporation in Los Angeles. It had a new security system with elements and components no one else had ever envisioned. To Pinola's mind, his bank and tower were as secure as Fort Knox, or at least as impenetrable.

Perhaps Giuseppe had managed to enflesh the myth of Midas after all. At the very least, the gods of mythology were aligning all the favorable stars. Neither he nor Yolanda knew it at the time, but she had just conceived their third child the same month that The Pegasus Group opened for research. On May 21, 1989, Leonardo was born, finally providing the family with the son Giuseppe always wanted. Yolanda quickly found that taking care of a baby boy was different than caring for a baby girl. Fortunately, Carmen was nearing four years old and she loved helping out and playing mommy to her little brother. She was a godsend for the real mommy. Still, with three children under the age of four, Yolanda was, at times, overwhelmed.

In 1988 Giuseppe had promised Yolanda a home of her own within four years. The rapidity with which The Pegasus Group developed, enabled him to fulfill his promise ahead of schedule.

On Friday, May 17, 1991, he arrived home earlier than usual.

"Anda", he said. "I asked my sister to come over and babysit tomorrow".

Yolanda replied by observing,

"I don't have any place to go tomorrow, Sep".

"You do now. I'm taking you to lunch".

Although Giuseppe and Yolanda tried to go out to dinner at least a couple of times a month, it had been ages since he had taken her to lunch. Nonetheless, she was not suspicious. She was thrilled. Giuseppe worked such long hours that they had precious little alone time. Time for just the two of them. Yolanda accepted it as part of the sacrifices he had always talked about.

"Do you mind if I pick the restaurant"?, he asked. "There is a little spot in Larchmont Village I want to try".

"No", replied Yolanda. "Any place is fine with me".

That was true. She would even have been happy with a picnic at the beach. But Larchmont Village fitted in perfectly with Giuseppe's plans. It is located at the edge of Hancock Park, a semi-exclusive part of Los Angeles, comprising many luxury homes. This is truly a hidden gem of a neighborhood. Some of the residences could just have easily been in Beverly Hills. The official mansion of the Mayor of Los Angeles is nestled in this enclave. A week earlier, Giuseppe had spoken to a real estate agent, requesting a list of homes to view the following weekend. So it was that, on the pretext of a luncheon date, the Lozanos started out in search of a new place to live.

The first home they viewed was a classic Brookside Estate on Rimpau Boulevard, after which Giuseppe took Yolanda to Le Petit Greek, located on Larchmont Boulevard in the heart of the Village. He feasted on the restaurant's signature rack of lamb, while she chose the daily fish special.

Giuseppe had always managed to keep a great deal of his profits hidden. Yolanda knew this. But it did not bother her, since she and the kids never wanted for necessities. Now, however, she was not sure how much they could actually afford for a new home. The houses for sale in Hancock Park that weekend were not inexpensive. They never were in that area. Giuseppe assured her that money was no object.

During lunch they discussed the type of home they wanted. Neither of them was particularly taken with the Brookside they had just seen. Giuseppe informed Yolanda that there were larger, more exclusive and more expensive homes on the list for that weekend. He also assured her that if she did not fall in love with something on Saturday, there were more to see on Sunday.

Giuseppe always kept commitments to himself, if not to others. He had previously decided that Yolanda would ultimately choose the home. He was more interested in the location than in the style of the house. And although Yolanda had a practical nature when it came to finances, her eyes sparkled at the idea of being able to choose any home she wanted.

Following lunch they took a close look at a Mediterranean Grand home, also on Rimpau Blvd. This came close to what Yolanda was looking for. She loved the veranda overlooking the front yard. But, since they were moving, and she figured this would be permanent, she wanted a home with at least 5 bedrooms. So it was that they were off to check out a French Normandy Style Estate on Beechwood. The kitchen was beautifully appointed, and Yolanda was very taken with the vaulted ceilings that created a spacious cooking area. Still, not quite what they wanted. They concluded the day by walking through a beautiful Craftsman inspired home on Irving. It was the most appealing of the day, except that it was smaller than Yolanda had hoped for. Though not disappointed with the days venture, she hoped for more success the next day. As it turned out, they needed only one appointment on Sunday morning.

Situated on Hudson Ave, was another French Normandy Style Estate with five bedrooms and six-and-a-half baths. There was a spacious kitchen along with dining, family and laundry rooms, even a quiet library that Giuseppe could use as an office. It also had a bonus guest or maids quarters and detached garage. For the kids, there was an expansive backyard and a pool. The Lozanos did not entertain much. Then again, the apartment they had been living in did not lend itself to large gatherings. This house would be perfect for parties, both for kids and adults.

They met with their realtor and directed him to make an offer. There was no haggling. In their desire to move, the owners wanted to make an expeditious sale. They accepted Lozano's offer, and the house sped through escrow. Yolanda could now awake from her dream. This was the house she always wanted.

Hancock Park was not a priority for the LAPD. In fact, the cops from Wilshire rarely went into the area. The official explanation was that there were no major problems, as opposed to other places. The Division included the Washington Boulevard corridor, where officers would regularly hang out due to the black gangs, prostitutes and the prolific drug dealing that operated out of the cheap motels. On the east side, cops took advantage of immigrants and other minorities, many of whom drove without licenses. This made it easy for the officers to make their ticket quotas. They also had to deal with the havoc created by MS 13 gang members in the Korea Town area.

Unofficially, the reason LAPD paid little attention to Hancock Park was that the officers were irritated by the rich folks. Many of them had installed alarm systems that tapped directly into the Wilshire Division. The problem was that these alarms frequently sent Code 30 alerts, which in turn almost always proved to be false, thus diverting the cops from real police work.

A private security company took up the slack left by the LAPD, and patrolled Hancock Park with relative frequency. This was sufficient for most of the residents. Giuseppe, however, was not so trusting of these rent-a-cops. So before allowing his family to move in, he installed a security system. Naturally, it was a Pegasus. It contained elements of the industrial system, but this was not a scaled-down, consumer version. It was in a class of its own and not available to the general public.

For outside security, Giuseppe focused his attention on general surveillance, embedding cameras around the roof, alternating between daylight and infrared lenses. These cameras shot continuous video that was stored on a hard drive. But it was the interior alarm that set his security apart from his neighbors. In fact, from anyone else.

As personal computing continued to accelerate, the R&D department at Pegasus had developed a system that worked with the soon-to-be ubiquitous home computers and wireless communications protocols that became the backbone of today's wi-fi internet. Unknown even to the U.S. Government, Pegasus was working with the Commonwealth Scientific and Industrial Research Organization (CSIRO) a government research group in Australia. Even CSIRO, however, was unable to foresee the extensive application of the wireless systems they were developing.

This joint venture with CSIRO put Pegasus' R&D at least as far ahead of industry as was the U.S. Government and military. In many ways, Pegasus outstripped them all, which is one reason Giuseppe wanted to procure government contracts. He had something to offer even they did not yet have.

Using the latest wireless technology, Giuseppe could operate his intrusion and alarm systems from his personal computer. The computer, itself, was password protected. An additional and highly complex encryption was used to set, monitor and disable the alarm. Indeed, once the system was armed, the Lozano family home was impenetrable.

After everything was installed, Giuseppe felt secure enough for his family to occupy the new home. He also had a custom, fireproof safe installed in the master bedroom. It was here that he kept his most valuable trade secrets. Only he, Yolanda and his lawyer, Christopher Coker, had the combination.

Yolanda spent several months decorating and putting personal touches on the home. Giuseppe left her to choose the paint colors and the furniture, even new plants for the gardens. These were the details for which he had neither the time nor the interest. Besides, he knew that she had superb taste. Life was good for the young Lozano family.

Once everything was in order, Yolanda decided to return to work. On this issue Giuseppe was not in disagreement. However, he felt that their new station in life would be enhanced if she did not return to a public school. As it happened, there was an opening at Mayfield Senior School, a private girls institution in Pasadena. This is as exclusive as girls' schools get, with all the children coming from families of privilege. While a number of the girls were pretentious and snooty, the majority were simply teenagers trying to find themselves in a world that was changing faster than they were.

Yolanda realized that her own girls could find themselves in this situation someday. Her approach was to respect the sensitivities of each child, but also treat them with resolve. It was the same approach she had used at Blair, and it worked. The girls participated with enthusiasm in the classroom, possibly due to the absence of boys. For whatever reason, Yolanda had once again succeeded in creating an interest in, even a thirst for, English literature among a new generation.

\*　　\*　　\*

I wouldn't call Giuseppe romantic, though he was always affectionate with Yolanda and the kids. At home he was considerate and tolerant. He was a different person altogether in his business dealings, displaying a near condescending contempt for his employees. Truly, he remained a study in contradiction. He attributed the fortunes of The Pegasus Group to his own ingenuity, personality and wit, conveniently forgetting where the true genius resided. He was authoritarian and very difficult to work with. Most of his employees remained, not out of loyalty, but because they were well paid. A few wondered if the salary was worth the abuse.

The Pegasus Group was successful beyond even Giuseppe's expectations. And he was correct about it becoming a household name. It did not hurt that he chose to eponymously designate his prized security system "The Pegasus Bolt". The name suggested the duality of a steel trap, and the task of the mythological divine horse delivering lightening from the god Zeus. Giuseppe had so completely conceived his business plan, that even as demand for Bolt exploded, it never outstripped the company's ability to deliver.

Unlike his days with Living Stereo, Giuseppe never tired of The Pegasus Group. To the contrary, he was in the processing of developing too many secret technologies. Security systems proved to be his launchpad. He developed a new research department specializing in communications technology, and another for developing guidance systems for unmanned planes and satellites. The Pegasus Group expanded his wealth exponentially. With wealth came influence. With influence, power. And with power the desire to dominate. His new target? The U.S. Government.

# Chapter 16

Giuseppe's turn to the political right may have begun with Reagan's presidential candidacy, but back then it was limited mostly to the fact that Reagan gave voice to Giuseppe's own self-centered musings. As time went on, he found himself becoming more involved with Republican politics on a practical level. I anticipated that this would be a bone of contention. No one in his family was Republican. His parents were deeply committed to the principles of the Democratic Party, and Giovanni, while careful to avoid partisan politics from the pulpit, was one of those clerics who still preached the common good and advanced the social principles embedded in the life of Jesus. Whatever differences he had with Church administration, Giovanni was committed to the "Preferential Option for the Poor", a bedrock Catholic teaching. Even Yolanda was a dyed-in-the-wool Democrat. But politics was not allowed to disrupt the harmony of Lozano family gatherings, and Giuseppe's activities remained outside the family. At least at first.

On the political landscape there are many wealthy Democrats, both among those who hold public office and those who support them. Giuseppe gravitated toward the wealthy Republicans. In that, there was more than a touch of irony. To a person they rejected the idea of the common good, but held firmly to what they, themselves, had in common, namely, money. And the desire to keep it for themselves.

Giuseppe discovered that he was not the only businessman whose wealth was dependent on the work of others. Sometimes that work was displayed in the sweat of manual labor, sometimes in the brilliance of the human mind. Sometimes it was a combination of both. He was pleased to have discovered comrades who managed to secure success and wealth for themselves under the cloak of hard executive work. Not they did not work. But really! Comparing executive meetings, travel and deal making with the work of laborers, stretches all levels of imagination. The working class are the people who actually create the products and make companies successful. The CEO's make the money. For Giuseppe and his new friends, the idea of profit-sharing was as anathema as atheism is to believers.

Since these new associates were not business partners, Giuseppe tended to be more honest with them. Actually, he had not felt this comfortable among his peers since his days at Harvard. Far from a novice at manipulating others, he was, to the contrary, experienced and ruthless, and Giuseppe applied those same skills to his political allies. His affability rivaled that of Ronald Reagan, which practically guaranteed him political success. Like Reagan, he was a master at obscuring the truth. He developed and solidified contacts among elected officials, hoping they would open doors and secure lucrative contracts for The Pegasus Group.

There was one problem that Giuseppe could not obviate. California is primarily a Democratic state, and all of his contacts were Republicans. After all, it was not as if he was in the defense industry. That part of the economy cut across party lines to provide jobs and income for millions of Californians. Giuseppe was trying to sell a concept of security that few could grasp. He, alone, seemed to understand the potential of the technology his firm was developing. Then, again, he alone realized that this technology would transcend the common concept of security. He was targeting the national level and beyond. But it was still in the developmental stages.

In 1992, Giuseppe was introduced to Robert K. Dornan, a boorish and boisterous Congressman from Orange County. Prior to 1973 Dornan had been a bit actor and talk show host. In the late 1970's he was elected by and represented a district in western Los Angeles County. As a politician Dornan never amounted to much. At least not outside California. Even within the state his political popularity was provincial. He unsuccessfully attempted to run for the U.S. Senate in 1982, finishing fourth in the Republican primary, a result that would have embarrassed a more modest politician. Instead, he moved to Orange County and managed to get himself elected to Congress again. Although there was reason to question Dornan's mental health, he was re-elected five more times. Eventually, his lack of ethics and integrity caught up with him. In his final successful run, he employed highly deceptive, and, as it turned out illegal means of intimidating minority voters. No matter. It worked. So it was, that in his capacity as a congressman, he met Giuseppe.

In the strongly Democratic state of California, Dornan was convinced that Giuseppe could fill a leadership vacuum in the state's Republican Party. Dornan wanted to be that person himself, but in a rare moment of honest self-reflection and stability, he realized that such a goal was beyond reach and the attempt would prove futile. Possibly even divisive. So he tapped Giuseppe, a person as resolutely arrogant, but far more subtle and sophisticated.

*　　*　　*

This increased activism within the Republican Party was of some concern to Yolanda. Ever since their days at Stanford, she had proved an intellectual match for Giuseppe. She was, more accurately, his superior, and a naturally skilled debater. She was quick witted and could easily craft clever and instant responses to most any argument he posited.

They engaged in numerous discussions about politics, but could not come to a meeting of the minds. And yet, Yolanda did not attempt to stifle Giuseppe's political activity or ambition. During one such conversation she informed Giuseppe that, as his wife, she would support what he wanted to do. But she could not change party affiliation or be an active participant in his politics. Her values were too strong and ran too deep. He tried the family values argument. To which she queried, "Whose values"? She had to admit that the Republican leadership employed cunning language in their attempts to convince the feeble minded. But it was clear that these politicians represented nothing remotely close to her concept of family values. She also objected to their duplicity.

A case in point was the abortion debate. As Governor of California, Ronald Reagan signed into law the nation's most liberal and permissive abortion legislation. As president, he did nothing to stem the tide of abortion. Yet he was a calculating politician. So during his presidency, he would speak against abortion, but did not attend one annual pro-life rally in Washington D.C., practically outside his front door. Instead he chose to address the attendees by telephone. And although "pro-life" and "anti-abortion" are not synonymous, most Americans think they remember Reagan as being both. They are wrong. On both counts.

Yolanda was far too intelligent to be taken in. Whereas the Republican Party continued to cast itself as pro-life, she consistently argued that all they really were was anti-abortion. Beyond that there was nothing at all life-giving about them. A classic illustration of this truth can be found courtesy of *The Los Angeles Times*. The newspaper had the exceptional fortune of employing Paul Conrad as its editorial cartoonist for almost thirty years. Of his many sophisticated and thought-provoking cartoons, one stands out as a prime example of the duplicity of the Republican Party.

Ronald Reagan is depicted standing at the presidential podium. He is giving an anti-abortion address. Beside him is a little boy tugging at his coat. The boy is dirty, disheveled and in tattered clothes. Reagan looks over at the child and the caption reads: "Leave me alone, kid. Once you're born, you're on your own".

There was a heartless, even inhuman dimension to the so-called values of the Republican Party that Yolanda simply could not embrace. She reminded Giuseppe of a Mass they attended one Sunday at Giovanni's church. The Gospel reading for that Sunday was taken from the twenty-fifth chapter of Matthew's Gospel, verses 31-46. Giovanni pointed out that there is only one criterion for entrance into the kingdom. It is not how often one prays or goes to church. It is not how many religious rules one observes. The only criterion is how we treat the least among us. As Jesus says, "Amen, I say to you, what you did not do for these least ones, you did not do for me".

From this perspective, in the Paul Conrad cartoon, the little boy is Jesus. Reagan's response, then, surfaces as beyond cold. It is unmasked for the hypocrisy that it is, totally devoid of the faith he so publicly proclaimed. It was precisely this Republican response to poverty and self-absorption with one's own self and wealth that caused Yolanda to question the family values rhetoric. Still, she could not choose Giuseppe's values for him or his political allegiance. They agreed to disagree.

*     *     *

At first, Giuseppe was content to be the power behind the throne, and in 1996 he was elected chair of the California Republican Party. He traveled the length of the state in an effort to bolster the party's prospects. Two things emerged during his two-year tenure. The first was that he became a much more recognizable figure in party politics. The second was that he grew increasingly frustrated trying to secure government contracts for The Pegasus Group. That was his true objective for political engagement. He realized that he needed to hold public office to make that happen.

In 1998 Giuseppe floated the possibility of running for the U.S. Senate. If need be, his personal finances were sufficient to finance a campaign. That would not be necessary, though, for he also had a cadre of Republican elite who advanced his cause and agenda with generous contributions of their own. The result was that in the March 2000 primary he faced minimal opposition from Ray Haynes and Bill Horn, and from the less-than-serious candidates, Linh Dao and James Gough. Giuseppe Lozano emerged as the Republican candidate for U.S. Senate from the state of California. The election would take place on Tuesday, November 7, 2000.

Over the summer, the campaign demanded more and more attention, and Giuseppe maintained a grueling schedule of events. As in all his endeavors, he hired a top-notch staff. Bill Morgan, who had long been a staple in California Republican politics was his campaign director. Catherine Stripling had been Giuseppe's executive secretary for years. She willingly took a leave from The Pegasus Group to serve his campaign in the same category. Between Morgan and Stripling, there were few hitches in campaign activities. Some events demanded Yolanda's presence. Since she agreed to support Giuseppe in his quest, she dutifully and gracefully attended. She did not have to play the devoted wife. She was that in reality. Morgan made certain that she never had to answer political questions. Her presence was to reinforce Giuseppe's image as a husband and father. It was easy enough to get a family member to watch the kids. They were well behaved and never caused any trouble. Still, when she could avoid it and was not absolutely needed, Yolanda skipped campaign activities and remained home with the children.

On Thursday night, September 21, a campaign fundraiser was held at the Los Angeles Biltmore Hotel on South Grand Street in downtown. Although this was a dinner event, it did not require Yolanda's presence, so Giuseppe went alone. This worked out well, anyway, since Los Angeles was experiencing a rare summer thunder storm. The three children were all old enough to handle the rain as well as the thunder and lightning, but at such times it is always comforting to have a parent around.

The Biltmore is one of Los Angeles' oldest hotels, having been built in the early 1920's. The elegance of its interior creates the impression of familiarity. Even large numbers of dinner guests are made to feel as though they are attending an intimate gathering. It was exactly what Giuseppe needed, given that he would ask everyone to fork over a fair amount of money. In fact, two hundred and fifty supporters were expected to attend, flush with cash. Therefore, the fundraiser was booked in an appropriate ballroom that could easily accommodate the size.

Morgan, Stripling, and Giuseppe's chauffeur, Andy Prescott, arrived at the house at 4:00 PM. After briefly greeting the family, the four of them got into the car and headed for downtown Los Angeles. With the afternoon traffic, it took thirty minutes to complete the drive from

Hancock Park. That was more than enough time to discuss any last minute details and make sure that Giuseppe's speech would stay on point. He, like his brother Giovanni, had raised public speaking beyond an art form. He was a very disciplined speaker, but with the election so near, the campaign was in critical mode. The polling indicated a close race and Giuseppe could not afford any gaffes.

Giuseppe knew how to treat guests. Even though this was a fundraiser, he was not averse to spending generously in an effort to make his supporters feel special. There was no rubber, banquet-style chicken on the menu. This dinner would be Italian faire: Ossobuco with a side of risotto or mashed potatoes. The wine was chosen with distinction to provide a perfect accompaniment to the meal--Fattoria Viticcio Chianti Classico Riserva Lucius, vintage 1997.

The evening was a prodigious success. Giuseppe played the crowd like a musical prodigy. He expounded on the Pasadena of his youth and the need to return America to a bygone era. He lent his voice to the chorus of Republicans who excoriated Bill Clinton for his sexual peccadillos while President. Paraphrasing George W. Bush, the Republican candidate for president, Giuseppe promised to restore honor and dignity to Washington.

Following his experience in Boston, Giuseppe had learned to camouflage his feelings, and since he never spoke out of turn, every thought was carefully gauged to conceal his true intent. He had so cultivated these skills that not one person in attendance that night was capable of deciphering what Giuseppe really stood for. And yet, they were all left believing that he affirmed their personal and collective values. In return, they were willing to pay handsomely to guarantee that position.

After all the guests had left the dinner, the core of Giuseppe's staff stayed behind. They met with him to analyze the effect of specific talking points on the audience, to share comments heard in discussion, and to tighten Friday's campaign schedule. By 12:45 AM everyone felt drained and called it a night. A successful one. Giuseppe climbed into the car, settled back and decided to close his eyes for the brief ride home.

# Chapter 17

A particularly risky and complicated job needs the best agents. The ones who leave nothing to chance. Vincent Gilmore and Gary Bass were two very professional operatives, accomplished in every facet of their work. Gilmore was the older and more experienced of the two. In fact, Bass started out as his apprentice, but had quickly risen to the height of his profession, himself. They each primarily worked alone, teaming up only on very special missions. This was one. It needed to be perfect, and Gilmore was in charge.

As with any expensive and elite assignment, they spent hours in preparation, which included providing for unforeseen variables, the weather being one of them. The rain this evening worked to their advantage. There would be fewer people out walking dogs late at night. And most important, it was a thunder storm with the potential for knocking out power and phone lines. This enabled them to pose as a repair crew for the utility company. No one on the street that night would have any reason for suspicion.

At 10:15 PM, they pulled up in front of the Lozano home in a telephone company van. At least it sported the "Pacific Bell" name and logo, as well as fake business license plates on both the front and back. There was need for precise timing, but they were not concerned. Like everything else, they had pre-planned and rehearsed each element of the crime.

The two men, each about six-feet one inch, exited the vehicle, placing orange construction cones on the street at the front and rear of the van. This suggested that they were engaged in official repairs, and would, therefore, draw little notice from pedestrians or drivers, even at that late hour. From within the van, Gilmore used a portable computer to tap into the Lozano family's wi-fi network. He had installed a sophisticated program to break the algorithms of Giuseppe's security system. This took slightly longer than anticipated, but still within the range of acceptability. Once Gilmore identified the correct passcode, he input the alphanumeric sequence, and the alarm system was disabled without anyone's knowledge.

At exactly 10:55, Gilmore and Bass approached the house. They were dressed all in black: shoes, pants, shirts, overcoats, leather gloves, and rimmed hats. Their long coats did not conceal shotguns, or uzis. This was, after all, not a Hollywood gangster film. In case they needed it, they each carried only one weapon beneath their coats. A semi-automatic Glock 9mm with a high-powered silencer. With the suppressor attached, the only audible sound was the slide of the chamber clip ejecting the bullet casing.

Gilmore and Bass could not risk entering the house through the front. There was still the possibility that a neighbor might appear walking some useless canine. Instead, they glided furtively along the concrete pathway that led to the backyard. They could not avoid the cameras, but the surveillance was easily thwarted and posed no threat. The long overcoats disguised any abnormality in their walks. This was particularly important for Bass. He had suffered a left knee injury many years earlier, that left him with a slight hitch in his step. Even though they knew the location of each camera, they kept their heads down. The brim on their hats obscuring any view of their facial features, and the all-black attire negated the value of night vision cameras.

The kitchen was dark. The only light on downstairs was in the empty living room. The door was securely latched. Bass picked the lock silently and swiftly. Having already disabled the alarm, they had no fear of security cops arriving unexpectedly. They paused to listen. No sounds downstairs. They drew their guns and with stealth-like precision ascended the stairs.

Each of the children had their own bedroom. Leonardo was already asleep. At eleven years of age he had the earliest bedtime, 9:00. Gina was sitting on her bed listening to music through expensive headphones. The kind that block all ambient noise. She was busy alternating between texting friends on her cell phone and reading a book for class. The book was clearly of secondary importance. Carmen was sitting at her desk in the midst of writing an essay for school. The girls's doors were both closed, Leonardo's partly ajar. The men passed the rooms in silence.

They entered the master bedroom. Yolanda had just completed a shower and was walking out of the bathroom in a full length terrycloth robe, her long hair still wet. She looked up and took a startled step backward. Before she could open her mouth, Gilmore said,

"Don't scream, or you're dead. And so are the children. You're only hope is to do as I say".

"How did you get in here", she asked a little less than demandingly?

"Never mind about that. Let's just say there aren't any security cops on their way".

"What do you want"? She was still terribly frightened, but sounded a bit more brazen. Yolanda had always been a strong woman. Now, however, she was caught unprepared. She could sense her own life and that of her children teetering. She instinctively knew that she had to cooperate.

"Open the safe", Gilmore replied.

Yolanda started to object,

"I don't...", she was quickly interrupted. Gilmore cut her off.

"We know where the safe is, and we know you have the combination. Don't even try to stall, or I send my partner down the hall to the other rooms".

There was a matter-of-fact tone to his voice, and an icy glare in his eyes. Yolanda could see the cold determination. Fearing for the safety of the children she decided to comply.

The safe was behind a floor-to-ceiling panel. It was not so much hidden, as disguised for interior design purposes. Yolanda was weak with fear, but empowered by her concern for the children. She opened the panel and exposed the six-foot high, fire-proof safe. Like everything else Giuseppe owned, it was state-of-the-art. Instead of a dial, it had a keypad, off-center left, next to the handle. Yolanda punched in the code and opened the safe.

"Now sit on the bed", Gilmore told her. Then he turned to Bass, "Keep your gun trained on her". He did not use Bass' name. True professionals never reveal their identities. It was enough that she saw their faces.

Yolanda sat down on the edge of the king size bed.

"Take whatever you want", she said. "Just get out of here and leave us alone".

Gilmore placed his gun on a shelf in the safe. It was not his style to rifle through folders or strew papers on the floor. He carefully flipped through the files. His deliberate pace made Yolanda increasingly nervous. She knew that the longer they stayed, the greater the chance that one of the children would interrupt them. Gilmore searched until he found the schematic for a highly secretive guidance system. He put the folder under his left arm and picked up his gun. Yolanda did not know their names, but she had a good look at both of them. Gilmore looked at Bass and with an imperceptible glance, gave him the O.K. "Thuup" was the only sound. The bullet entered Yolanda's skull through the forehead with dead center accuracy.

Almost instantaneously, Carmen called out to Yolanda as she entered her parents' room. She had almost finished her essay and came to ask her mother's help.

"Mom", she started.

"Thuup". Gilmore shot this time. Matching Bass' exactitude, he put the bullet straight through her heart. Carmen fell to the floor without ever entering the room or finishing her statement.

There was no need to rush. No one heard a sound, and their presence was still unknown. They quickly and easily stepped over Carmen's body. They could not take the chance that the other children might catch a glimpse of them through the window. Gilmore motioned to Bass to go to Gina's room, while he approached Leonardo's.

Bass opened the door. Gina did not even have time to be startled. She looked up. "Thuup". Another shot between the eyes. Since Leonardo's door was already open, Gilmore simply pushed it back enough to enter the room. He walked to the bed. "Thuup". Through the heart again. Almost casually, he breezed back into the hallway and the two men descended the stairs together.

Most habitual criminals have a modus operandi (M.O.), as the cops call it. Not Gilmore and Bass. They were too professional for that. The closest they came to an M.O. was leaving their guns and the bullet casings at the scene. But that was common practice among professionals. Since they never touched the guns or bullets with ungloved hands, they left no fingerprints. The weapons, themselves, were always stolen, and untraceable. At least the guns could not be tracked back to the killers.

In his own sick way, Gilmore decided to have some fun. They did not just leave the weapons behind. In a devious attempt to taunt the police, they placed the guns side by side, in plain sight, on the living room coffee table. He knew it would piss off the cops, especially since the police would know immediately that the guns would provide no useful leads in solving the crime.

Other than four dead bodies, nothing in the house was disturbed or out of order. Gilmore and Bass exited as quietly as they had entered. They encountered only one potential problem. During the murders, the rain had turned to a steady downpour. As they stepped onto the back porch, Bass slipped. He did not fall. It was more of a stumble. He managed to gain his balance as his left foot came down and nearly uprooted one of the azalea plants that framed the porch.

There was no one on the street when they returned to the van. They quickly picked up the cones, and put them in the vehicle. Then they took off their overcoats and hats. Gilmore stepped up and sat behind the steering wheel, while Bass entered from the passenger's side and rode shotgun. They drove off, heading south to Wilshire Boulevard, then turned left toward downtown Los Angeles. It was both the busiest street and the most natural direction for them to travel. In what appeared to be a Pacific Bell van, they would be even less likely to draw attention than when they had been parked on Hudson.

After crossing over the 110 Freeway, Wilshire Boulevard dead ends at Grand Avenue. Gilmore turned right and then made a quick left onto 7th St. This route runs right through the heart of Skid Row. They pulled alongside the curb and threw their gloves out of the window into the gutter. Most likely some homeless men would pick them up. That would terminate any connection to Gilmore and Bass. They each put on a pair of knit gloves so as to leave no fingerprints in the van and continued east on 7th Street, turning right onto Alameda. This placed them in a more industrial area enabling them to blend more effectively with their environment. Next, Gilmore turned left onto Hunter street where they abandoned the vehicle.

They put their coats and hats back on and walked east along Hunter Street, then right onto Lawrence. At Olympic Boulevard they made another left and walked to the parking lot of the Spearmint Rhino Gentlemen's Club where their own vehicle was parked. It was a 1995 Chevrolet Cavalier, light driftwood metallic color. Truly unmemorable in every way. Their assignment complete and their tracks covered, two of America's most lethal assassins entered the car and drove off. Gilmore was satisfied that the Pacific Bell van would not be found for at least a day. In any event, their was no forensic evidence to connect them to the vehicle. There was no evidence at all.

# Chapter 18

Andy Prescott drove Giuseppe, Morgan and Stripling back to the Hancock house from which they would all disperse for the night. At 1:00 the car pulled up to the Lozano home. Giuseppe asked Prescott to drop him off at the curb. He thought the crisp, post-rain air would be refreshing on the short walk up to the house.

He exited the vehicle. As he started up to the house, he was surprised to see lights on in the girls' rooms. He suspected Yolanda might be waiting up for him. But Carmen and Gina should be fast asleep. Still, it did not register as of particular concern. He went to the front of the house, took out his key, and opened the door. There was no signal alerting him to the ninety-second time frame for disabling the alarm. That meant the alarm was already off. That was very unusual. If he had drilled anything into his family's heads, besides the need to sacrifice, it was to always make sure the alarm was set. He called out.

"Yolanda, who left the alarm system disabled? I've told you all a thousand times how important it is".

There was no answer. The house was a silent as a tomb. Perhaps Yolanda was in the shower, although he did not hear any water running.

He started toward the stairs when he caught sight of the two Glocks on the coffee table. He immediately set out in a run, bounding up the stairs two and three at a time. He stopped cold at the first sight.

Carmen was laying on the floor, her upper body in the hallway, her feet protruding into the master bedroom. Giuseppe ran to her. As he knelt beside her, he could tell that she was not breathing. Then he looked into his own bedroom and saw Yolanda laying on the bed. They had each been shot one time. Yolanda in the head, Carmen through the heart. His panic began to expand exponentially as he ran to the other two rooms. There was Gina, one shot to the head. He went to Leonardo's room and what should have been a sleeping, careless child. Dead. One shot through the heart.

He knew there had to be two killers. A killer on his own, does not change his style or placement of shot unless he has to. And he had seen two guns. Gina and Leonardo evidently caused no disruption. For a moment or two he was stunned. This was no abattoir, no drug deal gone awry or bungled burglary. This was a coldblooded execution, a professional hit. He, too, was a professional. He knew what needed to be done, but he could hardly flip open the top of his cell phone. When he did, he dropped the phone and it slipped under the bed. He quickly went to the landline beside the bed and made two calls. The first was to 911 Emergency, even though he knew it was too late.

"911 Emergency, how can I help you"?

"My family has been shot. I think they're all dead. I need some help". His voice was understandably frantic. Still, he was making sense.

"Please calm down sir. Help is already on the way. Can you please tell me your name?"

The emergency dispatcher tried to be attentive, sensitive and understanding.

"My name is Giuseppe Lozano. I live on Hudson Avenue in Hancock Park".

"Yes, Mr. Lozano, your address shows up on the screen. I have dispatched the paramedics and the police. Just wait for them and do not touch anything. They'll be arriving any minute. I'll stay on the line until they do. Is there anyone else you can call, a family member perhaps"?

"Yes, thank you. I'll call my brother".

"Good".

Just then, he heard the sirens. The police turn off their lights and sirens two blocks from their destination, so they were at least that far away. But it was 1:00 in the morning, a quiet neighborhood, and the sound carried. He told the dispatcher, "I hear the police. Thank you. I'll call my brother now".

"All right. Mr. Lozano, I am very sorry about this". At least she really meant that last statement.

As soon as Giuseppe finished the call, he dialed Giovanni and woke him up.

"Gio", his voice was trembling now. Not as assured as it was with the 911 dispatcher. "You've got to come over to the house. Yolanda and the kids are dead".

"Sep, calm down and tell me what happened. How do you know they're dead?"

"They each have one bullet in them. They're not breathing. Gio, it's horrible".

"I'll be right over, Sep. And I'm calling Tom. I know it's not his division, but I think he should be there. Give me ten minutes." It would ordinarily take more time, but at that hour Giovanni knew he could fly through the streets. He was not concerned about the police. Even if they saw him speeding, they would not be able to stop him before reaching his brother's house. By then they, too, would understand his haste.

As Gio was getting dressed his fingers flew over the numbers of my cellphone. I had been working the late shift in RHD. I clocked out at 1:00 and went to my favorite bar. It was the one place I always went when I was alone, and I was alone often enough to call it a hang out. Tonight was like so many others. At first.

The 3 Clubs is located on Vine just north of Melrose. I walked in and moseyed on up to the bar to order a drink. Pete was the bartender Tuesday through Saturday nights, and we had come to know each other quite well over the last few years.

"Evening, Tom", he said.

"Hello, Pete".

"The usual"?, Pete asked.

"Nah. Let me think a moment".

I have always been primarily a scotch drinker. My usual is Pinch, chilled up. In my opinion Haig and Haig's Pinch, known outside the United States as "The Dimple," is the world's best blended scotch. Not that I have tasted them all. Nor do I think of myself as pretentious. My opinion about Pinch is not based simply on the fact that Haig is the world's oldest distiller of scotch. It is just that I have simply tried enough different blends to be comfortable in my judgment. Besides, it is neither an exact nor objective science. Not even for the so-called experts. Tastes in scotch are a personal preference. I know what my preference is.

That night, however, I was in the mood for a single malt, specifically Glenfarclas 17 year. Single malts I drink neat. When the glass arrived, I began to sip. No one downs a good scotch. I consumed this drink savoringly slowly, as other patrons engaged me in idle conversation.

I looked at my watch and noticed that it was 1:20 in the morning, and the bar was quickly approaching last call, which is always at 1:30. I ordered another just to be ready. As it arrived, I received a call on my cell phone. The screen indicated that it was Giovanni.

"Gio, what are you doing up so late"?, I asked.

"Tom". One word was all I needed to hear. As soon as Giovanni spoke my name, I knew something was wrong. He continued,

"Something terrible has happened". He could barely contain himself. "Yolanda and the kids have been killed."

I was stunned. Here I was, a seasoned cop, and yet this news was almost beyond belief. People do not joke about this kind of thing, so I did not ask the foolish question that so often comes to mind, 'You're kidding?'. Rather, my instincts as a detective took over.

I was filled with questions, almost as if I were already interrogating witnesses or suspects. My first thought was that they had been in an accident, and I wondered if anyone else was involved. I asked, "Where did it happen"?

"At home", Giovanni replied.

"I'm on my way", I said.

I left my drinks, threw some extra cash on the bar and said, "I've got to go, Pete. That should cover the drinks".

I was out the door like a shot.

*      *      *

The 3 Clubs is less than two miles from The Lozano home in Hancock Park and there was no traffic on Vine. It took me about four minutes, and when I arrived, paramedics, police and detectives from the Wilshire Division were already on scene. I identified myself to the cop standing sentry, and entered the house.

Giuseppe was sitting on a sofa in the living room. He looked dazed, as if he were in the middle of a nightmare from which he might never awaken. He didn't even look up.

During my years as a detective, I had developed a well-trained eye for detail. I was focused on Giuseppe, but as I approached, I surveyed the entire area. Nothing downstairs was disturbed or out of order. Yolanda employed a daily housekeeper, who kept everything immaculate, except while family and friends were milling around at a party. Across the room, about thirty feet, I saw the two weapons, and immediately knew that we were dealing with highly trained professionals.

Justin Blake was the detective on duty. I had never met him, so I walked over and introduced myself.

"I'm lieutenant Moran of RHD".

"I've heard about you", was the reply. "You used to be at Wilshire. What brings you here"?

"I received a call from Mr. Lozano's brother. He's a priest in a parish a few miles away".

"Well, I already put in a call to my supervising detective, Jack Gorman. He should be here any minute".

I thought to myself, 'Shit!'. I knew Gorman. We were not on the best of terms. He and I had been stationed together at Wilshire. Most of that buddy cop or partner stuff on television is bullshit. We're just like everybody else, and sometimes we have to work with assholes. That was Gorman.

I never felt unsafe around him. In that regard he was a good cop.

But I also never thought he had my back. He would have sold me down the river to advance his own career. And what a kiss ass! It was embarrassing to watch him try and cozy up to the lieutenant. Fortunately, the lieutenant did not suffer fools. He was only interested in making sure that the work was done and the cases solved. When I transferred to RHD, Gorman made D3. But that was the last I had to deal with him. Until now.

Gorman was already in a bad mood. He had been called to another murder on San Marino Street, just west of Vermont. This was the scene of gang violence, with an MS 13 gang member being killed by an 18th Street rival. He had been at the other location since 11:00 PM. It was a cold and wet night, and he hated being interrupted and called to Hancock Park.

To make matters worse, apparently someone had alerted Gorman to my presence. He walked into the house, ignoring Giuseppe and everyone else. He called out, "Moran, what the hell are you doing here"?

I thought to myself, 'Nice to see you, too', but I did not want to start any trouble. I simply repeated the answer I gave Blake.

"I received a call from Mr. Lozano's brother. He's a priest in a parish a few miles away".

At that moment, Giovanni arrived. I continued,

"That's him pulling up now."

"That still doesn't tell me why you're here. This is a Wilshire Division homicide".

"I came here because I am a close family friend. But I can tell you right now this is not staying with Wilshire. It's going to RHD".

"Bullshit", Gorman replied. "We can handle this investigation. Just because you think you're some hot shot RHD lieutenant, doesn't mean you can come in here and try to tell us how to run an investigation. This is still our division".

That was not a statement. It was a challenge. Gorman was like a rhinoceros, pissing on the boundaries of his territory. Still, this exchange was not just a warning or challenge to me. The moment the call went out about the murder, every commanding officer received a message on their Blackberries. As a result, The Chief Duty Officer, Jack Thompson, was already on site. Although he is a Commander, the CDO does not get involved or interfere with an investigation. He represents the Chief, and observes how a crime scene is handled. Gorman wanted to impress him, and challenging me over who should handle the case was just the ticket to show how tough he was.

In fact, Gorman was a real hard-assed cop. We may not have gotten along, but in his twenty years on the force he had proven himself and he was good at his job. But he was very territorial, and as the D3 detective, he was in charge. He liked it that way and wanted make sure he was noticed by the CDO. He probably saw this as the case that would really make his career.

"Not anymore", I said. "This case is going to RHD whether or not you like it ".

"That's not your call. You know you don't have the authority. Our captain will be here in a few minutes. In fact, here he comes now. Take it up with him. Right now I have some questions for Mr. Lozano".

"Hold off on the questions until I settle this with your captain". I turned to Giuseppe, "Sep, I'll be right back."

I went outside to head off the captain and speak with him out of earshot of the detectives. Of course, Gorman followed me. I made eye contact with the captain as he was walking up the drive.

Lyle Graham had been captain at Wilshire for almost five years, arriving two years after I transferred to RHD. We had never worked together, but knew each other by reputation. He was a hard working captain and respected throughout the department.

"Moran", he said. "What brings you out here"?

"Hello, captain", I responded. "I received a call from Mr. Lozano's brother. He's the pastor of St. Catherine Parish on Vermont. He arrived just before you. That's him standing with one your officers".

Just then, Gorman approached us and interrupted the conversation.

"Captain, Moran has no business here. He's already trying to cock block this investigation. He thinks he can run the division better than we can".

"I'm not telling you how to run your division" I said. "But, look. This is not a simple homicide".

"No shit", Gorman replied. "With four dead bodies I figured that one out for myself".

The officer standing with Giovanni called out to Gorman, "Detective, this is a priest. Mr. Lozano's brother. Can I let him through"?

Gorman gave the OK, and Giovanni came running up the driveway.

"Tom, where's Sep"?

"He's inside, Gio. Go check on him. See if you can do anything. I'll be right in".

"Wait", Gorman said. He signaled to an officer at the front door. "You go with him. Make sure he doesn't disturb any evidence".

Then he turned to me and said,

"You're not running this investigation, Moran. I'm still in charge".

How pathetic and trite. I think Gorman was already beginning to sense that he would lose this case to RHD. But that was still a ridiculous thing to say. I pushed on, addressing Gorman.

"You really have no idea what you're dealing with, do you"?

I was not trying to be a smart ass, nor was I implying incompetence. But I could see that I was beginning to irritate him, and I understood his reaction. Gorman was in charge of this crime scene and he did not like my interference, nor did he want to be overruled by his captain. I turned back to the captain and softened my approach.

"Listen, captain. I know that you and your guys do great work, but they are treating this like any other murder. I don't know how much information you have yet, but I've already been inside. We are not going to find any tangible evidence in that house. The guys who pulled this off were extremely professional. What's more, I think they want to embarrass the department. They did not just leave the weapons behind. They placed them on the coffee table, side by side, in plain sight. Two Glock 9mm pistols with silencers. It's as if they are daring us to try and find them".

Graham was a smart cop. He did not rise to the rank of captain just by putting in his time. Over and over in his career he proved himself a careful and effective detective and supervisor. And he knew how to listen. Even now.

"The point is, captain, this is going to be a high-profile case. Lozano is the Republican senatorial candidate. When news of this gets out, there will be a huge outcry to find the killers. This is going to be taken over by RHD whether I do it now, or we wait until daylight".

I could see caution begin to surface in him. He turned to Gorman and asked,

"What do you know so far"?

"Not much. I haven't been upstairs, but I don't think we'll find anything up there except the bodies. Moran is right about one thing. The placement of the weapons suggests that they made no mistakes. There is some digital video from the surveillance cameras, but we haven't got to it yet".

"Why don't we at least view the video together", I suggested? "I doubt we'll find much there, either. But it's a start".

We headed into the house. Meanwhile, Giovanni had gone straight to Giuseppe and sat beside him. He put his arm around him for comfort and strength.

"I'm here, Sep. So is Tom. Do you need anything right now? Water, scotch, gin, anything"?

He didn't speak. Just shook his head. Giovanni started to cry. This was his family, too, and he loved Yolanda and the kids as much as Giuseppe.

"I can't believe it, Sep. It makes no sense".

"I know, Gio. But it still happened".

"Well, Tom will figure it out. He's a good cop. As good as they come. You know that. He'll find the killers".

I don't know if he was trying to reassure Giuseppe, or himself, or both. Giovanni always had a lot of confidence in me, but he might have been promising more than I could deliver. For the moment, Gorman was easing off the control shit. Or, more accurately, he was letting me in on things. I asked Giovanni,

"Are you going to administer last rites"?

"The sacraments are for the living. The Anointing of the Sick is for those who might recover. I will go up, say a prayer and bless each body. Sep, do you want to come with me"?

He just shook his head.

* * *

Gorman, Giovanni, Graham and I all went upstairs together. We could observe the murder scene while Giovanni was doing his religious thing. Gorman told FIU (Field Investigation Unit) to leave the bullet casings where they were. For the time being, taking pictures of the crime scene was enough. Until we settled on which division would take the case, nothing was to be tagged or sent to the lab. Like the guns, however, we all knew the casings would be dead ends. The bullets can be found in any gun shop, and, like the guns themselves, they would have no fingerprints on them. The Firearms Analysis Unit would be of no help, either. Even if they could match the projectiles to a previous crime, there would be no connection to these killers. That is why professionals leave the guns at the scene. They are always stolen, and their history is useless. They also avoid the risk of accidentally being stopped with the guns in their possession.

The murder scene was remarkably clean. It was what the military likes to call a surgical strike. A term that has always bothered me. Mixing metaphors, in this case the saving of life through surgery with the destruction of it through military attacks, was part of the government's public relations campaign. It may be their most successful venture into the world of mass manipulation. In the process, though, it desensitizes people to the reality of war, of violence of any kind, and makes for a very cold citizenry. In this case, these were not messy or gory murders, but neither were they sanitary. Not even the military can coin an expression that expurgates such harrowing acts. As painless and instantaneous as these deaths may have been, this was still a violent intrusion into a world of tranquility.

As we looked at Carmen's body halfway in the hallway, it was a fair guess that the murders began in the master bedroom, and that she interrupted whatever was going on. Since we had to pass by the the kids' rooms, we looked there first.

Leonardo had never awakened or even opened his eyes. He was lying flat on his back. There was little blood on the front of his shirt. Only seepage around the entry point. In Gina's room, it was clear that she was awake and sitting on the bed when she was shot. Her body had fallen backward, her eyes remaining open.

We surmised that Carmen initially was an unexpected victim who was not supposed to have walked into her parent's room. There was a hint of startle in her expression. It was as if her eyes and muscles had been interrupted before she could complete even a simple look of surprise.

Yolanda appeared to be the first target. She had been sitting on her bed and had fallen backward with the shot. There was no question about her expression. She was frightened. Perhaps she knew she was about to be killed. But whatever she saw in her killers, it instilled fear. For herself and her children. Just seeing the guns should have been enough to accomplish that. We will never know what she read in their eyes.

There were many questions to be asked. Was this a burglary gone bad? Was Yolanda's death necessitated by something that happened in the room? Were the children an after thought? Were the intruders just afraid of being seen? Were the murders, themselves, the true reason for the break-in? And, of course, overarching all the questions was the profound "why"?

Near each body was a casing from the assassins' bullets. In the master bedroom, the safe was left open. Another question. It did not look disturbed. The shelves were neat. The files all appeared in order. Was something actually missing? We would need Giuseppe to determine that. But it could wait until after the bodies were removed.

After examining the bedroom scenes, and finding no obvious leads, Gorman, Graham and I went back downstairs. We were called to the kitchen. This was the apparent entry and exit used by the perpetrators. It was here that we caught our first break. Someone had left a footprint in the flower bed. Could it have been one of the murderers? As professional and careful as they had been throughout, was it possible that they actually made a mistake? If one of them had slipped on the wet porch, he may have thought the azalea broke his fall. Certainly the bush helped. But a significant part of his foot was imprinted in the wet dirt.

Maybe that passed by unnoticed, or they thought that taking time to erase it would be a greater liability. We did not know if this clue would pan out, but for now it was a lead, and the only one we had. The area was being dried so that the lab could get a cast impression.

Next the videos. We returned to the front of the house. Giovanni and Giuseppe were still sitting on the couch in the living room.

"Sep", I said. "Would you show detective Gorman where the security video is? We want to see if we can pick up anything from the rooftop cameras".

Just then one of the officers came in the front door.

"Detective, we have a news van outside".

"Fuck," Gorman said. "Which one"?

"Casper", came the reply.

Casper is an independent news service. It monitors police scanning radios twenty-four hours a day. This enables their reporters to be first on the scene of any unusual event, especially in the late night and early morning hours when the broadcast stations are either understaffed or closed. Casper then takes footage from the scene and sells it to various channels and networks, thus providing them with video to lead off their early news reports. We all knew that every local channel would be broadcasting this crime by 6:00 AM. One more reason a decision had to be made about transferring the case to RHD.

The officers who responded to the 911 call did a poor job of securing the area. That allowed the Casper van to get close to house even with the patrol cars and Rescue Ambulances there. I couldn't resist pointing that out to Gorman.

"Why didn't your guys block off the street with perimeter tape? Casper won't be the only news group to deal with. KFWB and KNX 1070 are probably already on the way over".

Gorman looked really pissed at this point. He called a couple of officers over and told them to block the entire street, move the Casper van and keep any other news crews at bay.

Graham turned to me and said, "Give your captain a call".

*　　*　　*

Erick Haskell is a good man to work for. He has been on the LAPD for over thirty years, has an unblemished record, and is an excellent commanding officer. He is tough, but fair. What's more, he is well like and respected throughout the department. Like all other commanding officers, he had already received the message on his Blackberry, but at this point he had no reason to suspect this would become a case for RHD. I did not relish the idea of calling him at this hour to tell him.

"Captain", I said. "This is Moran. We have a situation".

Haskell did not use trite expressions, so he skipped the 'it had better be important line'. His response was simple and direct.

"Go ahead, Moran".

I proceeded to tell him what I knew so far and filled him in on the conflict with Gorman. He agreed that it sounded like an RHD case, and said he would head right over. Haskell lived on the Westside, in Santa Monica. But his car is equipped with lights and a siren, so he would have nothing to slow him down. Besides, it was now about 2:00 in the morning and even the L.A. roads would be empty. It would take him no more than twenty minutes.

As I made the phone call, I watched comprehension slowly find expression on Gorman's face. So far, he was in charge of the case, but I could tell that he knew he was going to lose it to RHD. Still, he was not going to give up easily. He would at least need to find a face-saving way to surrender. Surrender! Now that's a word I would never associate with Gorman. And yet, he had to look good in front of his captain. He managed to maintain his composure, but wanted to take as much advantage as possible of the fact that he was in charge until a decision was made.

"Captain, let's take a look at those surveillance videos. Moran, you can join us".

That was not a gracious gesture on his part. It was image control. Besides, if the case really was going to be transferred, I might as well get in at the beginning of the investigation. Captain Graham and I followed Gorman into the library and watched the video recordings. They were taken from each camera that covered the front, side and back of the house. After we finished, Gorman gave his analysis.

"Well, we have two assailants. But we can only determine their approximate size, which I would guess as about six feet. They were dressed in very dark colors, probably all black. They seemed to have known where all the cameras were, because they kept their heads down. That makes these videos practically useless. The only thing we learned for sure is that the footprint was made by one of the killers".

My initial reaction was to agree with Gorman. There wasn't much there. But I saw something more. Or maybe it was nothing. It appeared to me that one of the men had an almost unnoticeable limp, as if he had injured his foot, or leg or knee. It had probably been a serious injury, but attended to by a skilled physician. It wasn't much to go on, so for the time being I kept that observation to myself. Over the next few hours, though, it kept gnawing away at me. I couldn't pin it down, but I couldn't let it go, either. I had seen that same walk before. But where?

Haskell arrived and was greeted by Captain Graham. They had known each other for years. They were classmates in the academy and rose through the ranks together. Over the years they had remained good friends.

"Hello, Erick. What a fucking mess we have here".

"Hello, Lyle. Yeah. It's a mess all right. I was filled in on most of the details on the way over. Is there anything specific I should know"?

"We don't know much yet. It's still too early to determine if the murders were the intention all along, or just a way to cover up some kind of burglary. Nothing in the house seems out of place. All we know for sure is that it was professional. But it's also high profile. That's why you're here. You noticed the Casper van outside"?

"Yeah. They don't bother trying to hide from us. You know, Lyle, they're going to send this national. The New York studios are just about ready to go live and they'll want to lead with this story."

"Like I said", Graham replied. "That's why you're here. The lead detective is Gorman. He's good, but he's already had words with Moran".

"Yeah. So I heard", Haskell said. "They are not on good terms. But they are both good cops. I guess Gorman feels he can handle this case and doesn't like Moran's interference. But it's not that simple. The profile is going to demand that it be taken over by RHD. And with the television cameras here, I think we should make that decision soon and let them know".

"Erick, sometimes I think you care too much about the media. But you're probably right. We should do everything we can to show that we are on top of this case. Internal conflict helps no one. Let's go inside and see what's going on".

The two men entered the house and were immediately briefed on the situation. As the officer in charge, Gorman took the lead. He pointed out the two Glocks on the coffee table and led them upstairs to view the murders. He also noted that they only had two potential pieces of evidence. The first was the fact that the safe was open. They would need Giuseppe's assistance to decide if anything was missing. The other bit of evidence was the partial footprint in the flower bed. Fortunately there was an awning over the kitchen door and windows. The flower bed was beneath the window and sheltered from the heaviest rains. But it was damp, and soft enough to leave an impression.

Captain Haskell called everyone together.

"I don't have to tell any of you that this is not a typical murder scene. It's further complicated by the fact that Mr. Lozano is the Republican nominee for the U.S. Senate. We need to make a decision about who will handle this and we need to present a united front. Gorman, you're in charge of this investigation so far. What do you have to say"?

"I say it stays with Wilshire. We're more than capable of handling it".

Who did he think he was kidding?

"Captain", I interjected. "I don't agree".

"We already know what you think", responded Gorman.

Graham intervened. "Take it easy, you two. With your history, I don't think either of you is capable of objectivity. But we are going to make a decision. Erick, it's your call. But my personal opinion is that you should take over".

"Fuck it", Gorman replied. "I don't give a shit. You can have the case. I have my hands full with that fucking gang murder anyway. And that's probably going to get worse". Then he turned to me and said, "You win, Moran". Except it wasn't a game.

Graham looked at Haskell. "Well", he asked?

"Yeah. It's RHD now", Haskell replied. "I'll go outside and handle the media. That way the morning broadcasts will be able to say that RHD has taken over and will be handling the case. Moran, call in our detectives. And don't leave. I want to talk to you".

Haskell and Graham walked out together. Graham patted Haskell on the back and said,

"I don't envy you, Erick". Then with a smile he added, "But you'd better not fuck this up or you'll find yourself assigned to a less than glorious division".

With that, Haskell headed over to the Casper van and briefed the media. When he returned, he said to me,

"Tom, you were right about this case. From the beginning. It's too high profile to stay local. But I don't like being caught in the middle. You and Gorman should have put your problems behind you for the good of the department. I'm not blaming you. I think Gorman's an asshole, too. But you're a lieutenant, for god's sake. You should have been able to handle Gorman better than that. Anyway, the case is ours now. You brief the detectives when they arrive".

According to department protocol, Gary Wharton would be the lead detective on the case. He would be assisted by Philip Rose. But I wanted to head the investigation. This would not be an easy sell, but it did not have to be decided now. Later in the day, I would take my opportunity to discuss the matter with Haskell. For now, I would leave it to the detectives. I had seen everything I needed to, and it was all embedded in my mind. The forensics teams could go to work without disturbing any information I had about the case. I would need to ask Giuseppe about the safe, but that could wait. I walked over to Giovanni and Giuseppe.

"Listen, guys. I'm going to be here awhile longer, at least until the RHD detectives get here. But I think you should leave. Sep, why don't you go home with Gio. That should keep you free from the media for awhile. I'll contact you later".

"Thanks, Tom", was Giuseppe's response. He left with Giovanni and I waited.

The Field Investigation Unit collected the evidence. The criminalists from FIU cast a stone impression of the footprint at the scene, just in case it turned out to be evidence from one of the assailants. The coroner also began his examination of the four bodies. I remained for a few more hours.

# Chapter 19

Giuseppe stayed with Giovanni. Neither of them slept that night or morning. They stayed up drinking coffee. They did not need it to keep them awake. Still, it was a hot beverage that warmed their bodies even though it gave no warmth to their spirits. Questions and uncertainties abounded. For now, at least, Giuseppe was secure in the presence of his brother.

In the midst of all the confusion, Giuseppe neglected to call his campaign staff. Since most of the inner circle were accustomed to getting little sleep, they were awake for the first news cycle.

Bill Morgan put on the radio as a matter of habit. He started to walk into the bathroom when the report came through about the murders. He froze in his tracks as he listened to the report. 'This can't be', he thought to himself. He immediately called Catherine Stripling to make sure she was hearing the report. It was on every broadcast, both radio and television.

"Catherine, have you heard the news"?, he asked.

"Just now", she replied. "Have you spoken to Giuseppe"?

"Not yet. I wanted to call you first and ask you to handle the staff. I'll call him now and get back to you as soon as I can. I can't believe this. I'm not even sure I know how to handle it, yet. But we'll have to put the campaign on hold. Cancel all events for today, and I'll call you back soon".

"OK, Bill. I'll take care of that now".

Morgan hung up and called Giuseppe on his cell phone. Giuseppe was still awake when the phone rang at 6:10 that morning. The readout on the screen told him it was Morgan.

"Hello, Bill. I guess you heard".

"Just now, with the morning report. Giuseppe, I don't know what to say. I'm very sorry".

"Thanks". Giuseppe's response was neither cold nor empty, but he was feeling numb. Besides, what else could he say? He did not really feel like talking to anyone, not even his campaign manager. At this point, the campaign was the least of his concerns. And yet, it was not going away. He would have to consider how this tragedy would impact his run for the Senate.

"Bill", he continued. "Right now I don't want to talk. Call me back in a few hours. I'm staying at the church with my brother. In fact, why don't you come over around 2:00 this afternoon? In the meantime, you can handle the media for me".

"OK, Giuseppe. For the time being, I will tell them that we have no comment. And I'll keep your whereabouts unknown. But you know they won't let up. I'm sure someone will show up at the church, if only to get a comment from your brother".

"Yeah. Well, he can take care of that. I'll see you this afternoon. Thanks, Bill".

He hung up, closed his eyes and tried to rest.

Giovanni was the consummate priest. He was scheduled to celebrate the 6:30 Mass that Friday morning. Rather than ask his associate to take his place, he headed over to the church. He was awake anyway. Besides, he probably would have gone to the church to pray. He always found solace in his God. During moments like these it is hard to sit in judgment on someone else's religion. If it worked for him, then fine.

After Mass he went back to the rectory to see if Giuseppe wanted something to eat. To his relief he found that his brother had dosed off.

Certainly not a peaceful sleep, but at least a little rest. He was careful not to awaken him. He closed the door and went to the kitchen.

The rectory telephone was already ringing. There were three incoming lines on a rotary system. All were lit up. It had to be the press. He heard the doorbell and decided to ignore it. But it kept ringing. Like the phone lines, it wouldn't stop. He said to himself, 'And so it all begins'. He might as well face them now.

He went to the office and opened the door. Before he could even say a word, the reporters started. Every reporter wanted to be first. The simultaneous questions created a typical media melee:

"Where's your brother"? "Is your brother here"? "How does your brother feel"? "Do you have anything to say"? "How do you feel"? "Who do you think killed them"? "When will your brother speak to the press"?

What a bunch of fucking assholes. Not one of them cared about the reality of the situation or the crisis that Giuseppe was going through. It was just another story to them and they all wanted their questions answered. They were backed up by cameramen, with vans parked out on Vermont ready to relay any footage and anything he said back to the studios.

"I have no comment". He started to close the door, when one of the reporters stuck his foot inside. Giovanni could feel the anger rising inside of him. He turned around and pushed the reporter back onto the porch and slammed the door. He knew they wouldn't leave, but at least they stopped ringing the fucking bell.

He went back to the living room where he had left Giuseppe and took a chair opposite him. He looked at his brother with profound sorrow. What could he say to him? What were they going to do now? Giovanni knew he was going to have to be strong. For both of them. But he didn't feel strong. At that moment even his faith was weak, though he would never admit that. Among the three of us, his was the faith that never wavered. At least not as far as we knew. Somehow he would draw courage. He believed that God could still be found in such tragedy. Whereas I had long ago stopped looking.

*    *    *

The two detectives who drew the case arrived at the Lozano home at about 3:30 AM. Gary Wharton, the lead detective, was accompanied by Philip Rose. They are both topnotch cops. More than capable of handling the investigation. My job was to supervise the two of them. But I needed to do more. I really wanted to head the investigation. To do the work myself. I had a vested interest in finding these killers. But that would not be an easy sell to my captain. Not only was it not my job, more importantly, Haskell would see me as too close to the case to maintain objectivity. I stayed at the house until 8:00 that morning. I kept going over the crime scene trying to fit the pieces together. Then there was that nagging video. I knew that I had seen that guy before, but still could not recall. Afterward, I headed to my office. I had to prepare my arguments.

Captain Haskell arrived at 10:00. He stopped by my desk and asked me to join him. We went to his office and he closed the door.

"I already told you, Tom, that I did not like the situation you put me in last night. You're supposed to be a professional. You should never have gotten into a pissing contest with Gorman".

"What do you want me to say"?, I replied. "You're right, of course. But Gorman is an asshole and it was obvious that this case could not stay with Wilshire. It had RHD written all over it".

"Sure. But that didn't have to be the first thing you said to him. You challenged him and did not give him an easy way out. The idea of transferring the case to RHD could have waited until after his captain arrived on scene. According to Gorman you tried to hijack it from the very beginning".

"I wouldn't put it that way. I just knew where it was headed".

"Well, forget about it. It's done with. It's our case now".

"Yeah, about that", I said. "Erick, I want to head the investigation".

"You're out of your mind, Tom. That's not your job. Besides, you're too close to the situation".

"I've been thinking about that, too. All night. My relationship to the family may work to our advantage. Look, we both know that in spite of what we say to the public, every case is not of equal merit or concern.

And this one is major national news. Giuseppe may be the next U.S. Senator from California. People are going to want this case solved, and in short order. What's more, I want these killers more than any case I've ever worked on".

"I can't do it, Tom. It's not just about protocol. And I certainly don't question your ability. You are the most redoubtable detective on the force. But I don't think you are objective".

"No. I'm not. I admit it. If that's what you're looking for, I can't provide it in this case. I know that. But, dammit, that gives me an edge. I don't know what went on at that house last night, but this is not just some random killing. It was too professional, too perfect. All my instincts tell me there's something more going on here. My personal connection to the case, will motivate me more than it will Wharton and Rose. I need to lead this investigation.

"Look, Erick. You want a promotion. You don't want to be a captain the rest of your life. You want to become a commander. If this case gets fucked up, your career is over. Not only will you remain a captain, but the chances are you won't stay in RHD. Both of us have a vested interest here".

I made my point and didn't want to overplay my hand. Haskell thought for awhile. I could tell he was thinking about the proposal, but I knew he still had serious reservations. Finally, he said,

"All right. But there are conditions. First, you work with Wharton and Rose".

I tried not to react or roll my eyes. Still, he could sense that I did not want to be hampered by anyone.

"I'm serious, Tom. You're not going solo on this. You're lead investigator, but I want you to keep them in the loop. Second, and most important, is that I want a daily report from you. Not in writing. But I want to know everything that's going on. Right now I have the chief breathing down my neck and the Governor and Attorney General are threatening to appoint their own investigators. Both our necks and careers are on the line. Consider yourself on a short leash. You can inform Wharton and Rose. Just remember. This is not you personal vendetta.

"By the way, I had a call from the FBI this morning. They offered their assistance".

"Hell no", I replied. "I've worked with them before, and they don't understand the concept of teamwork. They're like the black hole of intelligence. Information goes in and nothing comes out. I can assure that they wouldn't be of any help".

I started to leave when Haskell added, "OK, Tom. But you sure as hell had better know what you're doing".

I called Wharton and Rose into my office and told them of my meeting with the captain. It was clear that Wharton did not like the idea. This would have been his case. Not unlike Gorman, he saw this as an opportunity to make his career. The difference was that Wharton is not an asshole. Also, I am his superior. I assured them that we would share the investigation. I would give them a reasonably free hand.

"Wharton", I said, "The first thing I'd like to do is go over those videos. I know you've already seen them. So have I. But we should view them together. They've provided us with our only lead so far. Rose, you join us. Three sets of eyes might be helpful. The hard drive is over at TI (Technical Laboratory). Any questions"?

Neither of them said anything.

"OK", I continued. "Let's go".

No police department in the nation has a better Scientific Investigation Division (SID) than the LAPD. At the same time, few departments are as overwhelmed as Los Angeles. Still, we had no problem sitting down with a technician. We watched the videos several times and did not see anything new. It was just as Gorman had said earlier. The killers knew where the cameras were and kept their heads down. But there was still that annoying walk.

It was barely noticeable. I pointed it out to the others, but did not tell them that I had seen it before. Besides, I couldn't remember where. So I decided to keep that to myself until I could figure it out. The consensus was that the limp might have been the reason he slipped on the porch. We did not gain any new information from reviewing the videos. It was time to talk to Giuseppe about the safe.

"Rose, check on the guns and casings. They won't lead anywhere, but we need to cover all our tracks. Wharton, see if you can put pressure on FIU to speed up the investigation of that footprint. This case is big enough to move it to the head of the list. In the meantime, I'll go talk to Mr. Lozano. I'm not going to interrogate him. I just want to see how he is and get a feel for any information he might unconsciously know. If I learn anything, I'll tell you".

# Chapter 20

The media were still camped out in front of St. Catherine Parish. They must have known that Giuseppe was there. They would not be out in such force just to get a comment from Giovanni. I called to let him know I was there, then entered through the back door to avoid the press.

Giovanni met me.

"How's Sep"?, I asked.

"I guess he's holding up as well as can be expected. You know him. He hasn't really said much. He's in the living room. He's been there all night. He never went to bed. Neither did I".

"I need to talk to him, Gio".

"Come on. I'll go with you".

Sep was awake, but he looked like shit. They both did. I guess I did, too. We were all exhausted, and no one had slept.

"Hello, Sep". He didn't say anything. I sat on the chair across from him and just stared at the floor for awhile. Finally, I looked up. "I don't know what to say, Sep".

"That's OK, Tom. You don't need to try. I really appreciated your being there last night".

"I'm going to head the investigation. That means I'll be asking you some questions. The worst of it is, we have to go back to the house. Both of us. Not now. It can probably wait until Sunday, but no longer".

"I don't know if I can, Tom".

"Sep, we only have two possible clues. The first is a footprint in the flowerbed. FIU has already started working on that. They've already made the plaster cast. But even if we put pressure on them, it will take at least a couple of weeks to learn anything. The other lead is the safe in your bedroom. It was open, but nothing appeared disturbed. I need you to tell me if anything is missing".

"Tom," Giovanni interjected, "do you have to do it so soon"?

"Our best chance is to chase the leads as quickly as possible. Before they get cold. And we don't have anything else to go on. The coroner is completing his examination as we speak. But that's technical information. It's unlikely to reveal anything useful in finding the killers. The coroner will remove Yolanda and the kids shortly. Meanwhile, there is nothing else in the house of value to our investigation.

"By Sunday there should be minimal media presence over there. Officers will remain on the scene around the clock, and the house and yard will remain cordoned off with investigation tape. That will guarantee some privacy".

The secretary knocked on the door and informed Giuseppe that Bill Morgan had arrived. Giovanni asked,

"Tom, can we let him in now"?

"Yes", I replied. "But I'd like to stay. I won't interfere in any campaign stuff".

Giovanni told the secretary to show him in.

It had now been about eight hours since Morgan heard the news. He walked into the living room still bearing a look of shock. Giuseppe started to rise, and Morgan said,

"Don't get up Giuseppe. I'm so sorry about all this".

"Thank you", was his simple reply.

"I've canceled all of today's activities and will probably cancel events for all of next week. At least as far as your appearances. We might maintain some of the schedule and field substitute speakers. But we have to talk about where we go from here, Giuseppe. Gottesman's office called today. Actually, he made the call himself to personally express his condolences. He said he was pulling most of his campaign ads for the next week".

Anthony Gottesman was the Democratic nominee for California's U.S. Senate seat. Throughout the summer the campaign had been heated and feverish, but it was not particularly nasty. Gottesman had been mayor of Sacramento, the state capital of California. After that he served in the state legislature as a representative from the ninth district. Neither man was a household name throughout the state. Gottesman was well known in the northern part, Lozano in the southern.

Much of the summer's campaigning was an attempt by both candidates to expand their name recognition as well as make their case before the voters. Gottesman had practical experience on his side, having held elective office already. He continually emphasized this, noting that Lozano had never been elected to anything other than class president in elementary school.

On the other hand, Lozano had firmly established himself within the circles of California's Republican elite. He played up his business experience, including international contacts, as a way of building industry in the state and creating new jobs. Lozano felt that his experience evened the playing field, since Gottesman had no private sector experience.

Apparently, they were both right. Neither candidate was surging. Poll after Poll indicated a virtual dead heat, flipping the lead between them only two or three percentage points.

The murders had a profound impact on both campaigns. It led to a disquieting irony. Neither side could afford to be seen exploiting the tragedy for political gain. Yet the election was only six weeks away. How do you keep a campaign alive in these circumstances?

Out of deference and respect, Gottesman did not just pull his ads for the following week. He also canceled his personal appearances throughout the weekend. During that time he met with his staff to strategize how to resume campaigning on Monday. He was going to have to soften the attacks. The people of California would have a strong sympathy for Lozano, and it would be too easy for Gottesman to come across as insensitive. And yet, he had an obligation to the Democratic Party and to all Californians. The election would still take place on November 7th.

The Lozano campaign had bigger issues. Giuseppe was going to be in no condition to campaign actively for awhile. At least not until after the funeral. His ads would also have to be modified. If he stayed on the attack, he might be perceived as cold and heartless. People had to know that he was going through a serious trauma, and that would require easing his approach.

Both campaigns ended up changing their advertising to emphasize their own qualifications rather than negating the abilities of the other candidate. It was a rare experience in California politics. For years the media had suggested that people did not like negative campaigning, but it always worked. This year Californians were presented with an almost serendipitous opportunity to experience a positive campaign environment and find out how successful it could be.

"Bill", Giuseppe responded. I don't have much appetite for campaigning right now. I don't even want to meet with the staff. You can coordinate all meetings".

Giovanni interrupted.

"Sep, I think I know how you feel. And I certainly don't think you should be on the campaign trail right now. But I think meeting with your staff is a good idea. You need to keep yourself busy. Within limits. You can hold meetings here. When your staff is not here we can plan the funeral".

"Thanks, Gio. I'd like you to do the funeral planning. You know more about it than I do. As for meeting here, are you sure it won't put you out too much to have my staff around"?

"Not at all. I'll give you some office space, and the rest of the house is yours. Tom, how long before Yolanda and the kids are released"?

"I'm not sure, Gio, but I'm sure we can make this case a priority with the coroner. They finished their work at the house a couple of hours ago. Unfortunately, this will require autopsies. I'll ask them to bring in extra staff. I think they can finish by Monday. Tuesday at the latest.

"Sep, I think Gio's right about you staying busy. If you want, I can post some officers here to keep the media off your back. That way your staff can use the front door. It probably wouldn't help that much for them to enter through the kitchen anyway. The press would still manage to get in the way".

"That would be great, Tom. But I don't think I'll be going out much. Actually, I'll only stay here a couple more nights. Thanks, anyway, Gio. But I think I'd be better off at a hotel. Bill, can you get me a suite at the Bonaventure, beginning Sunday"?

"I'll work on it right away", he replied. "I'll head over to campaign headquarters now and brief the staff. If you need anything, call me".

With that Morgan left. Giuseppe turned to me and said,

"Tom, when we go to the house, I'll pack some clothes and move to the hotel. I think that's a better choice in the long run. Gio, if you don't mind, I'd like to go to the guest room and lie down for awhile".

"Of course, Sep".

Giuseppe left. Then Giovanni asked me,

"Tom, how did you convince Haskell to let you run the investigation"?

"Well, he didn't want to. He suggested I was too close to the situation. I used that argument to my advantage. Gio, I really want to find these bastards. This is not just another case. This one is personal, and I'll give everything I have to solve it".

Giovanni just nodded his head. I continued.

"Gio, I don't want to jump to any conclusions. There are all kinds of reasons why this might have happened. But something just doesn't seem right. For one thing, I know that I've seen one of the murderers before. I just can't remember where or when".

"Well, Tom. I trust you and I know you're a good cop. I just hope you can handle this. As you say, it's personal".

"Yeah. I'm going back to the office now. You know how to reach me if you need to".

"Thanks, Tom".

When I arrived back the office, Wharton and Rose were waiting for me. Wharton had some success at FIU. The entire SID (Special Investigations Department) is usually so swamped with cases, they dislike moving a new one to the top of the list. Murders, suicides and even accidental deaths in Los Angeles often rate national attention. However, SID understood the urgency of this case. As a result, each of its units, FIU, FAU and ESU moved as expeditiously as possible. Still, tracking the footprint back to a manufacturer, then to a store, and then to a buyer was going to take time.

Rose, on the other hand, came up empty with ballistics. There were no fingerprints on the guns or the casings. No surprise there. That's a mistake professionals do not make. If there were even the slightest chance, they would not have left them behind.

I finally decided to share with them my observations from the video. I still did not know where I had seen the guy before, but I knew where to start looking. The problem was, no one could help me with it. The only thing that might jog my memory free would be the Field Interview cards. Unfortunately, I would probably have to sort through hundreds of them.

Field Interview cards contain basic biographical data on individuals identified at the scene of some crime or incident. It includes name, address, phone number, social security number, driver's license or state ID. It also identifies a vehicle, if one is involved. The FI notes whether the person is a loiterer, prowler, solicitor, witness; whether there is gang activity; if the person has a record, is on parole or probation. It also contains information on other persons with the individual, as well as the officer's name, serial number and division.

I felt overwhelmed when I walked into the records department. The FI cards are not computerized. I thought to myself, 'Shit. It's 2000 and these damn cards are stored manually. City officials should have to come down and sort through this crap. Maybe then they would budget for a good computer system'. But I had to face reality. So I set about a task that would end up taking me days.

*　　*　　*

Giovanni agreed to take care of the funeral arrangements, and it brought relief to Giuseppe. He opted to use McCormick Mortuary in Inglewood. It was not the closest to the Lozano home, but over the years Giovanni had many services with them and had developed a good relationship with John McCormick. He trusted John and knew he could rely on his ability and discretion.

The size and political import of this funeral ordinarily would have dictated that the service be held in the Cathedral Church. However, Los Angeles has been without a Cathedral since 1995. So Giovanni contacted the pastor of St. Vincent Church on Figueroa and Adams, just south of downtown Los Angeles. He was most amenable to the use of the church. The burial would take place at Holy Cross Cemetery in Culver City. Making these arrangements was the easy part for Giovanni. He still needed confirmation from the coroner's office as to when the bodies would be released, but at least everything else was in place.

That night I had dinner with Giovanni and Giuseppe at the rectory. Giovanni decided to cook for us. He thought that preparing dinner would give his mind a rest. I certainly had no objections. I always welcomed the opportunity to taste his food. He had been cooking from childhood, learning the recipes that were traditional to the Lozano family, and I thought he was a good chef. He made gnocchi with pistou. As was often the case, I probably ate too much. But I had not eaten all day, and it was a good counter to the scotch that Giuseppe and I had while Giovanni was in the kitchen.

Even a wonderful meal could not distract us from the reality we were all confronting. Giovanni shared with us the funeral arrangements he had made, and I promised to pressure the coroner's office. When Giuseppe spoke, I was not prepared for his request.

"Tom, I would like you to give the eulogy. Gio's already going to preach, and no one knew my family better than you. Yolanda loved you and the kids adored you. You were just as much an uncle to them as Gio".

"Sep, I don't know what to say. It's a great honor, but it scares me. You two are both public speakers. I'm not".

"Please, Tom", he replied. "I don't care if you're a good speaker or not. The point is to share something with people that they may not know. To speak from your heart".

I looked to Giovanni for support. But he was no help.

"Sep's right, Tom. You're the perfect person".

"But I have the investigation to deal with, and it can't stop just so I can prepare a eulogy", I said.

"It doesn't have to be long", Giovanni continued, "or some oratorical masterpiece. Just say what you feel. Recall some story. Those should come to mind easily. In fact, the three of us can get together and share some of our recollections. That will make it easier for you. And when you speak, just pretend you are speaking to the two of us".

I agreed. And I knew Giovanni was right. Preparing the eulogy was not something I could do alone. We agreed to have dinner together again on Saturday and then just talk and remember. This would help me determine a direction for my personal thoughts and reflections.

# Chapter 21

Saturday night, Giovanni cooked again. This time he prepared veal parmigiana and a side of farfalle pasta topped with authentic bolognese sauce. Instead of scotch, Giovanni insisted that we all begin the evening with Pastis. He seemed to think it would better prepare our palates for the meal. He may have been right. Dinner was superb. But, then again, it always was.

During dinner we talked about Yolanda and the kids. It was an opportunity for the three of us to remember and share stories, many of which we had in common. It was also a chance for me to begin to gather my own thoughts, although I had no idea how I would mold them into a cohesive reflection.

As if the tragedy could possibly be any worse, we realized that both Carmen and Gina had just celebrated their birthdays. Carmen must have inherited some of her father's political ambitions. She had been elected class president and was almost certainly destined to become student body president. She had just met her first real boyfriend, and everything seemed to be going well. Gina was the perfect social butterfly. Incredibly popular among her peers, she still maintained excellent study habits and perfect A's on her report cards. That was fortunate, because if her grades had fallen, she would have lost telephone privileges. Little Leonardo was just coming into his own. Although he did not excel at the more common sports, he had developed a strong interest in judo. This martial art requires a keen and focused mind, and he possessed exactly the right concentration. What a waste! Three lives obliterated in moments. And for what?

Our memories of Yolanda took us all the way back to college and the first time Giuseppe came home and told us about this beautiful and intelligent girl at Stanford. Over the years we had shared many wonderful times together and they all came flooding back with powerful emotion. On the way home that night it occurred to me that we do not spend enough time doing that same remembering while people are alive. Whether out of anger or frustration, the common tendency is to focus on the troubled times and difficult moments. Until it's too late. Another waste!

During dinner, Giuseppe told us something about Yolanda that neither Giovanni nor I knew. She was an amateur poet. But there was a particular story he shared with us. It eliminated any attempts we might have had that evening to contain our emotions.

Giuseppe and Yolanda both loved the movies. It was in their Southern California roots. But Yolanda had been a teacher. For her, the movies were not just a diversion. The arts, in general, coursed through her blood and she made a practice of studying modern screenplays. Studying might be too strong a word, since most screenplays frequently left her disappointed and desolate. She often wondered how the Academy of Motion Pictures managed annually to cull five worthy nominees for the Best Screenplay Oscar. The classroom, however, was a different matter.

Yolanda's expertise was in English literature, including classic poetry on both sides of the Atlantic Ocean. She was a devotee of the romantic poets and was convinced that good, literary education included memorizing the works of Lord Byron, John Keats and Percy Shelley on the British side, and Emily Dickinson, Ralph Waldo Emerson and Walt Whitman on the American.

Yolanda lived that devotion in her personal life. She developed a method of cultivating and keeping alive her own poetic skills. Whenever she would go to a movie theater, she paid special attention to the soundtrack. Especially, the tracks with no lyrics. Not infrequently, such music becomes a recurring theme within a film. Whenever she heard a particularly moving piece, Yolanda would rush out to purchase the recording. Then she would set about to writing lyrics of her own. These were drawn from her exposure to the romantic poets and from the depth of her own personal experiences. Although Giuseppe often chided her about being too romantic, he was secretly thrilled with each song she composed.

One such set of lyrics was especially close to Giuseppe's heart, because it also served as an anniversary gift from Yolanda. This was far more precious than any item she could have acquired at a store. It originated with a surprise that he had given to her.

Giuseppe had firmly established himself in many areas of business, including the entertainment industry, installing The Pegasus Bolt at most of the major studios. His contacts paid off, and he managed to procure two tickets for the opening of the American Film Institute Festival on October 28, 1998. It was held at the Mann Chinese Theater. The opening night featured the premiere of "Life is Beautiful", an Italian film by Roberto Benigni.

This was the first trip to the AFI Fest for both of them. It would have been exciting even if Benigni's film were a disappointment. It was not. "Life is Beautiful" had already received the Grand Jury Prize at Cannes. In the United States it garnered rave reviews from critics. The public at large would weigh in with a similar verdict, and praise would quickly spread by word of mouth.

As Yolanda sat in the theater, she was swept away by Nicola Piovani's lush and emotionally powerful soundtrack. It was punctuated by the romantic "Bacarole" from Jacques Offenbach's "Les contes d'Hoffmann" (The Tales of Hoffmann). But it was Piovani's lyric-less theme that truly captivated Yolanda. Snuggling up to her husband, she felt overwhelmed. By the movie, the music and their love. It became clear that her next project would be to conjure lyrics that would attempt to do justice to the music and plumb the depths of the love they shared.

After the film, they stopped by the Cat & Fiddle restaurant and pub for a couple of drinks and a late snack of Scottish eggs, a house specialty. On their way home, Yolanda talked Giuseppe into stopping at Amoeba Music so that she could purchase the soundtrack from "Life is Beautiful". So was born her most personal anniversary gift. A testimony to all that he meant to her.

As it turned out, Giovanni also had the soundtrack. He put on the music and Giuseppe recited the lyrics he had committed to memory more than a year earlier. Giovanni and I were undone. Even without singing, Giuseppe managed break whatever levee held back our tears.

I managed to steady my voice and asked, "Sep, can I use that song at the funeral. In the eulogy"?

"Yes, Tom. I would like that. I think Yolanda would, too".

On the way home, I began thinking about what I would say at the funeral. It was still several days away, but the sooner I put my thoughts together, the better. Giuseppe gave me a good ending for the eulogy, but I would have to come up with the first part. And I still had the investigation. I began to doubt myself. I wondered if I could handle all of it. Not just the time and energy, but the emotion. For now, I needed a good night's rest. Or as close as I could come to one. When I arrived home, the emotion of the last couple of days overpowered me. I collapsed on my bed, too tired and enervated even to undress. I actually did sleep. Not exactly soundly, but enough that I felt more refreshed in the morning.

I got up, showered, shaved, put on fresh clothes and headed back to the church to pick up Giuseppe. On the way, I called Wharton and Rose and told them to meet us at the Lozano home.

By Sunday, much of the curiosity had died down. Everyone knew that Giuseppe was not living at home, so there was not much to see. Of course, that does not stop the imagination and we encountered a few onlookers. Mostly neighbors or nearby residents. They were kept at a distance and restrained by the investigation tape, and police officers were still keeping round the clock watch at the house. News teams were no longer using the house as a backdrop for their coverage. They had amassed sufficient archival footage and that seemed to serve their needs.

Giuseppe was clearly uncomfortable walking into the house again. Almost everything was exactly as we had left it a couple days earlier. The guns were no longer there. They had been taken to FAU (Firearms Analysis Unit) along with the bullet casings from the bedrooms. The coroner had removed the bodies on Friday. In the backyard, the casting of the footprint had been completed and was taken to the lab for examination. The only remaining evidence to be examined was the safe.

Giuseppe had an uncertainty to his step. His whole demeanor was one of unease and hesitancy. I knew it was difficult for him. Just being in the house was a problem. But the safe was upstairs, requiring us to move past the bedrooms of Leonardo and Gina, then into the master bedroom where it all began. I am used to crime scenes. For a brief moment I did not fully appreciate how Giuseppe felt. True, he had already been in the bedroom, having been the one who discovered the bodies. And they were now gone. But that did not pacify his emotions. Fortunately, searching through the safe would enable him to keep his back to the scene of the murders themselves.

The files were organized alphabetically. Giuseppe began a systematic search. He paused when he noticed the first missing folder.

"Tom, there is a file missing under the letter 'M'. But I don't understand. It is a coded file and would be meaningless to anyone just going through the safe".

"What was in it"?, I asked.

"It is a highly detailed schematic for a missile guidance system, with special focus on the design of the computer chips. It was filed under the title: 'Mercury, the Winged Messenger'. Not only would no one know the file name, I doubt anyone would take the time to read through it".

"Are there any other files missing"?, I asked.

Giuseppe continued his search.

"Nothing", he said.

"OK. Let's go. There's nothing else here of value to us. Do you mind coming back to the office with us? We need to talk about who might benefit from that file. And we need a list of your employees, past and present. We can get that from your office, tomorrow".

"Tom, let me pack some clothes. It will only take a few minutes".

"I'll wait with you, Sep, and give you a ride". Then, turning to Wharton and Rose, I continued, "You two head back to RHD. We'll join you shortly".

Giuseppe took out a couple of suitcases and packed the clothes and other items he would need at the hotel.

"Sep, I want you to hire a private security firm to provide personal protection for you. We still don't know the motives behind the murders. For all we know, you may be a potential target. Especially, it this was planned by a competitor".

He started to object. "Tom", but I cut him off.

"This is not really a request, Sep. I'm telling you. At least until I get more information on what happened. I want you to use Gavin de Becker. It is the best private security in the nation. Possibly the world. A number of guys who left the force now work there. And they can handle any kind of personal security issue.

"Back in 1988, Gavin de Becker provided protective security for Tina Turner's appearance at the Maracanã Stadium in Rio de Janeiro. That was the largest single-artist performance in history with some 200,000 people in attendance. No security threat is beyond them, and I want you protected. Besides, it will help keep the FBI off my back. They've already tried to move in on the investigation, but I won't work with them. And let's face it, Sep, you can afford Gavin de Becker".

"Fine, Tom. I promise to call them tomorrow".

"No. This afternoon, Sep. We can do it when we get back to headquarters".

When Giuseppe had finished packing, we headed back to my office. Once there, I gave him the number of the security firm and he arranged for them to begin providing protection at the Bonaventure Hotel.

# Chapter 22
## FUNERAL

Los Angeles has no shortage of churches, representing virtually every style of architecture from baroque to modern. Built in the early 1920's, St. Vincent's is a Churrigueresque church, Spanish rococo. It sits just a couple of miles south of downtown. A relatively large building, seating about 1200 people, it would serve the needs of the Lozano funeral as well almost any other. The major problem was parking, but that also would have been the case anywhere else, since most churches in the heart of Los Angeles were built prior to the automobile revolution.

This was more than a funeral. It was an event. As expected, the murders drew national attention, and the funeral was covered by every news outlet in the city. Never one to shy from cameras and the media, Cardinal Roger Mahony, Archbishop of Los Angeles, offered to be the celebrant. Giuseppe, however, insisted that his brother lead the service. So the Cardinal agreed to preside over the Mass. He was given a place of honor in the sanctuary, to the side of the altar. He also would lead the Prayers of Final Commendation at the end of the service.

I still don't know how Giovanni can celebrate funerals the way he does. It is not just a question of faith. I know he believes. It is the unique touch that he brings. He approaches each service with a fresh perspective. At least the funerals I have witnessed. He maintains a personal connection with the grieving. Something that I lost long ago in what may have been a misguided search for objectivity. Then again, my job is to investigate, not comfort. As a result death and funerals have become routine. At least most of them. Even for me, this one was different.

Not because the murders were so violent, but because they were so personally violent. I sat in amazement, deeply admiring Giovanni's dignity and outward calm. I was feeling the same internal turmoil that I knew was ripping at his own heart and soul.

The ceremony, itself, was not unlike other funerals, albeit with more coffins in the aisle, and more people in the congregation. As for me, I did not approach it with a deep and abiding faith. Nor was I concerned with which prayers and readings would be used to guide the faith of others. I was there to share my love, show my support, and deliver the eulogy. Most of all, I think I wanted to hear what Giovanni would say when he preached. I was sure that he would not disappoint and trusted that he could move even my fatigued heart. I certainly needed to find comfort somewhere.

Giovanni knew just how to begin the service. He welcomed everyone and thanked them for their presence and concern. Then he addressed the congregation with these words;

"Each of us has, at one time or another, suffered the loss of someone we loved. Sometimes it strikes quickly, as it did last week, in physical death. At other times, it approaches with stealth, as in a failed relationship, the gradual loosening of the heartstrings that once held someone so close. It is tempting to put the pain of loss behind us by forgetting. Today I ask you not to try to escape the pain, but through it to find love again".

Then followed the opening prayers and readings.

Giovanni had told me that he would base his preaching on passages from the Book of Sirach and from John's Gospel.

## Sirach 6:14-16

*A faithful friend is a sturdy shelter; he who finds one finds a treasure.*
*A faithful friend is beyond price, no sum can balance his worth.*
*A faithful friend is a life-saving remedy, such as he who fears God finds.*

## 1 John 4:16-21

*God is love. Whoever lives in love lives in God, and God in him.*
*In this way, love is made complete among us so that we will have confidence*
*on the day of judgment, because in this world we are like him.*
*There is no fear in love. But perfect love drives out fear, because fear has to do*
*with punishment. The one who fears is not made perfect in love.*
*We love because he first loved us.*
*If anyone says, "I love God," yet hates his brother, he is a liar. For anyone*
*who does not love his brother, whom he has seen, cannot love God, whom he*
*has not seen.*
*And he has given us this command: Whoever loves God must also love his*
*brother.*

## John 15:9-15

*"As the Father has loved me, so I have loved you; abide in my love.*
*If you keep my commandments, you will abide in my love, just as I*
*have kept my Father's commandments and abide in his love.*
*I have said these things to you so that my joy may be in you, and that*
*your joy may be complete.*

*"This is my commandment, that you love one another as I have loved*
*you. No one has greater love than this, to lay down one's life for one's*
*friends. You are my friends if you do what I command you. I do not call you*
*servants any longer, because the servant does not know what the master*
*is doing; but I have called you friends, because I have made known to you*
*everything that I have heard from my Father".*

## Homily

For a moment I thought I saw Giovanni falter. If so, his recovery more than masked it. He gathered himself together and began:

"For most of us, and I suspect for all cultures, family is one of our most treasured possessions, our primary bond. Whatever terms we use to define family, and whatever form it may take in the modern era it remains the bedrock of society. We often hear people speak of this importance by saying "family is everything". One popular phrase that emphasizes this sentiment is "Blood is thicker than water". Such utterances occur in film, on stage and in a variety of literature. And most likely similar expressions exist in all languages.

"A primary and often difficult task for parents is to help mold their children into a family—to instill in them those values that identify who they are and bind them together. I remember my parents telling me that I had to love my sister. This was often said in an effort to forge peace after we had been fighting. Although it did not always work when we were little, it did eventually take root as we matured.

"Unfortunately, the idea of family has frequently been corrupted in the larger society. In the U.S., some politicians, without any genuine interest in family values, have co-opted the term for their own political agenda and personal gain. In organized crime, it is not uncommon for members of the syndicate, particularly the Mafia, to speak of their employees as "family" while they order them into the streets to commit murder. On the heels of the Mafia, street gangs manipulate the idea of family to lure impressionable and unsuspecting youth into a world of drugs and violence.

"And yet, within many religious traditions there remains a profound commitment to family, with both the Old and New Testaments bearing witness. Among Christians we speak of being baptized into Christ Jesus, thus becoming a brother or sister to him. With God as our father, we are not just sisters and brothers to Jesus we are also brothers and sisters to one another. Clearly, in our tradition the family relationship has great import.

"Without in any way attempting to diminish the significance of family, I would like to suggest that there is a deeper and even more meaningful relationship in our lives that is also attested to in the Scriptures. The significance of this relationship is indicated even more by its economy of use in the Bible. It is friendship.

"People generally do not connect the idea of friend to their relationship with God. After all, in the Old Testament the use of friend is primarily confined to exhortations in the Wisdom literature, such as in today's first reading. Even in the New Testament it is used primarily in a generic and formal sense, as when Jesus says, "Friend, who has appointed me your judge or arbiter?" Indeed, this is far from the personal and emotional use we make of the word in our daily lives. However, there is something far more subtle and compelling at work here.

"In all of the Bible, only one person is ever called the friend of God. It is not Adam or Eve; not Sarah or Moses; not even David, who played music that pleased the Lord. The only person ever called the friend of God is Abraham. Why? Because God revealed to Abraham his plan of salvation: to form a great nation, Israel, and from that nation to call forth the savior of the world. Put simply, Abraham knew the mind of God. This is not just academic.

"Jesus' disciples would have been very familiar with the sacred writings of Israel and so would have known that Abraham alone was called God's friend. I don't think we can exaggerate how stunned they would have been to hear the words Jesus spoke in today's Gospel. The night before his death Jesus tells them, and for the first time, that they are his friends. What's more, as if to underscore his declaration, he also tells them why: "…because I have made known to you everything I learned from my Father." Remember, Jesus had already staked his claim to be one with the Father. So when he called the disciples his friends, it conjured the image of Abraham. The disciples may not have grasped the depth of their responsibility to continue the mission of Jesus. After all, even Abraham struggled in living up to his friendship with God. Still, the disciples knew what it meant when Jesus called them his friends.

"We can learn much from these Scriptures. First of all, calling someone a friend is a choice. We do not choose what family we are born into. I have joked in the past that if we did I would have chosen a different sister! Of course, I am pleased with the one I have and would not trade her for anyone. The point is that we do not have a choice about who will be our brothers and sisters, or even our parents for that matter. We do choose our friends.

"Second, we might consider that it is more than a little tragic that we use the word so lightly in modern day America. It is not uncommon for people to meet at a party, then an hour later introduce each other as a new friend, without knowing anything significant about each other, often nothing more than each others' names.

"A person becomes a friend when we let him or her inside. By sharing our mind. As God did with Abraham. It takes time and caution. Not everyone we meet will become a friend. In fact, few truly will. It seems that the prudence and exhortations of the wisdom literature are needed now more than ever.

"Third, there is a profound challenge presented in today's Gospel reading. At least for those of us who seek to live as followers of Jesus. What Jesus says of his disciples he says also of us. We are his friends. This might give us pause as to how we treat other people in our lives. It should certainly cause us to question whether or not we live as though we know the mind of Jesus.

"When I was in the seminary, one of our professors attempted to counter the phrase "Blood is thicker than water" with his own declaration that the "waters of Baptism are thicker than blood". It is modestly clever and does make his point that the bond created in Baptism is more inclusive than our natural families. But I think he missed the real point. For in calling another person friend, we extend the depth of our relationship beyond even our religious traditions and biases. Jesus did not call his disciples friends that night because they were Jewish. They had always been Jewish. He called them friends because he shared the fullness of his knowledge with them. They knew the mind of Jesus, and consequently the mind of God.

"Whether or not we know the mind of Jesus and are his friends is put to its greatest test this morning. We are confronted with a tragedy that is almost beyond belief. Both the violence and the utter senselessness leave us wanting. But wanting what? My guess is that most of us do not just desire the criminals caught, we require them to pay with their own lives. We call it justice. What it is, and what we really want, is revenge. But is that the mind of Jesus?

"At this point, I cannot speak for my brother, our sister, or our parents. I can speak for no one but myself. Yet I speak to all of you. The idea of revenge has no place in the Christian faith. Yes, my life has been shattered by these deaths. I am angry, and I will never be the same. And yes, I want the criminals caught. But I simply cannot call for their deaths. I cannot allow myself to be engulfed by a whirlpool of violence. I see no escape from that. So I look to God and to his Word.

"Arguably, the single most powerful scene in all of the Gospels occurs at the Crucifixion. Jesus, innocent of crime has been condemned to an unjust death. His response is to look at his accusers and simply say, 'Father forgive them'. The collision of perfect innocence and wrenching violence results in a plea for mercy. How can that be? Perhaps because Jesus knew the mind of God and so also knew that God's love is all-encompassing. It overarches every aspect of life, transcending the most egregious of crimes and the most heinous of criminals.

"I have committed my life and ministry to the belief that no one is beyond the redemptive power of God. That he forgives everyone. That everyone goes to heaven without exception or prejudice. To be honest, I do not know if I am ready to forgive. It is not the norm in human life. Yet, it is what we are called to do. Forgiveness, especially on this level, is never easy. It is, I think, made a little easier if we regularly make the effort to forgive on smaller scales. To forgive what others have done to us, choosing instead to see good in everyone, friend and foe alike. Perhaps that begins by not sitting in judgment on people who are different than we are.

"True friendships transcend any faith. Among us today are Christians, Jews, Muslims, other faith traditions. Even people who are non-believers. In my life, the one with whom I have shared the most, the one who clearly knows me better than anyone else, does not believe in God. Still, he is my friend, my closest friend. True friendship also transcends the other limitations of life: age, race, ethnicity, economics and sex. There are no restrictions on whom we call friends beyond the reality of who we know and who really knows us. True friends enrich us beyond measure.

"This was my experience of Yolanda, Carmen, Gina and Leonardo. Biologically, they were family, and I will treasure that always. The children were young and only beginning to explore the depth of what friendship truly is. Yolanda, however, was more than family. I believe that I will cherish most that she was also my friend. For as Abraham discovered, being God's friend was greater than being God's child. And as the disciples discovered, being Jesus' friends was greater than being his followers.

"Wandering through graveyards we see endless markers declaring that the one buried beneath us is a beloved wife or husband, son or daughter, etc. It might be a greater testament to write: 'Here lies my friend'".

At the conclusion, Giovanni sat down. He appeared overcome with emotion and took several minutes to compose himself before continuing with Mass. After Communion, Giovanni addressed the congregation.

"My brother has asked Lieutenant Tom Moran, a close friend of ours from childhood, to deliver the eulogy".

Then he motioned for me to come forward. I could feel my body trembling as I walked to the sanctuary and approached the podium. I was as prepared as I would ever be. Giovanni suggested that I not try to focus my attention on any individual with the possible exception of family members. That might ease my discomfort with the size of the congregation.

The first words are always the most difficult. How do you speak the obvious? I started.

## Eulogy

"Last Thursday night, the calm and routine of life was shattered by the senseless death of four wonderful people, three of them only in the earliest stages of their lives. For this past week, most of us have been caught up in this tragedy, and today we come together to celebrate their lives. It is in the context of tragedy and celebration that I now speak to all of you. And I ask you to remember.

"I have known the Lozano family all my life. We lived in the same neighborhood in Pasadena and our families were, and still are, very close. I had the pleasure of spending many happy hours at their home, as they did at ours.

"Giuseppe was best man at my wedding. I was best man at his. Giovanni officiated at both. When Carmen was born, I was asked to be her godfather. I watched her blossom as she began to emerge into a beautiful young woman. Only fifteen years old, with unbounded promise, she had a contagious joy of life.

"Gina had only entered adolescence two weeks earlier. Into this new phase of her life she brought the same effervescent personality that had made her popular and fun to be around. She was accepting and caring of everyone. And generous. She was particularly sensitive to people in trouble or need.

"And Leonardo. He was a treasure not just to his parents, but to everyone who met him. In some ways he was a boy out of time. He lacked the self-centeredness that defines so many children today. In its place, he possessed an under-appreciated sensitivity and awareness of others.

"The lives of these three children held unrestricted hope. A future that was bright beyond imagining. Who knows what that future might have been? Of this I am certain. Each of them would have had a profound impact on their own families, their friends and on society at large.

"Carmen, Gina and Leonardo were so much a reflection of their parents. Their personalities and gifts could have only come from a loving home and nurturing environment. They were Giuseppe's and Yolanda's greatest gift to all of us. Even in their absence, they continue to enrich those of us who knew them.

"Yolanda's life also was cut short, but she had already left her mark. During a life dedicated to teaching, she was regularly acknowledged with awards. But she accomplished much more than that. It was not just knowledge and ideas that she imparted. She exposed her students to the richness of language and taught them how to express their own deepest feelings. To speak and write of hope and fear, of love and loss. She taught them to trust and appreciate who they are. That they are diminished neither by their struggles nor by the rejection of others.

214

Through literature and her own personal example, she taught them to love and care about themselves. To love and care for all people.

"Last Saturday, I had dinner with Giuseppe and Giovanni. Much of the evening was given over to our memories of the family. Many of the recollections were ones that the three of us experienced together. But Giuseppe also shared something about Yolanda that most people do not know. She had a secret hobby.

"Yolanda did not only love the romantic poets. She was one herself. She regularly went to the movies, paying special attention to the film score. When she heard an instrumental track that she really liked, she would buy the recording and set about to writing her own lyrics.

"One such occasion occurred not quite two years ago, following the release of the movie 'Life is Beautiful'. Yolanda decided to put words to the theme. For their anniversary in 1999, she gifted Giuseppe with a new song. Track one from the movie soundtrack, titled, 'Buon Giorno Principessa'.

"Until today, this song has only been sung by Yolanda to Giuseppe. But like most of us, she had a favorite singer. Hers was Celine Dion. This morning we are fortunate to have Ms. Dion here at St. Vincent's Church. She has graciously agreed to share this song with all of us".

A single cellist sat in front of the choir. As the strings came to life, the congregation listened, then watched as Celine Dion walked out from the side of the sanctuary and stood beside him. With guided grace she began to intone Yolanda's gift to Giuseppe.

Life Is Beautiful
Track 1:
Buon Giorno Principessa

"You by my side
On the threshold of love do I stand.
Life lies beyond
I will cross if you just hold my hand.

Through all the years

Ev'ry dream ev'ry night was of you.
Lost in my fears
Never once did I dream you'd come true.

Just hold me close.

I cannot breathe
There are feelings inside I don't know.
Doubt wells within
I'm afraid if I breathe you might go.

Just hold me close
In your arms you can teach me how to live.

Once in a life
For a few there is someone like you.
One wish have I
To each day be that someone for you".

The song ended and Celine left as elegantly as she appeared. Not many eyes remained dry in the church. I certainly found my own vision blurred, but at least I did not have to speak again.

Giovanni continued to sit in silence allowing the congregation time to absorb the experience. When he spoke again it was to invite the congregation to stand for the prayers of final commendation over the four bodies. Giovanni then led the coffins toward the door, with Giuseppe, his parents and sister following behind.

As Giuseppe followed the caskets down the aisle, he looked up and saw Jackson at the end of one of the pews. Their eyes met and the recognition was instantaneous. Giuseppe could hardly believe it. Not only was Jackson present, but after all these years, his gaze was as piercing as ever. This could end up awkward. For both of them. Instead, to their relief, they both simply smiled. Faint, but genuine.

The procession to the cemetery included more than seventy automobiles and a half-dozen motorcycle escorts. The interment prayers, themselves, took no more than five minutes, but the service was extended with the addition of a couple hymns and one more brief speaker.

At the conclusion of the graveside services, Jackson walked up to Giuseppe to offer his condolences.

"Giuseppe. I'm very sorry about Yolanda and the kids".

"Thanks, Jackson. I never imagined you would be here. It means a lot to me. Listen, we can't really talk now. How long will you be in Los Angeles"?

"I'm staying through the weekend. I fly back to Boston on Monday morning".

Giuseppe took a deep breath and asked,

"Can we get together for lunch tomorrow"?

"I'd like that very much. Thanks. Where should we meet"?

"I haven't stayed at the house since it happened. I have a suite at the Bonaventure Hotel in downtown Los Angeles. Why don't we meet there? There's a good restaurant at the top of the center tower and several in walking distance. On second thought, I can't go anywhere without being recognized. Just come to my suite and I'll order room service".

"Thanks, Giuseppe. See you tomorrow".

As Jackson walked away, Giuseppe had to greet more people. He tried graciously to receive their condolences, but his mind was on his former friend. It was just like Jackson to show up for something like this. But what would they say tomorrow? A lot of time had gone by and a lot of feelings lost. Or were they?

# Chapter 23

The Bonaventure Hotel sits in the heart of downtown Los Angeles, just off the Harbor Freeway. It was built in the 1970's and has since become one of the city's most famous landmarks. Consisting of five round, glass towers, the 34th floor of the center tower boasts a revolving bar, allowing customers to relax any time of the day as the city gently glides past them. Giuseppe had been at the hotel for almost a week, and his room was comfortable.

He was staying in a two-bedroom suite, with plenty of privacy, yet room enough to conduct campaign work with his inner circle. He turned one of the bedrooms into an office equipped with computers, fax and copy machines. The living room was large enough for meetings with his staff. And, course, at my insistence, Gavin de Becker guards were outside the door.

So it was with some surprise that Giuseppe found himself ill at ease the next morning. Over breakfast he met with his campaign director and discussed events for the next several days. Most of the campaign had come to a halt over the last week. But he had a good staff, and trusted that they would get everything back on track. He wanted this day to himself, however, so he ended the meeting early. He wanted time alone to await his old friend.

When Jackson arrived, Giuseppe invited him in, and his thoughts flashed back to that long ago Saturday, and a reversal of roles when Jackson had opened the door for him. This would not be like the last time, still that was the memory that returned. It was, after all, the last one he had.

"Hello, Jackson. Come in. I didn't order lunch yet, but I have some coffee. Would you like some"?

"Thanks. I'd love a cup".

"It's not like that Louisiana stuff you used to make, but it's good".

"Actually, I don't drink it that strong anymore, either".

How is it that a conversation about coffee can ease discomfort between people? As awkward as this began, suddenly these two former friends sharing a cup of coffee seemed so natural and relaxing. As they sat across the table Giuseppe looked closely at Jackson. His eyes were less bright and lacked the excitement and innocence of youth, but they were just as piercing. His smile was a little grimmer, but still enchanting.

Goddam, Jackson. If he had ever called, Giuseppe would have kept his promise. He would have been there for him. But Jackson didn't call, and Giuseppe had spent twenty years forgetting. He had learned to isolate his emotions, and in the process had kept his promise to himself. No one ever got that close to him again. Not even Yolanda knew how he really felt. About anything. Giuseppe felt more secure keeping her at a safe distance.

Now he found himself in the presence of the only person who ever really knew him. The only friend he had truly trusted. Here he was, sitting across the table from Jackson, just as if they were back in Boston. And yet it wasn't really the same. It was simultaneously like and unlike the last time they met. Only today there would be no roundabout attempt to begin the conversation. Giuseppe got right to the point.

"Jackson, I was surprised to see you at the funeral yesterday".

As much as things had changed between them, he really did not want to sound cold. He couldn't anyway. Not with Jackson. He suspected that Jackson could still see through him. Much as he tried to hold them back, old feelings began to resurface. So he added,

"Surprised, and grateful".

"I figured I owed you that", he replied. "You were a good friend, Giuseppe, and this is a time when you need friends".

The implication of a continuing friendship and affection did not match the reality, but Giuseppe knew what Jackson meant. He was glad for the effort.

"It's been over twenty years", Giuseppe reflected. "I often wondered how you were. There were times I wanted to call, but you were pretty definite back then. I decided to wait for you to make contact. You never did".

"I'm really sorry about that, Giuseppe. That Saturday back in Boston was very difficult for me".

"For both of us", Giuseppe corrected.

"Yes. For both of us. I was very hurt".

"Again. We both were".

"You're not going to make this easy, are you"?, Jackson asked. "I don't blame you". He took a deep breath and continued, "You're right, we were both hurt. But for different reasons. I couldn't handle all the things you said. I couldn't face the truth. I thought there was too much on the line for me".

"Well", Giuseppe replied. "I have to accept some of the blame, too. I should never have said those things that Saturday morning. In fact, I should never have confronted you. Giovanni told me it would be a mistake and that the cost might be too high. I should have listened to him".

"No, Giuseppe. You were actually trying to be a good friend. Maybe better than I deserved. Besides, you were right. About everything. About Helena. About me. About me being naive, even a fool".

Giuseppe cocked his left eyebrow.

"Yeah", Jackson said with a smile. "I remember you calling me a fool. I remember every word you said.

"Even back then I knew I was not in love with Helena. I was only pretending, because it served a purpose and staved off something I couldn't face. Still, I should not have responded the way I did. There was only one thing you were wrong about that day, Giuseppe. I really did know what love was. Remember when I told you I thought I might be gay?"

"Jackson, I remember everything you ever told me, too".

"Well, the truth is I was gay. I am gay. I knew it back then. I think something inside of me despised Helena for what she was doing to me and what she let me do to myself. But there was a perverse comfort in being with her. It allowed me to continue to hide from myself as well as from everyone else. For a while".

"What happened"?, Giuseppe asked.

"Even though I was defensive at the time, I never forgot what you said. I tried to bury that conversation, but your words continued to play on my mind. I continued to date Helena for a few months, but eventually things fell apart. I gradually realized that she was using me. I discovered that she had lied to me about her past, her illnesses, everything. I don't think she loved her husband, but she never loved me, either, no matter how hard she protested. Eventually we both knew that it could not work out. I became dissatisfied with the relationship. I also realized that I couldn't be satisfied by any other woman, either, though I tried a few more times.

"Sep", the familiar name slipped so easily in his speech that he did not even realize he had said it, "I had such difficulty trusting people, and then the person I opened every part of my life to in therapy, turned all that knowledge into the worst betrayal ever. It was too much for me".

"Why didn't you call, Jacks? I told you I would always be there for you".

Giuseppe also found himself using the familiar nickname with ease and fondness. When two people have shared a truly deep friendship, the bonds withstand the tests of misunderstanding and anger; of hurt, even a loss of trust. Such friendships are able to survive pain, enduring both absence and time. Sadly, they are all too rare.

"I wanted to, Sep. But I was afraid. To tell you the truth, I was embarrassed. Not about being gay. I knew that would not matter to you.

But what I said to you that morning was cruel. I really wanted to hurt you. And I guess I did. Yet, it was not because of what you said to me.

"You see, Sep, when I say that I really knew what love was back then, what I mean is, I knew that I was in love with you. I also knew you were straight and that nothing would ever happen between us. But my feelings for you were real. So when you confronted me, the hurt did not arise from what you said. I was hurt because you were the one saying it. I thought to myself, 'How can someone I love so deeply hurt me so much'?

"But then, I guess that's the whole point. It's only the people we love who have the power to hurt us. The fact that you spoke truth, never entered into my mind. I was not thinking. I was feeling. I raised my defenses and struck back with as much venom as I could. Afterward, when everything fell apart in my life, I didn't think I deserved your forgiveness".

"It goes with friendship, Jacks".

"Probably so, Sep. But I couldn't forgive myself. I didn't have the courage to call you. Instead, I chose the path of a coward. I walked away and wanted to fade into memory. In fact, to fade beyond memory".

Giuseppe felt as though he was being vaulted backward in time. To a friendship that embraced, indeed, that engulfed every part of him. This was so reminiscent of that Saturday twenty-one years earlier. Both Giuseppe and Jackson seemed incapable of holding anything back. They spoke what they did not intend, because it came from the heart. They could not obscure the truth from each other. The main difference this time was that neither of them worked from a pre-planned script. Nor did either want to hurt the other.

"Jacks, over the years I've wondered how different things would have been if we had not had that talk. What if we had remained friends"?

"I've asked myself the same question. You know, I've actually followed your career. When you decided to run for the Senate, I wanted to say to people, 'That's my friend. He's a great guy and he'll make a great senator'. I ached with the reality that you were no longer my friend. Or, at least, that I was no longer yours".

"Yeah. Well, you might be just as well off. I'm not the same person

I was back at Harvard, Jacks. My life has not turned out the way I had hoped".

"This has been an unbelievable tragedy, Sep. Anyone would feel the same way".

"I'm not talking about my family. I'm speaking about the dreams we shared when we were young. Hell, I don't even know why I'm telling you this now. I guess it's like the old days, Jacks. Except, you don't really know me anymore. Even before the murders, I was not happy. My life was empty".

"What do you mean, Sep? You built a thriving and lucrative business. You had a beautiful family. You're the millionaire you always wanted to be. And now, you've got a good chance of being elected a United States Senator"!

"What you don't know, Jacks, is how hurt I was by what happened between us. Nobody, not even my brother, was as close to me as you were. When you decided to end the friendship, I vowed that no one would ever get that close again. And no one has. Not even Yolanda. I made a decision in Boston that I would never again trust anyone. So sure. I have a good business, I'm rich, and I'm running for office. I sacrificed a lot to get where I am. And you know what? None of it is fulfilling. Nothing I have accomplished means as much to me as you did".

"I feel sorry for you, Sep. And I regret if I'm the one who brought you to this. But I think I know how you feel. At least, in part. The same thing almost happened to me when Helena and I broke up. Unlike you, my trust issues went back further than graduate school. They went all the way back to my youth. Helena learned about them through therapy. Her betrayal was so momentous, I thought I would never trust again, either. But I was lucky. I met a wonderful guy, Jean-Paul Lecuyer".

"A Frenchman"?, asked Giuseppe.

"Actually, he's Belgian. He had come to do an internship in the same bank I was working in. I'm not militant about gay issues, and I hate it when people mock us by claiming to have 'gaydar'. Still, the truth is that the two of us recognized each other right away. And our personalities were very compatible. We just clicked.

"We began going out after work for dinner and drinks. The more time we spent together, the more we realized how much we had in common. At first we kept everything on the surface, because he would have to go back to Belgium, and we did not want anything to develop that was not permanent.

"Well, he did go back. I visited him several times in Brussels and we took side trips to London, Berlin and Paris. Those were great visits. Paris was my favorite. I don't think there is any city quite like it. Finally, my bank managed to help Jean-Paul obtain a permanent visa. That was a great day. When he arrived we moved in together and have been a couple ever since. It's been fifteen years now".

"And you're happy"?, asked Giuseppe.

"Very much so, Sep. I wish you could have met him".

"Why didn't he come with you"?

"He knows what transpired between us and that I had no idea what it would be like to see you again. He thought we needed time together and did not want to get in the way. He really is a very sweet and sensitive man. And I would like you to meet him some day".

"So, Jacks, you're still in Boston. Even with those horrible winters. Do you own a bank"?

"No, Sep. That dream dissolved for me years ago. Maybe if Jean-Paul had not come into my life. But he did, and I found life with him much more meaningful than wealth. We're comfortable. We're in love and happy. Life doesn't get much better. I wish you could have found the same".

"Well, I didn't. And here we are talking about a past we cannot change".

Jackson noticed a fatalism in Giuseppe's speech, but did not know its cause.

"Sep, tell me what happened. If you want to".

"It all started at Harvard, after we met. I had never encountered anyone like you. I don't think I ever told you that I always found your glance so penetrating. True or not, I felt as if you could look right through me. That was a new experience for me. I had always kept everyone at a comfortable distance, including my brother, Tom and Yolanda. You were different. Clearly, you got closer than anyone else.

"If we had remained friends, I think it would have continued to change my life. It would have altered the way I dealt with everyone. Certainly ending our friendship did. I made a complete about-face, maintaining a clear and distinct separation from others. Never telling anybody the truth. At least not the whole truth. I deceived my business partners and cheated my workers.

"I was not even honest with Yolanda and the kids. I emphasized how much we had to sacrifice in order to get ahead, but I exaggerated the facts. Little Leonardo was two years old before we moved to our current home. That meant five of us living in my old apartment. We could have moved years before he was even born.

"The truth is that after Harvard, I became more selfish than I had ever been. And why the fuck am I telling you this now? You break down my barriers, Jacks. I feel as though you can still see right through me".

Giuseppe began to shake noticeably, as if he were sitting in a freezer or caught in a blizzard. He seemed on the verge of sharing something that he had been holding back. He experienced a rush of emotions that he had trouble controlling. But under no circumstances would he break down. Now now. Not ever.

The truth is Giuseppe had never forgotten Jackson. But he locked away all recollections into a small corner of his mind where they would be neither disturbed nor awakened. This conversation threatened to unhinge that control. He understood the allure of memory and feared its power to entrap and enslave. What he did not realize is that attempting to forget can be equally paralyzing. Emotionally. He easily coasted through life, but he had become a man burdened with secrets. A man without love. He was afraid that Jackson was the one person who could get him to reveal what he had to keep hidden.

"I could never see through you, Sep", Jackson replied. "All I saw was a person of remarkable depth and potential. I actually wanted to be like you".

"You're lucky, then, because I don't like the way my life has turned out. I guess if we had remained friends, I would have been a different person and would have treated others better. But I was not going to get that close again. To this day, everything remains on the surface, where I can keep a tight rein. Anyone meeting me would think I have it all together. Anybody but you, that is".

"Are you blaming me, Sep"?

"No. Not really. We were only twenty-four, and had been in school since we were six. What the hell did we really know about life? We were just adolescents playing in an adult world. I suppose I actually blame myself. I let myself care too much for you. And when I saw your life in crisis, I wanted to step in and make it better for you. I should have stayed out of it. Just let you be. Then I could have been there for you if you needed me".

A noticeable tension surfaced in Giuseppe's voice.

"Jesus Christ, Jacks. I've never examined my life like this. It's been over twenty fucking years. Why can't we just have a light conversation"?

"I didn't come here to make things worse, Sep. If my presence is troubling you, I can leave".

"No. It's not you, Jacks. And yet it is. There are things that have happened, things I've done, that no one knows. I'm half-tempted to tell you about them, because you are like some light illuminating the darkness of my soul. You've always been like that. That's why I could never hide anything from you. But it's been a long time. Over the years I have trained myself and I refuse to walk that path again. You just make it more difficult for me to maintain my resolve".

"So, do you now regret my being here"?, Jackson asked.

"I wouldn't say that exactly. It's just complicated. I wouldn't have expected it to be like this".

"Then, let's change the subject", Jackson said. He attempted to ease the strain by saying, "Tell me about Yolanda and the kids. All I know is what I've read in the papers and heard on the news. And what your friend said at the eulogy yesterday. But nothing about them as individual persons".

Giuseppe welcomed the change. He ordered lunch from the room service menu, and they proceeded to talk all afternoon. It was a fluid conversation. Jackson filled in the missing years of his life, both before and after he met Jean-Paul. Giuseppe spoke about his life with Yolanda. About Carmen and Gina and Leonardo. He told Jackson about his business relationships, sharing both the good and the bad. But he kept secret what he did not want to share. There was still something trusting and trustworthy about Jackson, but Giuseppe was not about to go down that road again. Too many years had gone by. And too many secrets buried.

The late afternoon brought more memories as Giuseppe poured each of them a glass of scotch. Of course, this was better than the stuff they drank together as students. This was Dalmore 21 year old single malt. The distinctive bottle, adorned with the iconic royal stag's head taken from the MacKenzie family crest, practically spells expensive. This was a scotch they could not afford when they were younger. But it is the liquid inside that really matters. Indeed, Giuseppe had great taste!

For dinner, Giuseppe again suggested staying in the suite. Since it was likely they would never have another evening like this, he decided on the very best steaks from the hotel restaurant. As a special treat he opened his only bottle of 1987 Silver Oak Cabernet Sauvignon from Bonny's Vineyard in Napa Valley.

"Jacks, have you ever had Silver Oak wine"?

"I don't think so", he replied.

"Oh, you'd remember. It's one of the best wineries in Napa, especially for cabernet. That's all they make. This one is a single vintage release from Bonny's Vineyard. Since Gina was born in 1987, I bought this bottle intending to open it when she turned twenty-one".

The sadness in his voice was palpable and understandable. Jackson knew it was a great honor to share this wine. On this evening. With this friend.

Giuseppe proved himself more than generous. Even after all these years. Both meals were superb, and over all, their time together was relaxing. They talked for hours, steering clear of any troubling conversations, sharing only what was comfortable. Throughout, there was a sense of foreboding, their ease with each other descending into near melancholy. Their lives had taken such different turns, so many years had passed and so many opportunities lost. In spite of the ease with which they shared this day, Jackson instinctively knew Giuseppe was holding something back. He had no idea what it was. But there was something. Perhaps he would never know. As the years had passed, they had both found a way to live. One happy and fulfilled, the other sad and empty. He wondered if this opportunity would ever repeat itself. After all, occasionally there are chances to start anew. To enter that mythical "land of beginning again". Whatever future lay in store for Giuseppe and Jackson, today was a much better memory to treasure than the last time they were together.

# Chapter 24

Detective work is not nearly as glamorous as it seems on television or in the movies. It is tedious. For days I had been sorting through FI cards. Every time I sat down at the file I cursed the city officials who would not budget for the necessary computer equipment and personnel. Nonetheless, it was the task at hand.

FIU was still working on the footprint. They had moved the case to the top of the list, but identifying the impression made by the sole of a shoe is not a simple process, either. Particularly, if the imprint is uncommon and there is no record of a similar pattern on file.

Wharton and Rose took on the job of interviewing employees and ex-employees of The Pegasus Group, with special attention given to those who might have been disgruntled or might have wanted to exact some kind of revenge.

Since I could not stare at FI cards all day, I mixed that research with an investigation of Giuseppe's competitors in the world of micro-chips. That missing guidance system file had to be somewhere. So far, none of our investigations had produced results.

At the LAPD we do not compromise either our investigation or a potential court case by sharing details with the press. But, then, we did not have any real details, anyway. Still, the stations and networks always have reporters hanging around the division trying to pick up leads for potential stories. They know how to manipulate people in order to gain information. So, while the media were no longer hounding us on a daily basis, neither did they let the story lapse. Several times a week, reports were broadcast about efforts to solve the Lozano murders. There just wasn't much there.

Finally, on Wednesday, October 18th, I struck pay dirt.

I came across a 1984 FI card. This was the time I was working on the joint task force with the FBI, DEA and other Southern California agencies. Everyone had a common goal and purpose. Except the FBI. I discovered then, how fucking hard they are to get along with. They believe they are a cut above every other agency. As such, they are useless when it comes to any joint operation. Their lead agent was Rich Tomasek. The perfect agency asshole.

He and I did not hit it off very well from the beginning. He had an attitude of superiority and clearly held no respect for the LAPD. I had already been a cop for eight years, and did not need that kind of shit. I was also arrogant enough to let Tomasek know it. Still, it was not the personality differences that soured me to his agency.

A possible terrorist attack had been uncovered by FBI agents. They told no one. Although Los Angeles International Airport was not the target, the threat came through LAX. The FBI did not even alert the airport police. Rather than informing any other task force agency, they conducted their own secret investigation. They succeeded. Both in thwarting the attack and getting all the glory. So much for cooperation. This is the reason many law enforcement officers refer to them as the "FiBI's". They can't tell the truth.

The joint task force for the Olympics had a number of activities in play. One of them was an extensive surveillance operation. We kept tabs on possible suspects in a variety of criminal endeavors, and made a special effort to clamp down on illegal drugs.

One evening my team was keeping tabs on a man named Enrique Salazar. He was a known drug dealer. Mostly minor stuff that would have ordinarily kept him off our radar, or, at least, would not have garnered my attention. But this was the summer of the Olympic Games. Nothing was allowed to slip by. Salazar's territory included Exposition Park, next to the Memorial Coliseum where the opening and closing ceremonies were being held, along with various track and field events.

One night we were following Salazar from an unmarked car. The detective behind the wheel was expert at tailing suspects. We followed Salazar's car south along Figueroa Street, west on Martin Luther King Jr. Blvd (previously Santa Barbara Blvd, having been renamed MLK in 1983), then south again on Hoover Street, to the corner of Hoover and 40th. The area is not well-lit, and is relatively quiet. It was not a bad place to complete a drug deal. Unless you are being followed by the cops.

Salazar's car stopped and he got out to meet with his buyer. We cruised past them and around the block, giving him time to begin the transaction. We returned moments later, turned on our red police light, blocked his vehicle and exited, guns drawn. Everyone froze.

One of the people on scene was a tall man named Gary Bass. He had no weapon, drugs or cash on him. Still, he was an accessory. I physically searched him, roughing him a bit as I patted him down. When I got to his left knee, he said,

"Easy, Dick Tracy. I've got a fucked up leg. I don't think the city wants to pay my medical bills".

I took a good, close look at him. This was no drug dealer. I didn't even know why he was at the scene. There was something unusually cold and dark in his eyes. To me they reflected an even colder heart. I thought to myself, 'This bastard is capable of something very gruesome'.

I filled out the FI cards on Salazar and Bass. The following information was included on Bass's card: driver's license number, name, residence, phone number, date of birth, sex, height, weight, hair and eye color, clothing, social security number, description of the car. But it was the personal oddities that caught my attention. I noted that he a permanent, but slight limp from a previous knee injury. In the additional information section, I noted that he had no prior wants or warrants.

As soon as I read through the card that Wednesday, I knew I had the right guy. Tracking him, however, would prove to be another problem. We were able to locate a current address, in the city of Glendale. But he seemed to have disappeared from the world of crime. There were no records of arrests or even of him being a suspect. Whatever he had done after that night in '84, he had not been involved with the police again. The only thing I knew about his current activities, came from the Lozano murder scene. He had moved into a more highly sophisticated area of crime: Hired gun.

Even though he had no further conflict with the law, I was certain that he was the man I had been looking for. I moved forward on that assumption. There was, however, another killer that remained unidentified. The next course of action would be surveillance of Bass. The case was too important for sloppy investigative work, or any mistake in procedure. I made sure that we presented a detailed and accurate warrant requesting a wiretap. It was granted and the Technical Laboratory's Electronics Surveillance Unit (ESU) set up the audio surveillance of Bass's home.

Suspecting that Bass was one of the assailants also enabled FIU to make faster strides in identifying the footprint. At least it was a lead. They had already identified that the shoe was a special orthopedic design. If, indeed, it belonged to Bass, they would be able to identify the manufacturer, and the date and place of purchase more quickly.

*　　*　　*

Every Thursday after the murders, Giovanni, Giuseppe and I had dinner together. The next night they both noticed that I was in a better mood. Catching this first break in the case certainly eased some of the strain I was under.

"Hello, guys", I said.

"You seem to be in a good mood tonight, Tom", came Giovanni's reply.

"Well, maybe not good, but certainly better", I said.

"What happened"?, Giuseppe asked.

"From the beginning of this investigation I have been bothered by the video. I knew that I had seen one of the men before. I have been manually searching Field Investigation cards for days, and yesterday I figured out who he is. At least I think I did. That information should also help FIU identify the footprint. If I am correct, then we've got one man".

"What happens now"?, Giovanni queried.

"We put him under surveillance, hoping to identify the other man".

"Tom", Giuseppe asked, "Why not just bring him in for interrogation"?

"It's too soon. First, we have to make sure he's the guy we're looking for. And if we monitor him for awhile, we may be able to nail both of them and solve the first phase of the crime".

"First phase"?, asked Giuseppe.

"Yeah. I'm sure these guys were hired. But we don't know who's behind it. We're still trying to figure out who would most benefit from that file. The killers are almost certainly are not in the electronics business. So far, we don't have anything. However, it looks like your employees, both past and present, are off the hook".

Giuseppe responded,

"I told you before that was a dead end. I may not be the best employer. I might not be well liked, but even the people I've fired over the years don't fit the profile you're talking about".

"Well, it's all part of the investigation process", I replied. "We have to follow every possible lead. We can't take anything for granted.

"So, what's for dinner? Please don't tell me we're having pizza! I've had enough of that lately at division headquarters".

"How does pasta carbonara sound"?, Giovanni asked. "I'm going to use mini fusili. It's the perfect size for bacon and eggs".

"Sounds wonderful to me. But first, I've earned a scotch".

Even with the election only three weeks away, Giuseppe managed to keep Thursday evenings clear for Giovanni and me. Morgan was one of the best campaign managers in the country. He was adept at juggling events and making quick, but sound, decisions. He did his best not to interfere with these dinners. There were, however, occasional interruptions. Usually these involved some schedule change or activity for Friday that Giuseppe would need to know about.

California was not the only state having an election. November 7, 2000 was also a national election day. Bill Clinton was finishing his second term as President of the United States, and Al Gore was heir apparent. He was opposed by the Governor of Texas, George W. Bush. The national polls indicated a close race. They showed Gore in the lead, but Bush within striking distance.

California was a different story. Before the murders, the polls showed Giuseppe and Gottesman even. Since then, Giuseppe's numbers had risen by ten points. It was a sympathy vote. Nothing had changed in the messages of the two candidates. The only noticeable change was that both campaigns continued to be far less negative. In this post-murder environment, neither could run the risk of attacking the other. Still, Giuseppe knew that American voters are fickle and their passions unstable. He could not rely on their sympathy for him. He still had a message to communicate and a plan to implement.

The next morning he was catching a 6:00 flight to San Francisco, so we ended the evening early. At 9:00 Giuseppe and I left. He went to the Bonaventure Hotel, and I headed back to an empty house.

# Chapter 25

Bass did not have a very active social life. He received few phone calls, and there was nothing important or significant about the callers. However, on Wednesday, November 1, the phone rang at 3:45 in the afternoon, and Gilmore was on the other end. SID and ESU were monitoring Bass' calls. It did not matter, though. Gilmore never used his real name, and he had a non-traceable, disposable phone. Naturally, Bass would have recognized his voice, but they adhered to unbending rules and procedures. Their only safeguard was to guarantee that those rules were never violated. Gilmore had a code name and the call lasted only seconds. His message was simple: "Peregrine, 322".

Obviously, it was a coded message. Knowing that fact was of no help to SID, however. Yet it did raise their suspicions and unleash a flurry of new activity trying to decode what they heard. It was also reason enough to begin video surveillance. Within an hour ESU had a vehicle on site, but the techs were a long way from determining the code.

Bass, on the other hand, knew the exact interpretation. Peregrine was Gilmore. They were to meet at location "three". "22" stood for 10:00 PM in standard, twenty-four hour time. Since there was no code for a day of the week, they were to meet that same evening. Apparently they had been contracted for another job that required them to work together.

Location three was MacArthur Park on Alvarado Street in Los Angeles. The park has a checkered history. At one end is a lake, fed by natural spring waters, that was once part of the drinking reservoir system for the city. In the late 1800's the park was a luxury vacation destination. Wilshire Blvd originally terminated at the western edge, and the surrounding area was known as the Champs-Élysées of Los Angeles. The Park Plaza Hotel, now vacant and used primarily for filming, is one of the last remaining testaments to the area's former grandeur.

Long a victim of urban decay, MacArthur Park has, since 1985, been the scene of much gang violence. When the lake was drained in 1978, hundreds of firearms, mostly handguns, were discovered. Even today, it is not uncommon to find bodies disposed of in the water, frequently inside plastic bags.

During daylight hours the park is a mass of people and a convenient place to buy fake social security cards and other ID's. It quiets down by nightfall, but there is enough activity, that a meeting between two people would not draw attention.

*   *   *

Life as a hired killer is about more than just being able to pull a trigger. It requires detailed preparation and knowledge of one's environment. An assassin never knows when the police will be in visual pursuit. Bass was good at his job. Over the years, he had learned to be careful. He never forgot that night back in 1984. He had been driving the car for Salazar and was responsible for allowing the cops to apprehend them. Those are the kind of mistakes that professionals make only once. So he had learned to drive through his rearview mirror. His peripheral version was more than adequate for seeing the road ahead. He was more concerned about who might be behind him. No matter how good the driver of a pursuit vehicle, he must keep the suspect in his sights.

Bass had been staying at the Wilmar Manor Apartments in Glendale.

The complex is located on California between Pacific and Concord. He entered his car, turned on the ignition, and headed west on California. There was a car behind him. He turned left onto Concord and made another left on Wilson, sending him in the opposite direction from which he began. It was a quiet residential area. Bass looked through the rear view mirror. The car was still there. He knew, then, that he had company, probably the police in an unmarked vehicle. That was not a problem. Just knowing he was being followed was enough.

He next turned right onto Kenilworth, then made another right onto Broadway. He did not vary his speed. He was not trying to ditch his pursuit yet. He continued West on Broadway. As it crosses San Fernando Rd, Broadway becomes Brazil. It also crosses railroad tracks. On the other side, W. San Fernando Rd parallels both the tracks and the larger San Fernando Rd.

Bass had timed his arrival to coincide with a freight train. He was stopped at the light with the pursuit vehicle two cars behind him. When the guard rails descended, he paused only moments. Then he shot into the opposite lane, around the barriers and across the tracks. With the train quickly approaching, there was nothing for the police to do except wait.

When he crossed the tracks, Bass made an immediate left onto W. San Fernando Rd, through a small industrial area that took him past one of Baxter's manufacturing facilities. At Colorado Blvd he made a right turn that took him onto the Golden State Freeway (Interstate 5) south, toward Los Angeles.

Confident that he was in the clear, he exited onto the Glendale Freeway (Highway 2) south, into Echo Park. The freeway ends a quarter of a mile later, the traffic exiting onto Glendale Blvd. Bass veered right at Alvarado, and continued to Seventh Street. He made a right turn and then another left at Carondolet Street and parked his car. He was now only a block from MacArthur Park.

Even the process of ditching the police did not cause Bass to be late. He prided himself on his punctuality, and this night was no different. Gilmore had arrived early. His custom was to scout out meeting locations, just to make sure nothing was amiss. He waited near the boat dock, out of the light. When he saw Bass approach, he walked up behind him and fired one bullet. His aim was never off. It was as true from the back as it was from the front. Through the heart. Bass fell into the lake. Gilmore silently let the weapon fall from his hand and kept walking. The entire incident was quick and no one seemed to notice.

He figured someone would discover Bass' body later that night or by early morning and alert the police. That was expected and planned. Gilmore was sending the cops another message. He did not make mistakes. His trail back to the murders was now erased, as was the link to his employer.

On Sunday morning, October 22, police from the Rampart Division were called to MacArthur Park. It was 2:00. A body had been found at the edge of the lake. The responding officers checked for identification. It was Bass. When FIU arrived on the scene, they immediately alerted me.

"Fuck. I'll be right there". Then I called Wharton and Rose and told them to meet me. When I arrived on the scene, I approached the investigating officer.

"How did it happen"?, I asked.

"One shot. Through the heart. The bullet entered his back. No exit wound. The shooter dropped the apparent weapon, a Glock 9mm, beside the body".

Even without the gun, I knew this was no fucking coincidence. It had to be the second shooter from the Lozano murders. But why? No one knew we were on to Bass. Or did the media somehow find out about the footprint? I saw nothing on the news. Whoever ordered the original killings could not possibly have an informant inside the department. At least, not inside RHD. This brought us back to square one. We had no leads on identifying the second shooter.

*     *     *

Later that morning, Captain Haskell called me into his office along with Wharton and Rose.

"What the hell is going on? Can anybody tell me how we lost Bass"?

"Captain", I replied. "He evaded pursuit and got himself killed. Almost certainly by his partner from the Lozano murder. The MO was the same. Glock, 9mm, gun left at the scene".

"I suppose we have no leads at all, now"?, he asked.

"The only thing we have now is that damn file".

Haskell looked at Wharton and continued. "Wharton, have you found anything useful"?

"Not exactly, captain. We've checked all of Mr. Lozano's competitors. There does not seem to be anything unusual. From what we can tell, no one is working on a similar system. We've checked the work and shipping orders of various companies, as well as their supply chains. So far nothing to indicate any interest in guidance system chips".

Haskell continued,

"Tom, you're close to Mr. Lozano. I know he's in the last days of the election. But why don't you ask him what else those chips could be used for? Maybe we're on the wrong track as far as a missile system. They might have some other purpose".

"I'm having dinner with him tonight at his brother's. I'll see if he has any ideas that might help".

"What about bank records"?, Haskell asked. "If these guys were hired assassins, or even if this was a burglary gone bad, someone had to pay them".

That was Rose's job, so he responded.

"Bass was our only suspect. We scoured his records, but have come up with nothing so far. If he was paid, he had a very sophisticated method of hiding his money. It was not done under his name. At least not in this country. But we're still checking.

"We're also looking into the bank records of the CEO's of other computer companies and defense contractors, companies that The Pegasus Group worked with. Anyone who might have an interest in that file. We're narrowing the search. But it takes time".

"Well, there is a chain of command here. The chief's on my back. He's getting pressure from he governor, attorney general and mayor. You'd better turn up something soon, or your three asses will be on the line with mine. In the meantime, make sure the lid stays on this. I don't want the press finding out that our only suspect was killed".

"Captain", Wharton said. "They already know about the body".

"Yeah. Well, they don't know he was a suspect in the Lozano murders. Let's keep it that way".

*   *   *

With the election only five days away, I was surprised that Giuseppe still took time to have dinner with Giovanni and me. He assured us that the home cooked meals his brother prepared were better than anything he got on the campaign trail. In fact, outside of fundraising dinners, the food was pathetic. Usually something quick and easy, often fast food. In truth, I thought he actually enjoyed breaking free for a couple of hours with us. And Giovanni never disappointed either of us as a cook.

They could both tell I was not in a good mood that night. They probably thought I was turning into some kind of manic-depressive. Only a week earlier, I could not have been more pleased.

"What's wrong"?, Giovanni asked.

"I can't really talk about it. Let's just say we had a major set back in the case. Sep, we're still having trouble with that missing file. Can you tell me anything else about it"?

"Like what"?, he asked.

"We've been operating on the assumption that whoever took the file wants to get a jump on a missile guidance system. But what if that's not the goal"?

"Meaning"?, Giuseppe queried.

"Meaning that the chips could be used for another purpose. Do you have any idea"?

"Well, the chips are designed to increase the accuracy of a missile guidance system. That would mostly benefit the military. But they also have a civilian use. Let me explain it this way.

"In 1994 the DOD (U.S. Department of Defense) completed the installation of a full complement of 24 satellites for the Global Positioning System (GPS). Initially, it was conceived by and for the military. Things have moved very quickly since then.

"In 1996, President Clinton issued an executive order that GPS be a dual-use system, launching a whole new venture for civilian use. In May of this year, the U.S. Government discontinued its practice of selective availability, fully implementing Clinton's directive. That means that civilian use now has access to a non-degraded GPS signal. The issue now is one of accuracy both of the navigational systems and within various devices.

"The Pegasus Group has been working on a twofold assumption. The first is that the U.S. Government is going to modernize the entire GPS system, with an accuracy beyond anything now in operation. The second assumption is that we will soon see GPS services offered on consumer mobile telephones".

"You can't be serious", I said.

"I'm deadly serious, Tom. But more to the point is that the missing file contained information on a computer chip that is light years ahead of anything else. It would be of inestimable value to any number of people".

"Well, that is going to consume a lot of my time".

We proceeded to have dinner, then Giuseppe and I both left. He had a lot of campaign work ahead of him and I headed back to my office. I did not expect to get much rest for awhile.

# Chapter 26

I worked endlessly for the next several days, as did Wharton and Rose. But each hopeful lead got us nowhere. On Tuesday, November 7, we all needed a break. This was election day and the presidential race was turning out to be closer than anyone expected. In California, Giuseppe continued to maintain almost a double-digit lead. Still, he knew that as far as polls were concerned, he was still drawing sympathy from the electorate. Whether or not that would turn into actual votes was yet to be determined.

I had planned on watching the election returns at the 3 Clubs, but Giovanni called and invited me to the rectory. Neither of us is Republican, and as much as we cared for Giuseppe and wanted him to be successful, the site of his potential victory party was not a place either of us wanted to be. As usual, Giovanni fixed dinner, then we settled down in front of the TV to watch the returns from around the nation.

"Gio", I asked. "What do you think his chances are"?

"Well, Tom. He's my brother and I love him, but I didn't vote for him. It's not that I think he would be a bad senator. I think he is more than capable. But I don't see him bucking his own party. And the Republican Party doesn't stand for any of the values that are important to me".

"That's two votes he didn't get", I replied. "I'm one of the few cops who is a Democrat. I'd vote for a Republican if I thought he was the better person for the job, but I agree with you. The party, probably both parties, have too much control over the people we elect. I don't think many people elected to Congress can really stand on personal principles these days. Nor do they really represent their constituents".

"On the other hand, I do want to see Giuseppe win. For himself. He needs that kind of change now. And he'll be good for the state of California".

"I suppose. But tell me, Gio. If he wins, won't going to Washington just give him the opportunity to run from the reality of what happened"?

"How can I answer that, Tom? It's only been six weeks. So far he has survived, in part, because he's been so busy. But no matter where he is, or what he's doing, he can't really hide. There are those quiet moments when his thoughts must go back to Yolanda and the kids. Even in the midst of his work, memories intrude uninvited. They certainly have for me".

"And for me. I tell you, when I was sifting through those FI cards, it was so tedious, and I could not dispel my thoughts of the family. Of course, I was looking for one of the murderers. Still, it was difficult not to subside into daydreams at times".

"OK", Giovanni said. "Here we go. The polls are closing".

At 8:00 PM, the last votes were cast, and the polling locations closed. Almost immediately, the television news was predicting that Giuseppe had won by the exact polling percentage points indicated the day before. He rather easily cruised to victory. How much of that victory was due to his personal tragedy, we would probably never know. For now, he was senator-elect for the state of California. We called him, told him we had just seen the news and offered our congratulations.

Giuseppe had been living at the Bonaventure Hotel since the murders, so he chose to have his victory celebration in their 26,000-square-foot ballroom. Television cameras and reporters were already on scene and ready to broadcast his victory speech. This would not come until after Gottesman had delivered his own concession speech from his headquarters in San Francisco. Giuseppe waited in his suite.

Meanwhile, the most bizarre election in American history was unfolding on the other side of the nation. A combination of factors had left the outcome of the presidential race hanging on the returns from the state of Florida.

Through much of the summer, Al Gore had been expected to win. Handily. But a confluence of factors and events impacted the race in unexpected ways. Any one of them would have swung the election in Gore's favor.

The first was the Quixotic campaign of Ralph Nader. Actually, that is an insult to the fictional memory of Don Quixote. Nader was nominated by the Green Party, and campaigned on the premise that there is no difference between the two major parties. But there was no way he could ever have been elected president. However, he won enough votes, particularly in New Hampshire and Florida to swing the election to George W. Bush. Certainly, the vast majority of people casting their votes for the Green Party candidate would have chosen Gore over Bush. At least Gore shared with Nader a passion for the environment. Bush, on the other hand, seemed hellbent on destroying it.

The second factor was the poor campaign run by Gore, himself. During the summer, it was often said that the election was Gore's to lose. He did. The uproar, mostly among the religious right, over President Bill Clinton's sexual indiscretions made the United States a laughingstock throughout the rest of the world. It also led Gore to pander to the religious right. He would not allow Clinton to campaign for him. At least not until the end, and even then, not in key states. Clinton is still remarkably popular, and a powerful campaigner. Yet he was forced to sit on the sidelines. Gore lost Clinton's state, Arkansas, his own, Tennessee, and eventually, Florida.

That state gave us a fiasco of an election if there ever was one. Apparently, one of the state's ballots was not very user-friendly. A fair number of people found the "butterfly" design confusing, leading them to choose the wrong candidate. But it was another type of ballot used in parts of the state that caused the real problem. It was a punch card style. Because the initial outcome was so close, the Florida Supreme Court called for a recount. This led to even more problems.

First, the punch card ballot, itself. Over the next several weeks, an unfamiliar word was placed on the lips of every American: the "chad". A small piece of paper that should be punched out of the ballot during the voting process. A significant number of them were "dimpled", but not punched out, or "hanging", leading recount officials to question whether they could accurately determine the intent of the voter.

Second, the recount likely would have awarded the election to Gore. So the United States Supreme Court was brought in. It halted the recount, ordering the Florida Supreme Court to come up with new standards for counting the ballots. But time was running out to appoint the state's representatives to the electoral college.

Although everyone usually knows who the new president is, it is the Electoral College that makes it official. Each state appoints a number of electors, equal to their total number of members in Congress, both the House of Representatives and the Senate. The date for determining those electors is December 12. Legal experts question how absolute that deadline is, since the members of the Electoral College do not actually vote until December 18.

Although Gore won the majority of the national popular vote by a substantial margin, Bush was still elected president because of the Electoral College system. In over 100 years, no one has won the popular vote and lost the presidency. This leads many to question the relevancy of this electoral system. It had its place in the early days of the republic. Not any longer.

Six weeks after the election, it would all be over. The effective result of the U.S. Supreme Court's intervention handed the election to George W. Bush. He was declared the official winner of Florida's 25 electoral votes. Needing 270 to win, Florida's total put him over the top with 271.

No such problems existed in California, however. The state voted overwhelmingly for Al Gore, and also elected Giuseppe to the United States Senate.

*　　*　　*

Thanksgiving has long been my favorite holiday. Not as a child, of course. That was Christmas. In spite of my mother's religiosity, however, my fondness for celebrating the birth of Jesus had nothing to do with Jesus, himself. Christmas was all about the decorations and the presents.

When I became an adult, Thanksgiving rose to the top of the list. Ironically for me, this ascendancy had a religious root. Thanks to Hollywood movies, most Americans probably associate Thanksgiving with indebtedness to some kind of god. In reality, though, it is no longer a religious holiday. It has become simply another reason to gather family and friends in celebration, to officially begin the holiday season, and launch an irrational shopping frenzy the next morning. Still, most churches have some kind of service on Thanksgiving Day and many people attend.

For me it has been Mass at my local parish. I suppose one reason is a kind of compensation. In my adult years, I have not been very religious. Unlike so many Christians who make semi-annual trips to church on Christmas and Easter, I only go on Thanksgiving Day. Even after it lost its religious significance, I figured I owed that much to God. Besides, going to Mass one day a year is a way of hedging my bets. Just in case I'm wrong and there is a deity waiting in the wings.

But this was a very different Thanksgiving. I had already spent my one day in Church, and it was the most painful of my life. Although the funeral had been a beautiful service, as funerals go, it was not an easy experience to sit through. Comforting, somewhat. Pleasant, no. Nor did my efforts over the last seven weeks make things any easier. Not only was I immersed in these murders on a daily basis, but the investigation was no closer to a conclusion. No. This Thanksgiving Day I did not feel any gratitude toward a God who could have allowed four innocent people to die such a horrible death. I was not seeking to blame a divine being, but I was not feeling at all thankful. Always the unconditional friend, Giovanni made no judgment, and even seemed to understand my refusal to attend his Mass that morning.

Following the election, Giovanni and I continued our Thursday night dinners, but without Giuseppe. There was just too much for him to do as he prepared to take office. He made multiple trips to Washington,

D.C. Among other things, he needed to find a new residence in the capital. And moving across the country might provide a welcome relief from the new reality of life in Los Angeles. He also had to organize his Washington office and staff. However, Thanksgiving was still a time to be with family and friends.

My mother had always been the sensitive one in our family. She knew how difficult this holiday would be for Giuseppe and his family, so she insisted on inviting the Lozanos to her house for dinner. Both of our sisters were present, also, with their spouses and children in tow. It was a large gathering, but there was more than enough room at my parent's home.

There was no way to avoid conversations about Yolanda, Carmen, Gina and Leonardo. Sometimes it was collective. Other times it was an individual recollection. Mrs. Lozano recalled Carmen joining the school choir and her first solo performance at the Spring Concert.

My sister's son, Henry, was the same age as Leonardo and they took judo classes together. He remembered the first time he threw Leonardo to the mat. His eyes began to water. Bianca attempted to console him with reassurances that it was only part of the training. That Leonardo had not been hurt, and reminding him of the times that the situation was reversed. Still, it indicated for all of us, that emotions over the murders were still raw. It would take much more than seven weeks for life to achieve any type of normality.

# Chapter 27

While the nation understandably obsessed over the vote count and anxiously waited to learn who would be the next president, I had returned to the task of finding a killer. Wharton, Rose and I had been working exhaustively for weeks. The beginning of December found us frustrated and short on patience.

Bass had been killed on October 22, leaving us no clues as to the identity of the other assassin. We combed through every aspect of his life. But his disappearance from the official world of crime between 1984 and 2000, did not give us much to go on. His life was fairly quiet and uneventful. Bass had never married, nor could we find any indication of serious, long-term relationships. During those sixteen years, he had held two jobs. He first worked for a liquor store on Venice Boulevard until 1990. From there he moved to a Mens' Wearhouse clothing store. At the time of his death, he was manager of the Glendale store.

Bass had no family. He was an only child whose parents divorced when he was five and they were both dead. We interviewed everyone he had worked with as well as his neighbors. All to no avail. No one noticed anything unusual about him, other than that he kept to himself.

And yet he must have led a double life. The Lozano murders were not the work of amateurs. If he was a professional assassin, or worked within the underworld, it was masterfully disguised. It soon became clear that we would never find the other killer. He clearly did not make mistakes.

At the same that time we were sifting through Bass' life, we continued a detailed search for the missing file. In some ways this part of the investigation was more discouraging. At least with Bass's background we could talk to people who knew him, even if those conversations provided no helpful information. We turned up no leads whatsoever in terms of that file.

December 5, I sat at my desk mulling over all the information we did or didn't have. I kept thinking about that damn file. It had existed. It was real. We ascertained that much from Giuseppe's attorney and his research team. But what if it was just a red herring to throw the police off track? What if Giuseppe's family was the target all along? That thought had been discussed before. If killing his family was the true intent of the evening, he might also be a target. It was one reason I insisted that he hire Gavin de Becker to provide personal security.

Pursuing that line, we tried to determine who could possibly gain from such an act. Revenge was an unlikely motive. There was no passion in these murders. They were carried out in too polished a manner. Besides, the murder of an entire family is beyond the scope of personal revenge. So who else could gain? What other motive could there be? Could it be political?

The senatorial campaign had been close for months. We could not dismiss the possibility that Gottesman's campaign would benefit from the deaths. Not from the sympathy vote, of course. That would swing toward Giuseppe. But the scope of such a tragedy, losing one's entire family, might have the effect of causing Giuseppe to bow out of the race. It didn't. But then, Gottesman, or his people, could not know that ahead of time. Political intrigue was not the most likely scenario. Still, we did a thorough check of everyone associated with the Gottesman campaign. Once again we turned up nothing.

\*     \*     \*

As I sat at my desk, I began to feel a sick sensation and had to fight being overcome with emotion. There was a side to this investigation that was not fully explored. I had danced around the idea, but never faced it directly. What if Giuseppe knew more than he told me? What if he actually knew who the murderers were, or who had sent them? What if he was being blackmailed by someone? Perhaps Captain Haskell had been right all along. Maybe I was just too close to the family, to Giuseppe, to the case.

These were only conjectures, suspicions, uncertainties. But I was going to have to share them with Haskell. I needed information I would not be able to get from Giuseppe. I knew that his old friend Jackson had met with him the day after the funeral. Come to think of it, why had Jackson shown up anyway? After all these years. Was he involved? I was beginning to think irrational thoughts. My mind flying off in different directions almost simultaneously. This was not the mental process of a seasoned detective. I knew that they once had been very close friends, even if it ended badly years ago. From everything I knew of Jackson, he was a good, decent and sensitive person. There was nothing odd about his being at the funeral. I needed to get control of myself and get a handle on this. I went to see the captain.

"Erick", I said. I need to speak with you. Alone". I closed his door and sat down.

"What's wrong, Tom"?

"I've been thinking about the Lozano case. Hell, that's all I've been thinking about for two months. I can only come up with one angle we have not fully explored. I think Giuseppe may know something he's not telling us. I know it sounds crazy. Maybe he's the victim of some kind of blackmail scheme. I just feel that he knows something we don't.

"When I look back on conversations we've had since the murders, there seems to be something lurking. Something he hasn't said. Maybe that he is afraid to say. You know, he did not fight very hard when I suggested hiring Gavin de Becker to provide security".

"So, if he does know something, how do you propose to pursue it"?, the captain asked.

"There's a guy who lives in Boston. His name is Jackson Carver.

They were good friends back at Harvard. They had a falling out and lost contact over the last twenty years. In the past I know that Giuseppe had opened up to him in a way he never did with anyone else. Not me. Not even his brother.

"Jackson came out here for the funeral. They met the next day. The whole day. They had lunch and dinner. Jackson left about ten in the evening. That's a lot of time for conversation.

"I'm sure they had a lot to catch up on. Still, no one else had ever held Giuseppe's confidence on such a deep level. It may be that Giuseppe said something to him that he would not say to anyone else. He may even have revealed something unintentionally. Something Jackson might not have understood.

"I want to talk with him, but it is a conversation I cannot have on the telephone. I need to see him in person and gauge his responses. I want to fly to Boston and meet with Jackson, myself".

"And you want the department to pay for it", he said. More of a question than a statement.

"Erick, I'll pay for it myself if I have to. But I need the time. This is the only avenue we have left".

I sat there as Erick thought for awhile. It was not his style to make rash decisions. But he knew it was not mine, either. Finally, he said.

"All right, Tom. Take the weekend. Set up a meeting. The department will pay for it. But come back with something".

\*     \*     \*

I called Jackson to schedule a meeting for Saturday, December 9th, then booked a Friday flight out of Los Angeles. I have no trouble sleeping on planes, so I took the redeye, leaving LAX at 10:20 PM, arriving in Boston at 6:35 AM. This was only my second time in Boston. I definitely preferred the spring weather of my first trip to the snow and cold of this one. The people who write Christmas songs must be romantics at heart. Or masochists. Even covered in white, Logan airport and the city of Boston are anything but a winter wonderland. Fortunately, it was a short ride to the hotel, and at least I was not on foot.

Jackson had offered to come to my hotel, but I thought it would be more professional if we met at his house. It might also put him a little more at ease and disarm any apprehension. We scheduled our meeting for Saturday morning at 10:00.

He and Jean-Paul lived in the small town of Watertown, about a thirty minute drive from the city. They had a very comfortable home, within walking distance of the Charles River. I walked up the pathway and rang the bell. Jackson opened the door.

"Lieutenant Moran"?, he asked.

"Yes. I presume you are Mr. Carver".

"I am. Welcome. Come in. And please, call me Jackson".

"Thank you. Even though we've never met, I've heard a lot about you. When you were in graduate school, Giuseppe used to talk about you a lot. You made quite an impression on him. Believe me, that was not a simple task. We grew up together and he was not the most open of people".

"That was a long time ago", Jackson replied. "We did not end our graduate school days on good terms".

It was a matter-of-fact statement. There was no tone of regret or sadness to his voice. Perhaps the years had erased all that. Maybe it was because he was in a relationship and it fulfilled his need to care and be cared for. I was not. And I must admit that even today I feel remorse over the failure of my marriage. I don't think I am in love with Emily anymore. On the other hand, I still love her. I guess I always will. It was, after all, not a teenage romance. But that Saturday I could not allow myself to become distracted.

"No, I replied. But you went to the funeral in September. Only a real friend would do that after such an abrupt ending and so long a time. It meant a great deal to him".

"As I told Giuseppe, I thought I owed him that much. May I offer you a cup of coffee?"

"Thank you. Yes".

"How do you take your coffee"?

"Black", I replied. "One spoon of sugar, please".

Jackson disappeared into the kitchen. He returned a few moments later with a tray. On it was a pot of coffee, two cups, creamer and sugar. He poured one for me.

"Here you are", he said as he handed me one of the cups. Then he offered me the sugar, after which he proceeded to pour his own.

"But tell me, Lieutenant. What brings you here? You were very cryptic on the phone. And you can speak freely. Jean-Paul is not here".

"Well", I said. "I'm leading the investigation into the murders. It has been slow going, and the progress has been frustrating. I need to know what happened when you visited Giuseppe after the funeral. What he told you".

"That's private, lieutenant. Besides, it had nothing to do with the murders. It was just a time for us to catch up on our lives. To share what had transpired since graduate school. After all, we had not spoken for twenty years. Most importantly, it was an opportunity for him to tell me about his family. I had met Yolanda once. But that, too, was back in graduate school".

"I'm not trying to intrude, Jackson. But I think Giuseppe knows something about the murders. I don't know what it is, maybe he doesn't even realize he knows. Perhaps he said something to you, even in passing"?

"No. He didn't. And yet, I had the feeling that he wanted to say something. About what, I don't know. He seemed to be holding back. He said nothing specific, but there was something forlorn about the way he spoke. Honestly, lieutenant, I can't put my finger on it".

"I need you to try, Jackson. Tell me what he said and let me see if I can figure it out".

"Well, from lunch on, he talked mostly about his family. He told me about Yolanda's teaching career. He talked about the kids, their interests, what they were like when they little, how their personalities were developing. The kind of stuff that all parents like to talk about.

"He also told me about his business career and what led him into politics. When we were in school at Harvard, we both had dreams of success. He actually achieved his, although his business practices were not always ethical. It was not what I would have expected from him. You probably already know about that".

"Yeah. His business background is no secret. I'm looking for something less obvious".

"Now that I think of it, his demeanor and body language were unusual. At least before lunch. Maybe for the first hour or so. But we had not seen each other in years. I just figured he was a bit uncomfortable. That made sense. To tell the truth, I felt a little awkward myself. I thought that I would see him at the funeral, offer my condolences and leave. I did not expect him to invite me to lunch the next day".

I wanted to tread carefully, but I needed to push him a little more.

"Tell me what he said before lunch", I encouraged.

"We recalled our last meeting and our falling out years before. I suppose you already know about that, too".

"Yeah. Remember, his brother and I were visiting him when it happened".

"Of course. We actually should have met that weekend", he said. Then Jackson continued.

"After the funeral, I admitted that he had been right all along, and that I had over-reacted back in Boston. I admitted that I was hiding from myself and everyone else at the time. But that was really no secret to Giuseppe. He knew me better than I thought. It was when he started to ponder, that I noticed something.

"He said his life had not turned out the way he wanted. At first, I thought he was talking about the murders. But no. He was not happy even before that. He said his life was empty".

"Did he elaborate"?, I asked.

"Not really. He said that after our friendship ended, he decided not to allow anyone to get close to him again. He said he even kept Yolanda at a comfortable distance. He spoke about sacrificing to get where he was, but indicated even that had been dishonest. He said he demanded more sacrifice from Yolanda and the kids than was necessary.

"At the time, I thought he sounded fatalistic. He said that what happened between us had completely changed the way he related to everyone.

"At one point, he started to get somewhat emotional. I could see him shivering, and it was not cold in the room. I don't know what was bothering him. I half-expected him to say something. But he didn't. Whatever it was, he kept it to himself".

"Did he give you any idea at all"?

"Not exactly. It happened after he spoke about keeping everyone distant. About being less-than-truthful with his family. At the time, it seemed natural".

"In what way"?, I asked.

"Well, if he had lied to his family, or at least, if he had been unfair to them, he no longer had a chance to make up for it. They were gone. He couldn't make amends for anything he had done. At least not to them.

"But I really couldn't read him. I was unable to separate whatever feelings of loss he had because of the murders, from the regret he felt over his life".

Jackson was unique. No question about that. I could see why he and Giuseppe had been such great friends in graduate school. And I was beginning to understand why Giuseppe let him into the close quarters of his heart. I'm not sure I have met anyone as deeply genuine as Jackson. His sensitivity went way beyond compassion or empathy. He continued.

"I told Giuseppe that I had always admired him. That when we were in school I even wanted to be like him. He told me I was lucky not to be like him. That he had become superficial and was not nearly as together as people thought.

"I began to wonder if my presence was a mistake, especially at that time in his life. What with the funeral and all. That was when he came the closest to revealing anything".

"What did he say"?

"He said he felt as if I illuminated the darkness of his soul. That he had done things no one knew about. He considered telling me, but couldn't. It seemed clear to me that he needed to talk to someone, if only for his own peace of mind. But it would not be me. In fact, I don't expect him to talk to anyone.

"After that we changed the subject. He ordered lunch and we talked about our families and relationships. I told him about my life with Jean-

Paul. He spoke about his family and his move into politics. Important stuff, but nothing deeply secret and certainly nothing dark or sinister. It continued that way on into the evening until I left".

"Thank you, Jackson", I said.

There was not much to go on, but at least I knew that something very serious was on Giuseppe's mind. At least I could pursue the idea that he was not revealing everything. Of course, I not did not know if he was holding back information on the case. But how to find out? If he wouldn't tell Jackson, I knew he would not share anything with me. Certainly not directly or intentionally. I would have to figure this out some other way.

# Chapter 28

On the return flight from Boston, I was contemplating how I would proceed. I found myself struggling with, of all things, my religion. Or lack thereof. I had spent so many years content in my agnosticism, that I was more than a little uncomfortable wanting divine intervention. Then I recalled a belief found in Greek Mythology: "The gods are best served by those who want their help least." Or so it is presented in the film "Jason and the Argonauts".

How ironic. I had no desire to serve any god, and certainly did not wish to return to the absurdities of Myth. It was an interesting paradox for me. If the ancient Greeks were correct, then the more I depended on some kind of god for assistance, the less I was serving, or worshipping god. On the other hand, the more I looked to the heavens for help, the more I was implicitly acknowledging that there might actually be a god. But I was feeling desperate enough to seek assistance anywhere I could find it.

It was a long flight home, and my mind also wandered back to the details in the case. Ever since the murder of Bass, I had been trying to figure out who could have leaked information about the investigation.

The two killers must have known that he had slipped on the porch. Since it was a foregone conclusion that FIU would eventually identify the pattern, the manufacturer and subsequently, Bass himself, there was always the possibility that the second assassin was not willing to take that risk. Still, why had the second shooter waited a full month to eliminate him?

My thoughts took me back to the night of the murders. Only two civilians were present. Giovanni and Giuseppe. Both of them heard talk about the footprint. Then I recalled the day after, when I informed Giuseppe that he would have to return to the house with me to examine the safe. He was hesitant. I told him that the only other evidence we had was the footprint. And then there was that Thursday night dinner, the day after I had identified Bass as a possible subject. I never mentioned him by name, but I told Giovanni and Giuseppe that finding that FI card would help FIU make a clear determination if it was one of the murderers who had slipped into the flower bed. Two nights later Bass was dead.

The two common links were Giovanni and Giuseppe. Why had I not seen this before? Again I began to question my own objectivity. I certainly did not believe that either of them had anything to do with the murders, but I could not escape the fact that Giuseppe had been hiding some information from everyone. And according to Jackson, it was a deep secret. I could not help but wonder if Giuseppe was living under some kind of threat. Perhaps it had something to do with the defense department, or his being elected senator. There were just too many possibilities for me to investigate on my own.

My flight landed in Los Angeles at 8:15 PM. I wanted to stop by the 3 Clubs, but was too tired. I figured I would have a drink at home and then get some sleep. That proved more difficult than I thought. My mind was alert and wired. At that point it does not matter how weary the body is. Sleep becomes impossible. And yet, I did manage to doze off and on. But nothing approaching rest.

\*     \*     \*

On Monday morning, December 11th, I went to the office early and started putting my notes in order. Captain Haskell arrived at about 10:00.

"How did the trip go"?, he asked.

"Well", I replied. "I need to talk to you".

"Come into my office", he said. We sat down and he continued. "Now. What did you find out"?

"The meeting, itself, was not that productive. It appears that Giuseppe said nothing directly associated with the investigation. However, his friend Jackson felt that he was hiding something. Something of a very serious nature".

"But he has no idea what it was"?, Haskell asked.

"No", I said. "And yet it got me thinking more. Something about Bass' death has been bothering me for last two months. I mean, it makes perfect sense that he would get killed, after having left that footprint at the scene. But there are coincidences that concern me".

"Such as"?, Haskell queried.

"As near as I can figure, only two people outside the department knew about the footprint. Giovanni and Giuseppe. As it turns out, one night at dinner I let slip that we were on to Bass. I didn't mention his name, but I told them I had found an FI card that might lead to the murderer who left the print in the flowerbed. That was two nights before Bass was killed. Maybe you were right all along, Erick. Maybe I am just too close to the case".

"Don't beat yourself up too severely, Tom. Nobody else has come to this conclusion yet, either. Do you realize how dangerous a path you're treading? Lozano has done a lot of business with the U.S. Government. Now he is senator-elect. If he is somehow involved. Especially if he is being blackmailed, it could represent a national security threat".

"I've already thought about all that. But it seems that every other avenue of investigation has been depleted. I don't see that we have any choice".

"Tom, I know you. I know you've already thought this through. So what are you proposing"?

"We've already examined Giuseppe's business records. I think we should look at them again. From a new angle. Also, I want to search his personal records. Appointment calendar, financials, and telephone".

"I'm not sure we have enough for a search warrant".

"Look, we've already had access to the company records. That's not a problem. If we stress the fact that Giuseppe was one of only two civilians to know about the footprint, and that it came up in discussion two nights before Bass was murdered, we'll have no problem getting the warrant".

"OK", Haskell said. "Go ahead. I want you to fill Wharton and Rose in on everything. What about Lozano"?

"I want to talk to him myself. I won't let on that we are requesting a warrant. I just want to see if I can pick up any indications of what Mr. Carver said". I started to leave when Haskell added,

"And, Tom, pull more men if you have to. This case has been dragging. I want to see some results".

I called Wharton and Rose into my office and informed them of the plan. They were as frustrated as everyone else and eager to pursue a new approach. I told them about my meeting with Jackson and that I wanted to try to get some information from Giuseppe before we served the warrant. In the meantime, I asked them to get a team ready to search through the records.

Then I went to see Giuseppe. He still had Gavin de Becker providing security. He seemed to agree that it was even more important now that he had been elected. At least until after we caught the murderers and solved the crime. I met him at his office at The Pegasus Group. The room was spacious, well appointed. In Giuseppe's inimitable style, it was ornate, yet lacked pretense.

I had called ahead of time to schedule an appointment for noon, so Giuseppe was not surprised to see me. In fact, he seemed pleased.

"Come in, Tom".

"Hello, Sep".

"What brings you out here? I presume you have information on the case"?

"Not exactly. We're still working on it. It's just been slow going. We have no physical evidence and little else to go on. Actually, Sep, I came to talk you, indirectly, about the case".

"What do you mean, Tom"?

"I think you have some information. You may not even be aware of it. But you're about the last hope I have of getting a lead".

"I don't know how I can help you, Tom. I told you about the file and I have no idea who would steal it. I don't know what other kind of information you think I have".

"Sep, over the weekend I flew to Boston to meet with your friend, Jackson. I knew the two of you spent a lot of time together the day after the funeral. I thought you might have said something to him, maybe something that you did not even realize. Something that would help".

"Tom, I don't care about you going to see him. But not telling me sounds a bit deceitful. I'm not very happy about it. I don't have anything to hide from you".

"Well, now. That's just the point. According to Jackson, he sensed there was something you weren't telling him. Whatever you were holding back, he said it was very serious. Look, Sep. Nobody has ever known you as well as he does".

"Did", Giuseppe corrected. "That friendship ended years ago. Our lives went in different directions and we had not even spoken for twenty years before the funeral".

"Yeah. You lost contact, and you both changed. But you know as well as I do, that when two people are as close as you were, some connection survives. He still knows you better than anyone else. Better than Giovanni, even".

"Whatever, Tom. What did he tell you? What have I been holding back"?

"That's just it. He doesn't know. Whatever it is, you did not tell him. He just knew that you were keeping something inside. There wasn't a lot he could tell me. He said you were not happy with the way your life turned out and that you kept everyone, including Yolanda, at a distance. He said you made some veiled reference to a darkness in your life. In your soul".

"That was just a poetic expression, Tom", Giuseppe interjected.

"Who the hell do you think you're kidding, Sep? We've known each other all our lives. Look. I don't care if you broke any laws in your business dealings. I don't care who you might have cheated. I'm only interested in solving this crime. I need you to tell me what you would not tell Jackson".

"No. Instead, I'll tell you what I did tell him. Nobody will ever get as close to me as he was back in Harvard. And there are things in my life I will share with no one. Period. You're going to have to believe me, Tom. Whatever happened in my past, I did nothing to anyone that would have caused them to kill my family".

"That's not good enough, Sep".

Even before I went to see him, I knew it would be a fruitless venture. But there has always been a part of me that remains hopeful even when facing futility. It is something I need to believe in. I see myself as idealistic. Giovanni prefers to call me unrealistic. Perhaps it is a little of both. Regardless, I am also relentless.

I could tell I would not get any further with Giuseppe. I stood up and headed toward the door. As I reached for the handle I turned and told him,

"You should know me well enough to realize that I will not let this go. I'll be back, Sep. If nothing else, I am persistent".

I controlled myself enough not to slam the door. But goddammit. He pissed me off. I was beginning to remember why I did not like him in college, or most of our lives, for that matter. Giovanni and our families were all that kept us together. Ever since the murders, I allowed myself to think that we were getting closer. That the terrible bond created by sudden death was healing the differences of our past. Now, however, the truth was beginning to set with the finality of a winter night. Giuseppe and I could never be friends. He could not really be friends with anyone. He was as self-centered as ever. And I was now forced to be his adversary.

# Chapter 29

Later that same afternoon I returned to Giuseppe's office. Warrant in hand, accompanied by Wharton, Rose and a few other officers. I handed him the papers to read.

"Tom, you surprise me", Giuseppe said. "There was no need for a warrant. I would have given you access to anything you wanted".

"I'm afraid, Giuseppe, we've already passed beyond that level of trust".

The use of his full name did not go unnoticed.

"Are we being formal, now lieutenant"?

"We are", I responded matter-of-factly. "You have already withheld information, even if you do not consider it germane to the case. That's my call to make, not yours. I don't believe you would willingly provide us with what we need".

"You think you can find it by searching my telephone, calendar and financial records"?

"I don't know. But I'm prepared to do whatever is necessary. In fact, I'm more than prepared. I told you earlier that I don't care about any illegal business practices you may have been involved in over the years.

That's not my department. But I intend to find what I need to solve this case".

Giuseppe looked at me, then at the other officers and said,

"Take any files you need".

"Aren't you going to read through the warrant"?, I asked.

"No. I'm sure it's in order. You see, unlike me, I don't think you would do anything illicit".

"Well, when we finish here, I need you to accompany me to the house. We also need the files out of the safe".

"As soon as you're ready", he replied.

He was just a little too confident. Following the murders, Giuseppe had displayed a certain weakness, or at least a need for other people. People like Giovanni and me. Since the election, however, that weakness had disappeared. In its place was his customary, unmistakable air of being in control. Of being able to manipulate any person and every event. He did not get in the way or interfere with the officers. In fact, he acted as if the entire process of gathering files and information was a challenge.

I have never been able to fully comprehend Giuseppe. When we were kids, he always seemed to be looking for something. Something that did not attract either me or Giovanni. It was not just wealth. Or even recognition. Although they were part of the equation. I think Giuseppe wanted power. Wealth and recognition can each exist on their own. And for most people, either of them is sufficient. But power provides and guarantees a bond that holds them together. Nor is it about corruption.

Lord Acton may have been insightful, but he was also wrong. It is not so much that "power tends to corrupt", as he so famously wrote. That may have been true in Acton's 19th century England. In modern day America, however, corruption is not a result. It is a cause. It is the foundation that pre-exists and serves the exercise of power. Most people do not rise to the highest levels of authority and control unless they have already proven themselves corrupt. It is most evident in institutions like politics and religion. There are, of course, exceptions. However, Giuseppe was not one of them.

I did not think of it at the time, but neither lofty rhetoric nor great social principles led to his election. He had amassed phenomenal wealth, was considered a visionary and acknowledged as an astute businessman. But his success itself was the result of having already succumbed to corruption. He lacked only power to provide the zenith to his life. And yet, that afternoon, there was something more to his confidence. Something that defied definition.

*　　*　　*

Over the next couple of weeks teams of detectives poured over the records we had seized. We came up empty with the telephone logs. No unusual or extraordinary communications. If they existed, they were not to be found on any of Giuseppe's official phones.

I took the lead in reviewing Giuseppe's calendar. Like many executives, he used a certain kind of shorthand to make appointments, the most obvious being the use of initials. A list of his associates and other business contacts helped to decipher the codes, but, again, nothing appeared out of the ordinary. His financials, however, were a different matter.

Forensic accountants examined both Giuseppe's personal records, as well as those of The Pegasus Group. He had established several offshore accounts. In Switzerland, Cayman Islands, The Bahamas, and even one as far away as the Republic of Seychelles. Unfortunately, obtaining information from these banks is next to impossible. They pride themselves on guaranteeing privacy for their customers. One thing was certain, no money had been transferred from any of them into Giuseppe's U.S. bank accounts. We were not able to find anything illegal about his financial activities. If he was being blackmailed, there was no paper trail of payments.

It was clear that Giuseppe had learned from the mistakes of his railroad heroes, the Central Pacific's "Big Four", particularly their near brush with imprisonment. All his records were sterile. Almost beyond imagination. No wonder he was so cocky. I was not about to surrender, however.

It occurred to me that only Giuseppe, Yolanda and Coker had the combination to the master bedroom safe. I also knew that Giuseppe kept Yolanda in the dark regarding the extent of his finances. It was a fair assumption, then, that he entrusted only Coker with access to his offshore accounts. Although we would not be able to retrieve that information from the banks, we could at least check both of their travel records.

Giuseppe had not been out of the country for over six months. Coker, on the other hand, flew to Grand Cayman on September 23rd, only two days after the murder. Even though the flight had been booked in July, it seemed odd that he would not have rescheduled, given the magnitude of the murders. My next visit was to see Coker.

*　　*　　*

Coker had a plush office on the 50th floor of the Wells Fargo Tower in Los Angeles, offering a magnificent view of the Los Angeles basin. Throughout the week of Christmas, the city experienced a near perfect weather pattern. Tuesday, December 26th was a smogless day with temperatures reaching a mild 71°. Catalina Island rose with sparkling clarity out of the Pacific Ocean some fifty miles distant, and a number of freeways ribboned a pathway out of Los Angeles into Orange County and beyond. It was easy to see why he chose this office.

Coker had only two clients. He was in-house attorney for The Pegasus Group, and on permanent retainer as Giuseppe's personal lawyer. As such, he was aware of the search warrant we had executed on December 11th, and of the files that had been removed from Giuseppe's premises.

The receptionist announced my arrival and showed me into Coker's private office.

"Welcome, Lieutenant. How may I help you"? He stretched out his hand. I shook it and replied, "Mr. Coker". Then he said to his secretary,

"Ms. Reed, please bring us some coffee". Turning to me he asked, "How do you take your coffee, lieutenant"?

"None for me, thank you", I replied.

"Then never mind, Ms. Reed", he said. "I won't have any, either". She left and closed the door.

"Well, lieutenant, let's get right to the point, shall we"?

I accepted the invitation and wasted no time on pleasantries.

"As you know, RHD has been searching through Mr. Lozano's personal records".

"I am, indeed, aware, lieutenant. However, I do not know what you expect to find. Certainly, you do not consider him a suspect".

"I'm not calling him a suspect. I am simply trying to uncover any information that might lead us to the assailant. In fact, that's what brings me here.

"We know of Mr. Lozano's offshore bank accounts and that only you and he have access to them. I would like to ask you about a trip you took to Grand Cayman on September 23rd of this year".

"You know that's privileged information, lieutenant".

I knew he would bring this up at some point, but I was prepared. I had already decided that I would bluff my way through the conversation, if necessary. So I responded.

"I'm not concerned with any client confidentiality. But it seemed rather strange that you would go two days after the murders".

"That trip had been planned for months", Coker replied. "There were a number of financial transactions I had to handle. Besides, the funeral would not take place for several days, your investigation was in its initial stages and there was nothing for me to do".

"You know that we are trying to locate a file taken from the house on the night of the murder. It may be the key to solving this crime. We know you took a large envelope with you to the Cayman Islands and left it in a safe deposit box at the bank. I want to know what was in it. Or at least where the envelope came from".

The truth was that I knew nothing about any envelope. But it was the only logical explanation. I had put together all the information I had.

A file was missing from the crime scene. That much was not a ruse. Giuseppe could have denied its existence from the beginning. But his self-assurance would have brooked no deceit about that. Whatever he did or did not know, he would have been confident that he could remain in control of the situation. In fact, from his way of thinking, telling the police about the file would only serve to distract and possibly confuse us.

It worked. For months we had combed through the records of every conceivable competitor in the computer, security and defense industries. There was no link to anyone. We dissected the lives of his employees, both past and present. Nothing. We chronicled the history of his former business partners and current associates. Again. Empty.

Next, there were two murderers. One of them had been killed, apparently because the police had discovered his identity. From him we might have been able to learn the identity of the other killer, and the person who had hired them. He was a liability that had to be eliminated.

We found no unusual telephone communications on Giuseppe's part, and his calendar held nothing suspicious. His financial records were in order. Even though he had several offshore accounts, they did not appear to be illegal, nor could we determine any unlawful activity. I had reason to believe that Yolanda did not have access to them, leaving his attorney as the only other person likely to possess such entrée.

Giuseppe had done no significant traveling in the last several months. Our investigation turned up one single anomaly. The trip that Coker took to the Cayman Islands. It was of particular note because it occurred only two days after the murders. He must have been carrying and depositing that file. But I did not know if he placed it in Giuseppe's safe deposit box or his own. And I certainly had no idea how much information Coker actually had.

"Lieutenant, what makes you think that I know anything about that missing file"?

"Counselor", I responded, "Let's agree not to play games. Our sources in Grand Cayman have informed us that you walked into the bank with a large envelope, accessed a safe deposit box, and exited the bank empty-handed. Now, what was in that envelope"?

"If you had any real evidence, you would not be sitting here so casually. You obviously have no witnesses. No one to prove that I took

268

any such envelope to Grand Cayman. At least no one who can testify in a court of law. And I certainly admit nothing. But I'll tell you, lieutenant, that if such an envelope did exist, I have no idea what was in it".

As a detective, I have spent my life reading people. While humility is not my strongest suit, it is not boastful to admit that I am an expert at manipulation techniques. Breaking down the resistance of people under interrogation. Getting them to reveal what they do not intend.

There I was matching wits with another expert. His particular skill was causing people to break down and reveal information while under oath on a witness stand. It was similar to my work, but the rules are not the same. Witnesses are protected both by their own lawyers and by court procedures. Police interrogation is different, especially when it is done off-handedly, as I was attempting to do that day.

I can tell when someone is holding back. In the same way that I knew Giuseppe withheld information, I was convinced that Coker did not. There was definitely an envelope, but sitting there in his office, having this discussion, I did not believe that Coker knew what was in it. He had an exclusive and limited law practice. He worked for a man with questionable business ethics. But that did not mean that he was a crooked lawyer.

"Mr. Coker", I continued. "I have a hunch that Mr. Lozano is being blackmailed. Perhaps by the very person who ordered the killings. That's the one we want to find. It's very possible, that besides being blackmailed, Lozano is running scared. He has been guarded by Gavin de Becker ever since the murders. It's a good precaution, but no guarantee of safety. The assassins were highly trained professionals. Even with bodyguards there are ways of getting to him. If you know something, don't you think you owe it to your client to tell me"?

"Lieutenant, I have nothing to say. Even if I did know something, that would still be privileged. I keep all client information confidential, and I would never risk disbarment simply because you have a hunch. So if there's nothing else, I do have other work to do. I'm sorry I couldn't be of more help".

With that he stood up, walked around his desk, extended his hand and offered to show me the exit.

"Thank you. I know the way out", I said.

The meeting had not been a total loss and I left with mixed feelings. I was certain that Coker had taken an envelope to Grand Cayman and left it in a bank vault. I had reason to believe that he did not know the contents. And I had a reasonable suspicion that it contained the missing file. That brought my investigation back to Giuseppe again. I headed back to the office and set about planning my next move.

# Chapter 30

After I left Coker's office, he made a phone call. It was to Giuseppe, but not to one of his listed numbers. This call was not traceable. It was a precaution, just in case we had set up wiretaps.

"Giuseppe, I just had a visit from your friend, Lt. Moran. He knows about my trip to Grand Cayman and he claims to know about the envelope I left in the safe deposit box. He seems to think that it contained the missing file from your house. He also believes that you are being blackmailed by someone".

"He's been on my case about that stuff, too, Coker. He thinks I know something about the murders that I'm not telling him. It's just a crazy theory. I mean, hell, we're talking about my family, for god's sake. I'd tell him anything that was relevant".

"Giuseppe, I never asked you what was in the envelope. The trip to the Caymans had been planned for months, and there were a number of transactions I had to take care of. So I never thought twice about it. But now I wonder. And, of course, anything you say is confidential. The police have come up empty trying to track that file. So, tell me. What did I deliver"?

"Now, Coker, don't let your imagination run wild, too. I've given the police everything they've asked for. I'm not holding anything back".

"That's an evasive response, Giuseppe. I'm your lawyer, not a cop. I'd like a truthful answer".

"You're right, Coker. You're not a cop. You're a lawyer. Mine. I decide what I want to tell you. I'll say this much. You do not need to know what was in the envelope and that's my last word on the subject. As for Moran, you need not worry yourself about him, either. You have no information that will help his investigation".

They had known each other for years, not just professionally, but also personally. This was not Giuseppe's most open conversation. And his assurances were of small comfort to Coker. He was left with the same type of questions that troubled me. Still, Coker had a legal obligation. He was Giuseppe's lawyer, and it would be a violation for him to express his doubts or uncertainties to me. He, also, was destined to remain in the dark.

Even with only two clients, Coker was a busy attorney who had a tendency to work long hours. He left his office at eight o'clock in the evening. It was already dark, but a clear night. The temperature had dropped precipitously from its afternoon high, to a low of 43°.

Coker lived in a posh neighborhood in the Los Feliz district of Los Angeles. At that time of night, the evening traffic commute had calmed down. This made his trip home no more than a fifteen minute drive up the 110 Freeway, then north on Interstate 5 to the Los Feliz Boulevard exit. His house on Aberdeen Avenue, bordered Griffith Park, the nation's largest urban parkland with a combination of both landscaped and wilderness areas.

Griffith Park itself, is a popular destination for entertainment and outdoor exercise. Activities include camping, golf, hiking, horseback riding, swimming and tennis. The L.A. Zoo is located at the northeast corner of the park. The world famous Greek Theatre and Griffith Observatory are both located within the park, as is the Gene Autry National Center.

In spite of all the activities and events at Griffith Park, and the fact that it is only minutes from downtown Los Angeles, and the movie studios of Hollywood and Burbank, the Los Feliz district is a pleasant and mostly quiet place to live. The hills, canyons and natural forestation make it possible to forget that one is still within the city limits. It is truly a world of its own.

Coker pulled up in front of his home and exited his car. Aberdeen is a semicircular cul-de-sac. Most evenings he would take a short stroll west along Aberdeen to Vermont, then south to the other end of Aberdeen and back up to his house. That evening he was feeling particularly energetic and chose to walk east to Inverness, then to Hillhurst, back up Vermont to Aberdeen and home again.

Two of the streets, the residential ones, were quiet. No traffic to speak of and few neighbors out for a walk. As he returned home, Coker passed another pedestrian. Although it was not a very cold night, the man was dressed in a long overcoat. As they met, Coker looked up to greet him. "Thuup". One shot through the heart. Gilmore dropped the gun and walked to Vermont, where he had inconspicuously parked his car. He got in and drove off.

At five o'clock the next morning, a neighbor noticed the body on the sidewalk and called 911 emergency. Paramedics and officers from the Northeast Division arrived almost immediately. The paramedics pronounced Coker dead at the scene and the officers identified the body.

*   *   *

I had been up late the night before. Like countless other nights I was alone, so I went to the 3 Clubs. Pete was not just an excellent bartender, he was also a reliable conversationalist, even if the other patrons were not. It took no great effort to stay until closing, and the last thing I needed was an early morning wakeup call. Nonetheless, that is exactly what I received.

It was 5:30 and Rose was working an early shift at RHD. As soon as he got the word, he phoned me.

"Tom", he said. "This is Rose. You're not going to believe this. We just received word about a body. It was found on Aberdeen Avenue in Los Feliz. It's Coker".

That startled me awake and into what passed for reality. My first words were an exclamation.

"Un-fucking-believable! When did it happen"?

"Rough estimates are about ten o'clock last night. Some neighbor found him about a half-hour ago. He was shot once", I quickly interrupted him.

"Don't tell me. Through the heart, right"?

"You guessed it".

"It didn't take much guess work", I replied. "I suppose there was a Glock 9mm left at the scene"?

"Sounds like you were there", Rose said.

"I was. Not physically, of course. But this is a replay, and I've been through it before". Then, with a passive resignation I continued. "I'll get dressed and head over to the office. In the meantime, I want you to find out who Coker called yesterday. Start with calls he made after I met with him".

I hung up and for a moment continued to sit on the edge of the bed. There wasn't really any rush. All I could do downtown was think, and I could do that just as easily at home. I got up and put on a pot of coffee. While it was brewing, I took a shower.

As the water engulfed me, I realized that I was rather calm. There were no thoughts racing in my head. My response was not the same as the night Yolanda and the kids were killed. Nor was it like the morning after Bass' body was discovered. Something cold and calculating was at play here and I would have to be just as artfully cunning if I was to succeed. Three murder scenes, one crime. But what was the heart of the crime? That's where the solution was to be found.

I got dressed and poured some coffee. I didn't feel like eating breakfast. I had filled up on bar snacks only a few hours before. I took the time to evaluate what had transpired since that catastrophic night in September.

Killing Bass made sense. He had inadvertently left evidence at the original murder scene. His identity could have led to the other assassin and to the one who had hired them. Executing Coker, however, was a different matter. As a lawyer, he would have had access to privileged information, including the possibility of blackmail. But as far as I could tell, he was not corrupt. He would have preserved the confidence of his clients. As a matter of both ethics and law. On the other hand, if I was correct about his trip to Grand Cayman, that he deposited the missing file from the Lozano safe, then he might conceivably be a co-conspirator. But with whom?

I was beginning to doubt the theory of blackmail. Everything I had learned inexorably led in one direction and to only one person. Giuseppe. I was still at a loss, however, as to what his connection was. Or how to extract from him the information I needed.

I arrived at the office at about 8:00. When Captain Haskell arrived, he did not look too pleased. He glanced in my direction and nodded for me to enter his office. He did not even wait for me to sit down.

"This is out of hand, Tom. You met with Coker yesterday and now he turns up dead. What happened"?

"No one knew I was meeting with Coker", I said. "He must have informed somebody on his own. Whether before or after the meeting, I don't know".

"Tom, I didn't tell you, but I had a call from the FBI last week. They have been particularly concerned since Lozano won the election. They're not impressed with what they consider our lack of progress. They offered their assistance again. I assured them that RHD is handling the investigation properly and that we don't need any outside help. This latest death raises serious questions".

"We are doing everything we can, Erick. The FBI would fare no better. There's very little evidence. The odd thing is, Coker didn't reveal anything helpful".

"What did you find out"?

"Not much. I played a bluff. I'm fairly certain he took the missing file to the Cayman Islands. But I'm also sure that he knew nothing about it. If I'm right, he lost his life for nothing".

"Do you have any ideas now"?, Haskell asked.

"Two", I said. "So far the press has not made the connection between the original murders and Bass. They will undoubtedly find out that Coker was Lozano's attorney. But we still have a little time on our side.

Lozano is in Washington, but he's returning today. I want to tap his phone and I want to put a tail on him".

Haskell started to interrupt, but I continued.

"Listen, Erick. Giuseppe is the only person connected to this case who isn't dead yet. If he's innocent, he's in danger. If not", my voice trailed off and I looked away.

Haskell could see the toll this was taking on me.

"I want to get Wharton and Rose in here", he said.

He opened the door and called out for the two of them to join us. They came in and sat down.

"Tell them what you have in mind, Tom".

"I don't need to summarize the case for you guys", I started. "As I see it, our investigation has gone pretty much nowhere. Our only link is Lozano, himself. I don't know what that link is, but I'm tired of watching as each piece of evidence evaporates. I want a warrant to tap his phone and I want to tail him. I want to know everywhere he goes, everyone he sees, and everyone he talks to".

"That's a tall order now that he's been elected and is preparing to move to Washington", Wharton noted.

"I know what I'm suggesting", I replied. "Does anyone else have a better idea"? No one did. So I continued.

"Here's my plan. Lozano is due back from Washington later this afternoon. He will probably know about the murder. Coker's secretary will have already called him. After all, Giuseppe and his company were the only clients Coker had. By the time he gets back, we should have the taps in place. Then, I'm going to go speak with Lozano, alone. I want to give it one more shot. I'm not sure what I'm going to say, yet. I don't want to script it too carefully. But I hope to instill a little concern, if not genuine fear.

"Wharton and Rose, you two go with me, but in your own cars. Wait outside and keep watch. After I leave, you follow Lozano. Everywhere. And report back regularly". I looked at Haskel and asked, "Captain"?

"It's still your case", he said. "But this is treacherous ground. Tread cautiously. And keep me informed".

# Chapter 31

Giuseppe had moved back into the family home at the beginning of December, and that's where he headed after his plane landed. I called and told him I needed to meet with him alone. I arrived at 7:00 PM. He had already dismissed his staff, including his campaign manager who had assumed the role of directing the transition team. Giuseppe opened the door.

"Hello, Tom. Come in".

I was not feeling very warm or friendly. I guess it showed in my expression. Giuseppe observed, rather dryly, "You looked displeased, Tom".

"I am. I'm sure you've heard about Coker".

"Yeah".

"Did you also know that I met with him yesterday"?

"He told me".

"When", I asked.

"He called right after you left his office. One of the privileges of being his only client, is that he does not have to take time from anyone else".

Damn! His arrogance really pissed me off. He continued uninterrupted.

"He said you were looking for the missing file. That you seemed to think he had something to do with it. Maybe even took it to Grand Cayman. He said you were still going on about me being blackmailed. That was about it. I told him not worry".

There was something disturbing in his tone. His recitation of events contained not the slightest of emotions. I found myself speaking unprocessed thoughts.

"Did you also tell him he was going to be killed"?

Giuseppe froze. I had not intended to ask that question, but I clearly struck some kind of nerve for his face lost all expression. He said tersely,

"I know this case has stressed you out, Tom, but that question's out of line".

"Is it, Giuseppe? It occurs to me that you are the only person involved in this case who's not dead".

I found myself giving voice to months of frustration, compounded by Giuseppe's lack of cooperation.

"I also don't believe that the missing file has anything to do with the murder of your family. I know it existed, but I think the theft was concocted to throw the police off track".

"And you think I had something to do with it"?, he asked.

"I'm really not sure. However, the more I think of it, the less I think you're being blackmailed. I believe you have some kind of involvement. I just don't know what it is, yet. But you can bet I'll find out. Unless, of course, you're willing to tell me now", I suggested.

"I've told you everything I intend to", he replied. "It looks like you're going to leave empty-handed". He had accepted my challenge, so as an after thought, he added, "Again".

He was right. But I was leaving with even less than that. Ever since the election, actually, ever since his meeting with Jackson after the funeral, Giuseppe's attitude had changed. It had bothered me for some time. I knew that he was holding back information, but I had no idea what that information was. Planned or not, the die was now cast.

Our conversation that night would prove to be my Rubicon. From that point forward, Giuseppe and I were engaged in battle. I found myself channeling the courage of Julius Caesar and wondered if I could also muster his confidence.

*    *    *

ESU had already tapped Giuseppe's phone and were monitoring all calls, incoming and outgoing. As far as I could tell, I had not managed to instill concern or fear in him. But maybe I touched something even deeper. As soon as I left, he called his brother.

"Gio, this is Giuseppe. Can I come over and talk to you"?

"Of course, Sep. What's wrong"?

"It's not that anything's wrong. You're probably going to think I'm joking, but I want to go to confession".

"Come off it, Sep. That's not funny".

"I know it's been a long time, Gio, but I'm serious. There are some things I need to talk over with you".

"Sep, you can talk to me without going to confession. I'll keep your confidence".

"I know you will. But I need a guarantee beyond that. There are some things I need to share with you, and I cannot risk your being forced to repeat them. And I know that even Tom could not get you to break the seal of the sacrament".

"It sounds ominous, Sep. Of course you can come over. When will you be here"?

"Is 8:00 good for you? It will take me about twenty minutes to finish things here and get to the church".

"I'll be waiting".

"Thank you, Gio".

*    *    *

ESU informed me the moment Giuseppe completed his call. Wharton and Rose were also notified, but they were already on scene and prepared to follow him. At least for now, we knew where he was headed. We did not want him to know that his calls were being monitored, or

279

that he was being followed. It was, therefore, necessary to let him play out the scenario with Giovanni.

In the meantime, I thought about my conversation with Giuseppe, wondering what might have occasioned an immediate need to seek his brother's counsel. The only thing I could come up with was my suggestion that he was involved in the murder of Coker. It was only an innuendo, but he responded as if it was an accusation. If I was even close to the truth, then it was possible that his fabled control was beginning to unravel. That would certainly necessitate speaking with someone, and Giovanni was the perfect choice.

I decided to head over to St. Catherine Parish, wait for Giuseppe to leave, then speak with Giovanni myself. I did not know what to expect. Giovanni would not reveal anything his brother told him in confession, but he might tell me something else, or let slip some helpful information without even realizing it.

St. Catherine Church had been growing almost from the day Giovanni became pastor. People dissatisfied with the conservative direction of other parishes were happy to call it their home. They found his theological perspective fresh and liberating. It was a comforting environment, even for those who disagreed with his politics. In fact, that disagreement led to many opportunities for ongoing discussion, adult education, and a variety of other programs to serve the larger community. Indeed, there was always something going on at the parish. As a result, it was one of the few churches that maintained office personnel until 9:00 PM.

Giuseppe stayed in the rectory only thirty minutes. Apparently, whatever he needed to talk about did not require any lengthy counseling on Giovanni's part. He walked out the door, entered his car and drove off. Wharton and Rose discreetly pursued.

I waited about ten minutes, then walked up to the rectory and rang the bell. Haley Navarro was the receptionist. I had been to the rectory so many times since the funeral, that she had come to know me well. Or at least to recognize me. As she opened the door, I quickly brushed past her, asking: "Is he in"?

"Yes, Lieutenant. I'll announce you."

"Never mind, I'll announce myself."

Giovanni looked up as I burst into his office, slamming the door shut behind me. He did not seem surprised to see me, although he was put off by the question I posed.

"How could you"?, I asked.

"How could I what"?

"Don't play games with me. You're a priest, for God's sake! How could you hear your brother's confession, knowing what he would say"?

"What makes you think I heard his confession"?

Giovanni was never very good at playing coy. But I realized he wasn't even trying. I was so irritated when I arrived, that I did not notice his own state. His face was ashen and I could see his mood shifting before me. Even his question lacked the normal lift of inflection. He was clearly a man dejected. I was almost ashamed of my own single-mindedness. Still, as unpleasant as it might be, I had a job to do. I reduced the intensity of my voice and continued.

"Look, Gio. I already know for a fact why he came here. My question is how you could do it"?

"Tom, you know that if Giuseppe came to me for confession, I can't tell you anything about it. You and I may be friends, but I'm not violating the confidentiality of the sacrament for anyone. Besides, I never know what someone is going to say beforehand. And even if I suspect, it is precisely because I am a priest that I would hear anybody's confession. To try to help lift someone out of torment".

"But he committed murder".

"You don't know that".

"I know that he went to confession".

"Come to think of it, how do you know that"?

"That's the reason he came to see you tonight. I had been to see him first, and something I said caused him to call you immediately after".

"So, you bugged his telephone? That's unbelievable, Tom. After all these years, and everything the three of us have been through"!

"I had no choice, Gio. Look, you know there has always been a certain distance between Giuseppe and me. The truth is, he's been holding back information. He knows details that will help our investigation. And I can tell from your demeanor, that whatever he told you was devastating".

"You have no idea what he told me. And I can't say anything".

"There must be some way you can put me on the right track", I persisted.

"Tom, you're wasting your time. If you want to know anything, you'll have to ask Giuseppe".

"I've tried. A couple of times. Why do you think I went to see him tonight? But he gave me nothing. All I know is that I said something that caused him to come running to you".

I was trying to be sensitive to whatever Giovanni was going through. But I needed information. And even though he was my friend, and I cared about him, I was becoming impatient. My memory flashed back to our youth.

"Shit, Gio, you never change. It's always been like this. Ever since we were kids. You've always defended Giuseppe and covered for him. But we're not kids anymore. And this is serious business".

"I'm not defending him or covering for him. The fact that you would even say that, suggests that you have a problem with religion and the church".

I was pursuing a murder investigation and could not allow myself to be deterred by my feelings for Giovanni. I sensed a fierce determination rise within me.

"I don't have a problem with religion", I replied. "But I do have a problem with a church that would protect a murderer under the guise of some religious practice. Your problem, Gio, is that you live in a world of illusion, shrouded by risible ritual and magical incantations".

Giovanni's voice took on a stern, almost defensive tone. He sat up straight and glared at me.

"That's an unfair judgment, Tom. Whatever your beliefs are now, we were both raised Catholic. You know what the sacrament stands for. And you know my commitment to my faith. How can you dismiss it so callously"?

I did not have a ready answer. Giovanni looked at me and continued.

"Tom, we've been friends all our lives. But I have never felt as sorry for you as I do now. How sad it must be to have nothing to believe in. No place to find peace. Does anything matter to you anymore? Anything besides your job? From where do you draw inspiration"?

'Damn, Giovanni', I thought to myself. He always had the ability to see beneath the surface, and he knew me better than anyone. But I could not let him distract me from my purpose.

"Nice try, Gio. But this case is not about me or my lack of faith or what you might consider my emptiness. It's about finding a cold-blooded killer. About solving a murder. A murder that is as important to you as it is to me".

"Well, I have nothing more to say", he replied.

"We both know that Giuseppe holds the key to unraveling these crimes. I suspect that he told you he had Coker killed. I just don't know why, but I'm sure it is a question you would have asked him. If you won't give me the answer, I will find it another way. But let's be clear about this much, Gio. I will bring Giuseppe down".

Those words returned him to the melancholy I saw when I first arrived. He, too, knew something I did not. Even though he would not tell me, the trip was not a waste. I was now as certain as I could be, lacking any tangible evidence, that Giuseppe ordered Coker killed. I still needed to figure out the motive.

*　　*　　*

Giuseppe returned home after meeting with his brother. He made a few phone calls that night, each having to do with his transition to Washington. He spoke with his manager and called a couple of other senators. Although this was Giuseppe's first foray into politics, it was a successful one. Already there were those who viewed him as a rising star in the Republican party.

The next day he headed to his office at The Pegasus Group. He had been winding down his personal involvement with the company. He had already made the necessary arrangements to place Pegasus into a trust during his time in the U.S. Senate. Since he wanted his company to secure government contracts, he would at least have to try and avoid the appearance of a conflict of interest. Not that the law or ethics ever got in his way before.

Most of the time, detective work is a laborious piecing together of evidence. It requires patience and determination. Sometimes it involves luck. But there is another, often under-appreciated element that evolves with years of experience--intuition. Solving the Lozano murders, as well as those of Bass and Coker, would take all the skills I had learned from twenty-four years on the force.

I walked out of Giovanni's office that night with a firm resolve. There would be no more killings in this case. One way or another, I was going to bring it to an end.

# Chapter 32

Instead of returning to the office, I went home. I really wanted to stop by the 3 Clubs. But I needed time alone. No company, no distractions, no scotch. Just me, my notes and my intuition.

There was a master plan at work behind these murders and whoever designed it was brilliant. Rarely are a set of murders so clean, and carried off with such precision that the police are left clueless. At this point I was less interested in finding the other murderer than I was the person who hired him. The person who hatched the entire scheme.

From the beginning, there was only one piece of valuable evidence. The footprint. That was sheer luck. Given the efficiency and expertise of the assassins, it was more the result of accident than sloppiness. However, once we identified the person who left it, he himself became a victim. The only other possible clue was tenuous, at best. That was Coker's trip to Grand Cayman. To make use of it, I had to bluff my way through a conversation with him. Immediately after, Coker was killed, too.

In the solitudinous silence of my apartment, my mind began to wander. Doubting the existence of God is one thing. Doubting oneself, quite another. Those two uncertainties, disbelief and disquiet, briefly collided. Inexplicably, I found myself calling out to a God I no longer believed in, as if he were the only one I could engage in conversation.

"God, how could I have spent, how could you have let me spend, three months chasing ghosts? Not the ghosts of friends, but of non-existent suspects. How could I have misdirected this investigation from a pursuit for truth into a world of malice and illusion? Maybe I should never have taken over the case. Captain Haskell was right. I was too close. Too close to Yolanda and the kids. Even too close to Giuseppe".

I paced around the floor wondering if Wharton would have been any more successful. He had the same evidence I did, and he never suggested a different avenue of investigation. But, then, he didn't tell Giuseppe about Bass, either. I did that. Had he not been killed, we might have solved this two months ago. I put the burden on myself to find the killers and solve this crime. And I failed. I was the one who made the mistakes.

"What happens now, God? What do I tell the captain? How do I explain this fiasco? Will people accept that this is just another unsolved mystery? Will they allow it to become one more 'cold case'? How is the FBI going to view the LAPD now? And what about my career?

"You know, I don't give a shit anymore. I don't care about the department or my future. I only care about four innocent people. My friends. In a very real sense, my family. So tell me, God, if you really exist, if you really care about people, how could you have let this whole fucking mess happen"?

The ringing of the telephone startled me. I looked around. If there was a god, he was not present. Nor was he listening. I was alone. The call was from Wharton, informing me that Giuseppe had returned home. It did not appear he was going out again that night.

I knew I was going to have to confront Giuseppe once more. But I would need to be better prepared than I was the last time. So I set about to formulate the sequence of events into a convincing narrative.

I had suspected for sometime that Giuseppe possessed pertinent knowledge of the events. At least those following the murder of his family. He was the only link to each part of this crime. I had proceeded on the assumption that he was being blackmailed. However, I could not prove that. And yet...

He knew that the police had identified Bass. I inadvertently let that information slip one night at dinner. Twelve days later, Bass was dead. He also knew that I suspected Coker of hiding the missing file in a bank located in the Cayman Islands. I told Coker as much in a conversation. He called Giuseppe and informed him. Hours later the lawyer was dead.

When I met with Giuseppe and suggested that he knew ahead of time about Coker's death, his reaction did not ring true. At least not for an innocent man. He was not nearly as defensive as he should have been. His reaction was more cold and calculating than it was shock or surprise. He did not deny the suggestion. Typical of his arrogance, he began to engage in mental jousting, undoubtedly believing it would be easy to outwit me. But I still did not know what his connection was, or why he did not divulge what he knew.

I had come to believe that the file itself was merely a distraction. A successful one, for it caused us to waste untold man hours hunting down non-existent suspects, from employees to competitors. It led nowhere. Except to the death of Coker.

I no longer believed the theory of blackmail. Once his family was killed, Giuseppe would have no reason to succumb to threats. Other than to save his own life, of course. But there was no evidence to support that. There was no evidence at all. If not blackmail, then what?

No matter what direction my thoughts took me, I kept coming back to Giuseppe and wondering what he knew. Our investigation had exhausted every other avenue. The first time I reached this conclusion, I felt sick inside. Regardless the problems we had over the years, the alienation that had grown between us, I shared with Giuseppe the profound loss of Yolanda and the kids. I saw the distress and agony that consumed him. And with Giovanni I stood beside him and helped him through his greatest tragedy. I did not want to believe that he could in anyway be involved, or withhold knowledge that would help me solve this crime.

But things change. After our last encounter, I found the two of us diametrically opposed. Locked in a struggle for truth from which only one of us would emerge the victor. I puzzled over how a search for assassins had turned into a competition between two old friends. At the same time I could not allow sentiment to deter me. I focused my attention and braced for the next day. I was going to speak with Giuseppe one last time.

*　　*　　*

From the outside, the headquarters of The Pegasus Group looked the same. There were no indications that Giuseppe was handing over control and administration for his sojourn in the nation's capital. Only his office had changed. His personal items had all been removed. Some sent to Washington, others to his home for storage.

To me, it all seemed eerily comfortable. Almost pleasant. Especially given the events of the last three months. The last time I was in that office was the day we served the search warrant. Oddly, it actually seemed more funereal this time. I figured that was the effect of Giuseppe's self-centered existence. In any case, I was unprepared for the relaxed atmosphere and his calm disposition.

"Hello, Tom". Giuseppe's manner was almost buoyant. And distasteful.

I nodded and simply replied, "Giuseppe". I perused the room, then turned back to him and said, "I'm surprised you could make time for me".

"I can always make time for a childhood friend, especially one who is trying to solve my family's murder".

Maybe it was only my imagination, but he sounded insincere. Almost mendacious. At that point in my career, nothing surprised me. Nonetheless, Giuseppe's cavalier attitude was unexpected and off-putting. It drew a slightly sarcastic response from me.

"I see you're packing for Washington. I suppose I should congratulate you again on winning the senatorial race, but I don't think congratulations are in order—at least not for the people of California".

"Well, that's a little snarky, especially coming from a childhood friend".

It was difficult for me to maintain a cool demeanor and control my temper. I had always held a great deal of affection for Yolanda and the kids. And I was Carmen's godfather. That made Giuseppe's attitude even more repulsive.

"We haven't been children for a long time. As for our friendship, it faded beyond memory years ago. Anyway, I didn't come because of the election. I came to talk you about your family".

"Then you have news"?, he asked. Somewhat disinterestedly.

I shifted my posture, my gaze sharpening into a glare. "I have. But let's begin with your visit to Giovanni. I know what you told him in confession".

Giuseppe's response was emotionless, as if he had just heard the weather report. "Not from him, you don't".

"No, of course not", I replied. "Though I do find your visit to him frightfully, if not diabolically clever. In truth, it disgusts me. I tried to get Giovanni to reveal what you said in confession. I guess I knew it was futile. Unlike you he is not corruptible. He maintains your secret, and always will. But don't forget. Giovanni and I really are friends. While he would not speak the words, I could read what I wanted to know in his eyes. That's why I'm here".

Giuseppe remained distant, but could not keep himself completely in check. His interest peaked a little. "Just what is it you think you know"?

"That you killed your wife and children". I raised my hand as I continued. "Oh. You were too cautious and cowardly to do it yourself. You enlisted someone else for that. Still, you were the puppeteer and it was your hand at work".

"You got that from looking in my brother's eyes"?, he asked. His tone contained a combination of mockery and disdain.

"No. What I learned last night is what I already suspected. You had Coker killed. Working backward, everything fits into place. You knew the police had identified Bass, so you had him killed. The only reason to eliminate the two of them was to protect the mastermind behind the murders.

"Even the missing file was a clever ploy to throw us off track. And it worked. Coker took the file to Grand Cayman only two days after the murders. One of you had to be in contact with the assassins. But after I corrected that misdirection, and confronted Coker, you were the last man standing. I pointed out once before that you are the only person connected to this case who isn't dead. What I still don't know is why, Sep. What possible motive could you have had"?

"That's what I was going to ask you".

There was no anger, no defensiveness. Still, he was not fully without expression. His eyes were blank, but it was precisely their emptiness that betrayed him. The eyes always unveil the feelings of the heart. Dante depicted Satan trapped in a lake of ice formed from his own tears. But Giuseppe had no tears to freeze over. I felt as if I was face to face with impenetrable evil. I saw before me a man I no longer knew, and I wondered if I had made a mistake. Not about my reasoning or my conclusions. But about confronting Giuseppe alone.

I had not planned on pleading for the truth. I had intended to demand it. Without even knowing it, my words seemed almost plaintive in my pursuit of a confession. Indeed it was a plea.

"I'm giving you a chance to confess, Giuseppe. This time without the secrecy of a sacrament or the protection of a church. Rather, for your own peace of mind. We may not be friends anymore, but we once were and I want you to admit the truth to me".

"You may be asking too much, Tom. You presume that I'm guilty".

"Cut the fucking games, will you? I know you're guilty. We both know it".

Giuseppe had become intrigued, and he believed that like every other event in his life, he was in control of this situation. He knew that if I had any real evidence I would already have him in custody. This meeting was an unexpected opportunity to continue the cat and mouse game he had been playing for months. So he toyed a little more.

"Even if that were true, why would I admit it to you"?

This was no game for me. It never was. My years in the department, first on patrol, then as a detective had toughened, but not fully hardened me. Despite my doubts about God, doubts that had led to my own descent from faith, I still wanted to believe in people.

"I've given that some thought", I replied. "I want to believe that somewhere deep within the recesses of your being there is still goodness. That you still possess the desire to do the right thing".

"You were always such a fool, Tom—you and Giovanni, both. When we were kids, there was one thing that our parents, the sisters at school and the priests in church repeated over and over. But its constant repetition made it no less untrue".

It was my turn to be intrigued.

"What was that"?, I asked.

"Simple. They told us 'crime does not pay.' Maybe that's true for someone stupid enough to hold up a liquor store or a bank. But the deeper truth is that carefully crafted crime, executed with precision and passionless accuracy—that kind of crime always pays. You and Giovanni were just too naïve to realize that. And, therefore, too impotent to grasp its full potential".

"You mean neither of us possessed your unbridled ambition".

"Everybody has ambition, Tom. Unfortunately for you and Giovanni, you did not know what to do with it, and so it waned. Has it never occurred to you that you could have been Chief of Police? Or that Giovanni could have been a bishop, maybe even a cardinal? I studied the deeper forces behind ambition, and, as with the great leaders of history, I learned how it morphs into power".

Giuseppe sat down behind the desk in his leather executive chair. He leaned back, placing his hands behind his head as if lilting through a casual conversation. "How well do you remember Alexandre Dumas' 'The Count of Monte Cristo'"?, he asked.

I had always been fascinated by the stories and characters in Dumas' works. Like many little boys, Giovanni, Giuseppe and I often pretended to be 'The Three Musketeers'. Sometimes, I would choose instead to play the part of D'Artagnan. On other occasions Giovanni and Giuseppe alternated being the twins from 'The Man in the Iron Mask'. But my personal passion was for the 'The Count of Monte Cristo'. As a child I used to dream of finding a treasure like the one Edmond Dantès discovered. I did not need to fashion a response to Giuseppe's question. It came most readily.

"I read the book, saw the movies, pretended the part. I know all the characters and am intimately familiar with the story. Why"?

"Then you remember that the Abbé Faria was imprisoned in Le Chateau d'If because he opposed Napoleon Bonaparte, while years later Edmond Dantès was confined to the same prison for supporting Bonaparte. Political fortunes wax and wane like the moon!"

With a somewhat exasperated expression, I queried, "Your point"?

"Good is not an absolute. It is a shifting horizon of pragmatism, power being its exclusive avenue of approach. Edmond Dantès grasped that concept and pursued it after escaping from prison and discovering the treasure of Monte Cristo. I am not unlike Dantès".

"You're delusional, Giuseppe. You are no Count. Edmond Dantès promised to use the treasure for good".

Giuseppe's countenance suggested that I did not understand. He continued.

"Yes, but first he exacted revenge on those who wronged him".

"And just how did your wife and children wrong you"?

Giuseppe suppressed a laugh, but mockingly responded,

"You surprise me, Tom. I expected more. I knew you would not approve, but I thought you would at least understand".

"Understand what"?

"Everyone is expendable. That is obvious in the pursuit of revenge. But it is even more notable in the pursuit of power. In spite of last summer's polls, the race was never really close. I knew that there was no way I was going to win the election. I needed an edge. My family provided it".

He spoke with such detachment. Balancing the contradictory emotions of sorrow and elation would be difficult for anyone. Then again, Giuseppe experienced no real loss, at least not emotionally. In pursuit of his career, his family was disposable, the death of his wife and children merely being a means to an end.

"There are people who live for others", he continued. "For family and friends. For them that is their whole purpose and their true treasure.

They do not care for money. I am not one of the them. Family and friends do not bring wealth. And wealth is a means to power. We have always seen life differently, Tom. It's not about caring for people, or about relationships. They only led to pain".

"And what about Jackson", I asked? What about those years in Boston"?

"A mistake, Tom. We all make them. For awhile I thought maybe it was possible to care, to be close to someone. That experience led to pain, a pain I did not want to suffer again. It cured me of the illusion. That was when I first realized that everyone is expendable".

At this point my frustration became undeniable and the intensity in my voice strained. I shouted back.

"You sacrificed four people's lives to advance your career and all you can say is that they were expendable"?

Giuseppe maintained an almost diabolical ease and replied, "No. I said everyone is expendable. My family, you, even I am expendable. That is why I had to reach out and grasp power while I could. It does not mean I did not love them. If there was one truth I shared with Yolanda and the kids, it was the need to sacrifice. I did love them, Tom. But I was willing to sacrifice them".

I did not respond. I was speechless and bewildered. He continued.

"Why do you look so surprised? Do you really think that anyone actually matters? Or do you actually think that you matter"?

"I do possess some values, Giuseppe".

"Values. You still don't get it, do you? You may think of me as a despot, but I'm not. The problem throughout history has been that too many leaders did not know how to harness the power they possessed. The ones we now consider to be tyrants were the ones who fell into it accidentally. Sometimes they inherited the power from their parents, as in the case of royal families. At other times they were heralded into command as the victor of a war or the leader of a revolution.

"The truly great men of history were the ones who planned and plotted to achieve their dominion. They did not creep into authority, nor exercise power in the shadows. They understood that only the public and relentless demonstration of control would enable them to set the direction for social and political development. To achieve the greater good, some people must always die".

This was not ambition morphing into power. I realized for the first time that my childhood friend was a sociopath. Even so, I could not restrain the question to which I already knew the answer.

"Have you no social conscience, no sense of moral responsibility"?

By this time Giuseppe knew that he was in control of this conversation. I would never understand, never grasp the great deeds that only the ruthless can accomplish.

"Moral responsibility and social conscience are no more absolute than good'" he replied. "They are perfected when one exercises sufficient power to vanquish all enemies and direct the path of social progress. I have a vision to share with America".

"You call that a vision? If you have no love and allegiance for family and friends, how can you love a nation? How can you lead a people? The nation is people. And none of them is expendable".

For the first time Giuseppe demonstrated exasperation.

"Can I not make you understand? There is a contingency of events at work here, a set of links in a formidable and unbreakable chain. There is no time to sit around and talk about how to make things better. The people need simple answers. They need a leader who can tell them what to do".

For a moment, I found myself transported back to a conversation I once had with Giovanni. I recalled him saying that we can only conquer the evil we see. The world rises up to fight against invasions, torture and genocide, but what if malice cannot be seen? We are warned of evil lurking around dark corners and in dimly lit alleys. Giovanni believed that the greater evil is not to be found in the shadows. It hides in plain sight. Tragically, Giuseppe missed the true lessons of history. His so-called vision arose from the very thing Giovanni cautioned against—darkness masquerading as light.

If I had expected to achieve a meeting of the minds, to rescue some last remnant of humanity in the newly elected senator, I knew now that expectation would never be fulfilled. The only hope left was to get the confession.

"Giuseppe, I know what you're saying, but I think you're wrong. You're selling the people short--both the people of California and the rest of the nation. They are fully capable of charting their own future. What they need is a leader with a genuine vision, not a dictator with a complex".

"Now who's selling the people short, Tom? Do you really think they care about a vision? Besides, I don't want to replace the ballot box. In today's world voting is another means to an end. What good are my plans if I am not elected? I justify everything that serves that singular end".

"Then you did have your family killed"?, I asked. "A simple yes or no will suffice".

Giuseppe's features became cold and heartless. He looked at me and took his time to answer.

"Ever since you walked in here, you've been trying to get that confession out of me. Very well. Yes, I had my family killed in order to secure my election. I found it a necessary maneuver to garner the sympathy vote. I needed it to put me over the top. Now that you know, what difference does it make? We are alone here, and I will never repeat that statement outside this room. So what are you going to do? Draw your gun and shoot me"?

"I have a pretty good reputation among investigators, Giuseppe. Did you really think I would come here unprepared"?

As I reached into my pocket, I retrieved a digital recorder, and continued.

"I did not come here in a rush. Nor did I want to hurry this conversation. I was willing to take whatever time was needed. Every word spoken between the two of us is right here. Your confession is now on record. You're finished, Sep".

Giuseppe began to chuckle. Quietly, at first. Then it turned to laughter. Not quite hearty, but full-throated. As it grew louder, his eyes darkened and his countenance glowed a fiendish color. His laugh, itself, grew almost demonic.

"You're so predictable, Tom. That's one of the things I like about you. Unfortunately, the cops are always three or four steps behind when it comes to technology. How could you think to get the better of me? I built this company into an electronics giant. Not even the U.S. Government can equal our research and development.

"I can afford the best minds and I pay them well. In return they have created the best products. Look around you. You don't see anything, but you are standing in the most confidential room in the world. There is an electronic signal that blankets every inch of this office. No one else has achieved this level of technological development. Not even the Oval Office of the White House is as secure. And here's the best part. We named the device 'The Silencer'. Surely, you can appreciate the irony in that. You will find your recording quite blank, I assure you".

I began to wonder if I had stumbled into a world of comic books and science fiction. A place where a superman cannot see through lead and spaceships are protected by invisible shields. Could recording devices really be nullified by some unseen barricade?

"As I said, I will never repeat that admission outside this room. So it turns out, you don't have enough evidence to arrest me, or even hold me for questioning".

He was right, of course. Without his confession, I had no cause to place him in custody or detain him. His attitude indicated that any additional appeals would go equally unheeded.

Clearly, I would not emerge the victor in this battle. But surrender was not something that came easily to me. Even in my agnosticism, I could not shake off the influence of Giovanni. Damn! My friend the priest. I might have turned my back on God, but I could not forgo the years of friendship that had inseparably bound us. A part of his soul had attached itself to mine. It held stronger sway over me than years of police work. As a result I believed that some element of good was to be found in every person. I deeply desired that to be true of Giuseppe. If there was no pathway available to elicit an admission of guilt, then perhaps there was a corridor that led to his conscience.

"Don't you feel any remorse at all, Giuseppe? You're like a man trapped within a maze of tombs, unable to find an exit. How can you live in a world of such darkness"?

"It's not that I can't find the exit, Tom. What you don't realize is that there is safety in the tomb. It is not a trap. It is the final refuge. Within the tomb, no one can be hurt. Emotions are safely guarded and the human heart is secure. As for darkness? Sometimes darkness is preferable to the light".

I had gone there searching for some piece of my childhood friend. Something that might have survived the shattering course of corruption. I also hoped to right a most grievous wrong. That was no longer possible. I had allowed myself to be the victim of a naive illusion. What I experienced was a classic case of heart and mind being out of sync. Untold years of police work told me that there was no human redemption in people who traversed so evil a path. But my heart held out. Until reality swept over me.

I had one play left. My legs began to shake and I felt energy and purpose drain from me. I needed to muster all the force within me, for I could not allow Giuseppe to see the internal struggle that was so affecting my physical strength. That was a victory I would withhold from him. I drew my gun.

"Go ahead, Tom. Take your revenge. It is the only way you can make me pay for what I've done. Of course, in the end you will be no better than I am."

For a few moments, images flashed before my eyes. Yolanda and Carmen, Gina and Leonardo. Memories flooded back from birthdays and holidays. From a baby's first steps to family parties to summer barbecues. It took great effort to wall back the tears. I could feel my finger tighten around the trigger.

Giuseppe sat opposite me, continuing to lean back in his chair, his hand still behind his head. There was no fear in him.

I holstered my weapon.

"Giuseppe, I stopped believing in God and Church a long time ago. I don't know what I believe in now, but I know what I don't believe in. I came here today driven by a great deal of anger, and I thought I could do whatever was necessary to bring you to justice. But I don't believe in revenge".

Giuseppe was ready with his response. It was measured, but not rehearsed.

"You're wrong, Tom. It's not that you don't believe in revenge. On some level we all do. But you share a common problem with Giovanni. Neither one of you can cross the line when you need to. He would not tell you what I said in confession, and you cannot bring yourself to shoot me. I was counting on that. I entertained this conversation today so that when you walk out of here you will know two things. First, you will never be more than a lieutenant. And second, someday I will be president".

I turned and headed for the door. As my hand reached out for the handle, I turned my head and said.

"Actually, Giuseppe, you're not worth the bullet".

The last thing I heard as I closed the door was laughter.

# Epilogue

A strange conflict waged within me. Was my decision not to fire, a sign of commitment to valued principles, to law and order? Or was I just impotent?

For only the second time since graduating from the academy, I wished I were anything but a cop. It's true that Giuseppe was not worth the bullet. I wanted to kill him anyway. If I had not been a cop, or if I had been a little more self-indulgent, I might have pulled the trigger. Not just for Yolanda and the kids, but for myself. I had been bested by Giuseppe most of my life. In matters that were unimportant. This was different. Justice was at stake.

I also had serious reason to be concerned about Giuseppe's megalomania. History abounds with stories of people consumed by power and self-importance. People who left only death, destruction and chaos in their wake. Emperors, kings, presidents, prime ministers. To that generic list I added the personal. Giuseppe. If I were to find solace anywhere, I would have to turn to my best friend.

I think Giovanni was expecting me. He must have known that my last words to him would go unfulfilled. I was not able to bring

Giuseppe down. I recounted my conversation with Giuseppe, including his admission of guilt. Like the night before, Giovanni disclosed nothing of what he had heard in confession. But I watched him display an unmistakable mix of desolation and despair. Once again, his eyes revealed what he could not speak. He knew.

Neither of us could undo what Giuseppe had done. Nor could we prevent what he would become.

CPSIA information can be obtained at www.ICGtesting.com
Printed in the USA
LVOW060123050612

284624LV00003B/1/P